C-4471 CAREER EXAMINATION SERIES

This is your
PASSBOOK for...

Information Technology Specialist III

Test Preparation Study Guide
Questions & Answers

COPYRIGHT NOTICE

This book is SOLELY intended for, is sold ONLY to, and its use is RESTRICTED to individual, bona fide applicants or candidates who qualify by virtue of having seriously filed applications for appropriate license, certificate, professional and/or promotional advancement, higher school matriculation, scholarship, or other legitimate requirements of education and/or governmental authorities.

This book is NOT intended for use, class instruction, tutoring, training, duplication, copying, reprinting, excerption, or adaptation, etc., by:

1) Other publishers
2) Proprietors and/or Instructors of "Coaching" and/or Preparatory Courses
3) Personnel and/or Training Divisions of commercial, industrial, and governmental organizations
4) Schools, colleges, or universities and/or their departments and staffs, including teachers and other personnel
5) Testing Agencies or Bureaus
6) Study groups which seek by the purchase of a single volume to copy and/or duplicate and/or adapt this material for use by the group as a whole without having purchased individual volumes for each of the members of the group
7) Et al.

Such persons would be in violation of appropriate Federal and State statutes.

PROVISION OF LICENSING AGREEMENTS – Recognized educational, commercial, industrial, and governmental institutions and organizations, and others legitimately engaged in educational pursuits, including training, testing, and measurement activities, may address request for a licensing agreement to the copyright owners, who will determine whether, and under what conditions, including fees and charges, the materials in this book may be used them. In other words, a licensing facility exists for the legitimate use of the material in this book on other than an individual basis. However, it is asseverated and affirmed here that the material in this book CANNOT be used without the receipt of the express permission of such a licensing agreement from the Publishers. Inquiries re licensing should be addressed to the company, attention rights and permissions department.

All rights reserved, including the right of reproduction in whole or in part, in any form or by any means, electronic or mechanical, including photocopying, recording, or by any information storage and retrieval system, without permission in writing from the Publisher.

Copyright © 2024 by
National Learning Corporation

212 Michael Drive, Syosset, NY 11791
(516) 921-8888 • www.passbooks.com
E-mail: info@passbooks.com

PUBLISHED IN THE UNITED STATES OF AMERICA

PASSBOOK® SERIES

THE *PASSBOOK® SERIES* has been created to prepare applicants and candidates for the ultimate academic battlefield – the examination room.

At some time in our lives, each and every one of us may be required to take an examination – for validation, matriculation, admission, qualification, registration, certification, or licensure.

Based on the assumption that every applicant or candidate has met the basic formal educational standards, has taken the required number of courses, and read the necessary texts, the *PASSBOOK® SERIES* furnishes the one special preparation which may assure passing with confidence, instead of failing with insecurity. Examination questions – together with answers – are furnished as the basic vehicle for study so that the mysteries of the examination and its compounding difficulties may be eliminated or diminished by a sure method.

This book is meant to help you pass your examination provided that you qualify and are serious in your objective.

The entire field is reviewed through the huge store of content information which is succinctly presented through a provocative and challenging approach – the question-and-answer method.

A climate of success is established by furnishing the correct answers at the end of each test.

You soon learn to recognize types of questions, forms of questions, and patterns of questioning. You may even begin to anticipate expected outcomes.

You perceive that many questions are repeated or adapted so that you can gain acute insights, which may enable you to score many sure points.

You learn how to confront new questions, or types of questions, and to attack them confidently and work out the correct answers.

You note objectives and emphases, and recognize pitfalls and dangers, so that you may make positive educational adjustments.

Moreover, you are kept fully informed in relation to new concepts, methods, practices, and directions in the field.

You discover that you are actually taking the examination all the time: you are preparing for the examination by "taking" an examination, not by reading extraneous and/or supererogatory textbooks.

In short, this PASSBOOK®, used directedly, should be an important factor in helping you to pass your test.

INFORMATION TECHNOLOGY SPECIALIST III

DUTIES

As an Information Technology Specialist 3, you would perform such activities including, but not limited to: technical and agency program support; information technology activities related to network and system design, configuration, maintenance, and network/information security; customer support; project support; business/systems analysis and design which may include mainframe, client/server and n tier (e.g., three tiered) web or browser based applications systems; and the design, development, and administration of enterprise storage, backup, and database systems.

As an Information Technology Specialist 3 (Programming), you would perform such activities including, but not limited to: technical activities related to writing instructions (code); applications program development, program and system testing, and business/systems analysis and design related to computer systems, systems maintenance, and implementation in such areas as the design and development of database systems; dynamic, transactional, or interactive websites; and agency specific applications programs.

As an Information Technology Specialist 3 (Database), you would perform such activities including, but not limited to: activities associated with the design, development, installation, and performance of agency databases.

As an Information Technology Specialist 3 (Data Communications), you would perform such activities including, but not limited to: data communications network design, analysis, capacity planning, installation, monitoring, performance evaluation, tuning, and/or maintenance.

As an Information Technology Specialist 3 (Systems Programming), you would perform such activities including, but not limited to: systems programming and implementation, maintaining, and managing an agency's hardware and systems software environment or major component of it.

For all titles, you may supervise Information Technology Assistant, Information Technology Specialists 1 or 2, Information Technology Specialists 1 or 2 (Programming), and support staff.

SUBJECT OF EXAMINATION

The written test is designed to test for knowledge, skills, and/or abilities in such areas as:
1. Logical reasoning using flowcharts;
2. Understanding and interpreting a manual;
3. Preparing written material; and
4. Systems analysis.

HOW TO TAKE A TEST

I. YOU MUST PASS AN EXAMINATION

A. *WHAT EVERY CANDIDATE SHOULD KNOW*

Examination applicants often ask us for help in preparing for the written test. What can I study in advance? What kinds of questions will be asked? How will the test be given? How will the papers be graded?

As an applicant for a civil service examination, you may be wondering about some of these things. Our purpose here is to suggest effective methods of advance study and to describe civil service examinations.

Your chances for success on this examination can be increased if you know how to prepare. Those "pre-examination jitters" can be reduced if you know what to expect. You can even experience an adventure in good citizenship if you know why civil service exams are given.

B. *WHY ARE CIVIL SERVICE EXAMINATIONS GIVEN?*

Civil service examinations are important to you in two ways. As a citizen, you want public jobs filled by employees who know how to do their work. As a job seeker, you want a fair chance to compete for that job on an equal footing with other candidates. The best-known means of accomplishing this two-fold goal is the competitive examination.

Exams are widely publicized throughout the nation. They may be administered for jobs in federal, state, city, municipal, town or village governments or agencies.

Any citizen may apply, with some limitations, such as the age or residence of applicants. Your experience and education may be reviewed to see whether you meet the requirements for the particular examination. When these requirements exist, they are reasonable and applied consistently to all applicants. Thus, a competitive examination may cause you some uneasiness now, but it is your privilege and safeguard.

C. *HOW ARE CIVIL SERVICE EXAMS DEVELOPED?*

Examinations are carefully written by trained technicians who are specialists in the field known as "psychological measurement," in consultation with recognized authorities in the field of work that the test will cover. These experts recommend the subject matter areas or skills to be tested; only those knowledges or skills important to your success on the job are included. The most reliable books and source materials available are used as references. Together, the experts and technicians judge the difficulty level of the questions.

Test technicians know how to phrase questions so that the problem is clearly stated. Their ethics do not permit "trick" or "catch" questions. Questions may have been tried out on sample groups, or subjected to statistical analysis, to determine their usefulness.

Written tests are often used in combination with performance tests, ratings of training and experience, and oral interviews. All of these measures combine to form the best-known means of finding the right person for the right job.

II. HOW TO PASS THE WRITTEN TEST

A. NATURE OF THE EXAMINATION

To prepare intelligently for civil service examinations, you should know how they differ from school examinations you have taken. In school you were assigned certain definite pages to read or subjects to cover. The examination questions were quite detailed and usually emphasized memory. Civil service exams, on the other hand, try to discover your present ability to perform the duties of a position, plus your potentiality to learn these duties. In other words, a civil service exam attempts to predict how successful you will be. Questions cover such a broad area that they cannot be as minute and detailed as school exam questions.

In the public service similar kinds of work, or positions, are grouped together in one "class." This process is known as *position-classification*. All the positions in a class are paid according to the salary range for that class. One class title covers all of these positions, and they are all tested by the same examination.

B. FOUR BASIC STEPS

1) Study the announcement

How, then, can you know what subjects to study? Our best answer is: "Learn as much as possible about the class of positions for which you've applied." The exam will test the knowledge, skills and abilities needed to do the work.

Your most valuable source of information about the position you want is the official exam announcement. This announcement lists the training and experience qualifications. Check these standards and apply only if you come reasonably close to meeting them.

The brief description of the position in the examination announcement offers some clues to the subjects which will be tested. Think about the job itself. Review the duties in your mind. Can you perform them, or are there some in which you are rusty? Fill in the blank spots in your preparation.

Many jurisdictions preview the written test in the exam announcement by including a section called "Knowledge and Abilities Required," "Scope of the Examination," or some similar heading. Here you will find out specifically what fields will be tested.

2) Review your own background

Once you learn in general what the position is all about, and what you need to know to do the work, ask yourself which subjects you already know fairly well and which need improvement. You may wonder whether to concentrate on improving your strong areas or on building some background in your fields of weakness. When the announcement has specified "some knowledge" or "considerable knowledge," or has used adjectives like "beginning principles of…" or "advanced … methods," you can get a clue as to the number and difficulty of questions to be asked in any given field. More questions, and hence broader coverage, would be included for those subjects which are more important in the work. Now weigh your strengths and weaknesses against the job requirements and prepare accordingly.

3) Determine the level of the position

Another way to tell how intensively you should prepare is to understand the level of the job for which you are applying. Is it the entering level? In other words, is this the position in which beginners in a field of work are hired? Or is it an intermediate or advanced level? Sometimes this is indicated by such words as "Junior" or "Senior" in the class title. Other jurisdictions use Roman numerals to designate the level – Clerk I, Clerk II, for example. The word "Supervisor" sometimes appears in the title. If the level is not indicated by the title, check the description of duties. Will you be working under very close supervision, or will you have responsibility for independent decisions in this work?

4) Choose appropriate study materials

Now that you know the subjects to be examined and the relative amount of each subject to be covered, you can choose suitable study materials. For beginning level jobs, or even advanced ones, if you have a pronounced weakness in some aspect of your training, read a modern, standard textbook in that field. Be sure it is up to date and has general coverage. Such books are normally available at your library, and the librarian will be glad to help you locate one. For entry-level positions, questions of appropriate difficulty are chosen – neither highly advanced questions, nor those too simple. Such questions require careful thought but not advanced training.

If the position for which you are applying is technical or advanced, you will read more advanced, specialized material. If you are already familiar with the basic principles of your field, elementary textbooks would waste your time. Concentrate on advanced textbooks and technical periodicals. Think through the concepts and review difficult problems in your field.

These are all general sources. You can get more ideas on your own initiative, following these leads. For example, training manuals and publications of the government agency which employs workers in your field can be useful, particularly for technical and professional positions. A letter or visit to the government department involved may result in more specific study suggestions, and certainly will provide you with a more definite idea of the exact nature of the position you are seeking.

III. KINDS OF TESTS

Tests are used for purposes other than measuring knowledge and ability to perform specified duties. For some positions, it is equally important to test ability to make adjustments to new situations or to profit from training. In others, basic mental abilities not dependent on information are essential. Questions which test these things may not appear as pertinent to the duties of the position as those which test for knowledge and information. Yet they are often highly important parts of a fair examination. For very general questions, it is almost impossible to help you direct your study efforts. What we can do is to point out some of the more common of these general abilities needed in public service positions and describe some typical questions.

1) General information

Broad, general information has been found useful for predicting job success in some kinds of work. This is tested in a variety of ways, from vocabulary lists to questions about current events. Basic background in some field of work, such as sociology or economics, may be sampled in a group of questions. Often these are principles which have become familiar to most persons through exposure rather than through formal training. It is difficult to advise you how to study for these questions; being alert to the world around you is our best suggestion.

2) Verbal ability

An example of an ability needed in many positions is verbal or language ability. Verbal ability is, in brief, the ability to use and understand words. Vocabulary and grammar tests are typical measures of this ability. Reading comprehension or paragraph interpretation questions are common in many kinds of civil service tests. You are given a paragraph of written material and asked to find its central meaning.

3) **Numerical ability**

Number skills can be tested by the familiar arithmetic problem, by checking paired lists of numbers to see which are alike and which are different, or by interpreting charts and graphs. In the latter test, a graph may be printed in the test booklet which you are asked to use as the basis for answering questions.

4) **Observation**

A popular test for law-enforcement positions is the observation test. A picture is shown to you for several minutes, then taken away. Questions about the picture test your ability to observe both details and larger elements.

5) **Following directions**

In many positions in the public service, the employee must be able to carry out written instructions dependably and accurately. You may be given a chart with several columns, each column listing a variety of information. The questions require you to carry out directions involving the information given in the chart.

6) **Skills and aptitudes**

Performance tests effectively measure some manual skills and aptitudes. When the skill is one in which you are trained, such as typing or shorthand, you can practice. These tests are often very much like those given in business school or high school courses. For many of the other skills and aptitudes, however, no short-time preparation can be made. Skills and abilities natural to you or that you have developed throughout your lifetime are being tested.

Many of the general questions just described provide all the data needed to answer the questions and ask you to use your reasoning ability to find the answers. Your best preparation for these tests, as well as for tests of facts and ideas, is to be at your physical and mental best. You, no doubt, have your own methods of getting into an exam-taking mood and keeping "in shape." The next section lists some ideas on this subject.

IV. KINDS OF QUESTIONS

Only rarely is the "essay" question, which you answer in narrative form, used in civil service tests. Civil service tests are usually of the short-answer type. Full instructions for answering these questions will be given to you at the examination. But in case this is your first experience with short-answer questions and separate answer sheets, here is what you need to know:

1) **Multiple-choice Questions**

Most popular of the short-answer questions is the "multiple choice" or "best answer" question. It can be used, for example, to test for factual knowledge, ability to solve problems or judgment in meeting situations found at work.

A multiple-choice question is normally one of three types—
- It can begin with an incomplete statement followed by several possible endings. You are to find the one ending which *best* completes the statement, although some of the others may not be entirely wrong.
- It can also be a complete statement in the form of a question which is answered by choosing one of the statements listed.

- It can be in the form of a problem – again you select the best answer.

Here is an example of a multiple-choice question with a discussion which should give you some clues as to the method for choosing the right answer:

When an employee has a complaint about his assignment, the action which will *best* help him overcome his difficulty is to
A. discuss his difficulty with his coworkers
B. take the problem to the head of the organization
C. take the problem to the person who gave him the assignment
D. say nothing to anyone about his complaint

In answering this question, you should study each of the choices to find which is best. Consider choice "A" – Certainly an employee may discuss his complaint with fellow employees, but no change or improvement can result, and the complaint remains unresolved. Choice "B" is a poor choice since the head of the organization probably does not know what assignment you have been given, and taking your problem to him is known as "going over the head" of the supervisor. The supervisor, or person who made the assignment, is the person who can clarify it or correct any injustice. Choice "C" is, therefore, correct. To say nothing, as in choice "D," is unwise. Supervisors have and interest in knowing the problems employees are facing, and the employee is seeking a solution to his problem.

2) True/False Questions

The "true/false" or "right/wrong" form of question is sometimes used. Here a complete statement is given. Your job is to decide whether the statement is right or wrong.

SAMPLE: A roaming cell-phone call to a nearby city costs less than a non-roaming call to a distant city.

This statement is wrong, or false, since roaming calls are more expensive.

This is not a complete list of all possible question forms, although most of the others are variations of these common types. You will always get complete directions for answering questions. Be sure you understand *how* to mark your answers – ask questions until you do.

V. RECORDING YOUR ANSWERS

Computer terminals are used more and more today for many different kinds of exams.

For an examination with very few applicants, you may be told to record your answers in the test booklet itself. Separate answer sheets are much more common. If this separate answer sheet is to be scored by machine – and this is often the case – it is highly important that you mark your answers correctly in order to get credit.

An electronic scoring machine is often used in civil service offices because of the speed with which papers can be scored. Machine-scored answer sheets must be marked with a pencil, which will be given to you. This pencil has a high graphite content which responds to the electronic scoring machine. As a matter of fact, stray dots may register as answers, so do not let your pencil rest on the answer sheet while you are pondering the correct answer. Also, if your pencil lead breaks or is otherwise defective, ask for another.

Since the answer sheet will be dropped in a slot in the scoring machine, be careful not to bend the corners or get the paper crumpled.

The answer sheet normally has five vertical columns of numbers, with 30 numbers to a column. These numbers correspond to the question numbers in your test booklet. After each number, going across the page are four or five pairs of dotted lines. These short dotted lines have small letters or numbers above them. The first two pairs may also have a "T" or "F" above the letters. This indicates that the first two pairs only are to be used if the questions are of the true-false type. If the questions are multiple choice, disregard the "T" and "F" and pay attention only to the small letters or numbers.

Answer your questions in the manner of the sample that follows:

32. The largest city in the United States is
    A. Washington, D.C.
    B. New York City
    C. Chicago
    D. Detroit
    E. San Francisco

1) Choose the answer you think is best. (New York City is the largest, so "B" is correct.)
2) Find the row of dotted lines numbered the same as the question you are answering. (Find row number 32)
3) Find the pair of dotted lines corresponding to the answer. (Find the pair of lines under the mark "B.")
4) Make a solid black mark between the dotted lines.

VI. BEFORE THE TEST

Common sense will help you find procedures to follow to get ready for an examination. Too many of us, however, overlook these sensible measures. Indeed, nervousness and fatigue have been found to be the most serious reasons why applicants fail to do their best on civil service tests. Here is a list of reminders:

- Begin your preparation early – Don't wait until the last minute to go scurrying around for books and materials or to find out what the position is all about.
- Prepare continuously – An hour a night for a week is better than an all-night cram session. This has been definitely established. What is more, a night a week for a month will return better dividends than crowding your study into a shorter period of time.
- Locate the place of the exam – You have been sent a notice telling you when and where to report for the examination. If the location is in a different town or otherwise unfamiliar to you, it would be well to inquire the best route and learn something about the building.
- Relax the night before the test – Allow your mind to rest. Do not study at all that night. Plan some mild recreation or diversion; then go to bed early and get a good night's sleep.
- Get up early enough to make a leisurely trip to the place for the test – This way unforeseen events, traffic snarls, unfamiliar buildings, etc. will not upset you.
- Dress comfortably – A written test is not a fashion show. You will be known by number and not by name, so wear something comfortable.

- Leave excess paraphernalia at home – Shopping bags and odd bundles will get in your way. You need bring only the items mentioned in the official notice you received; usually everything you need is provided. Do not bring reference books to the exam. They will only confuse those last minutes and be taken away from you when in the test room.
- Arrive somewhat ahead of time – If because of transportation schedules you must get there very early, bring a newspaper or magazine to take your mind off yourself while waiting.
- Locate the examination room – When you have found the proper room, you will be directed to the seat or part of the room where you will sit. Sometimes you are given a sheet of instructions to read while you are waiting. Do not fill out any forms until you are told to do so; just read them and be prepared.
- Relax and prepare to listen to the instructions
- If you have any physical problem that may keep you from doing your best, be sure to tell the test administrator. If you are sick or in poor health, you really cannot do your best on the exam. You can come back and take the test some other time.

VII. AT THE TEST

The day of the test is here and you have the test booklet in your hand. The temptation to get going is very strong. Caution! There is more to success than knowing the right answers. You must know how to identify your papers and understand variations in the type of short-answer question used in this particular examination. Follow these suggestions for maximum results from your efforts:

1) Cooperate with the monitor

The test administrator has a duty to create a situation in which you can be as much at ease as possible. He will give instructions, tell you when to begin, check to see that you are marking your answer sheet correctly, and so on. He is not there to guard you, although he will see that your competitors do not take unfair advantage. He wants to help you do your best.

2) Listen to all instructions

Don't jump the gun! Wait until you understand all directions. In most civil service tests you get more time than you need to answer the questions. So don't be in a hurry. Read each word of instructions until you clearly understand the meaning. Study the examples, listen to all announcements and follow directions. Ask questions if you do not understand what to do.

3) Identify your papers

Civil service exams are usually identified by number only. You will be assigned a number; you must not put your name on your test papers. Be sure to copy your number correctly. Since more than one exam may be given, copy your exact examination title.

4) Plan your time

Unless you are told that a test is a "speed" or "rate of work" test, speed itself is usually not important. Time enough to answer all the questions will be provided, but this does not mean that you have all day. An overall time limit has been set. Divide the total time (in minutes) by the number of questions to determine the approximate time you have for each question.

5) **Do not linger over difficult questions**

If you come across a difficult question, mark it with a paper clip (useful to have along) and come back to it when you have been through the booklet. One caution if you do this – be sure to skip a number on your answer sheet as well. Check often to be sure that you have not lost your place and that you are marking in the row numbered the same as the question you are answering.

6) **Read the questions**

Be sure you know what the question asks! Many capable people are unsuccessful because they failed to *read* the questions correctly.

7) **Answer all questions**

Unless you have been instructed that a penalty will be deducted for incorrect answers, it is better to guess than to omit a question.

8) **Speed tests**

It is often better NOT to guess on speed tests. It has been found that on timed tests people are tempted to spend the last few seconds before time is called in marking answers at random – without even reading them – in the hope of picking up a few extra points. To discourage this practice, the instructions may warn you that your score will be "corrected" for guessing. That is, a penalty will be applied. The incorrect answers will be deducted from the correct ones, or some other penalty formula will be used.

9) **Review your answers**

If you finish before time is called, go back to the questions you guessed or omitted to give them further thought. Review other answers if you have time.

10) **Return your test materials**

If you are ready to leave before others have finished or time is called, take ALL your materials to the monitor and leave quietly. Never take any test material with you. The monitor can discover whose papers are not complete, and taking a test booklet may be grounds for disqualification.

VIII. EXAMINATION TECHNIQUES

1) Read the general instructions carefully. These are usually printed on the first page of the exam booklet. As a rule, these instructions refer to the timing of the examination; the fact that you should not start work until the signal and must stop work at a signal, etc. If there are any *special* instructions, such as a choice of questions to be answered, make sure that you note this instruction carefully.

2) When you are ready to start work on the examination, that is as soon as the signal has been given, read the instructions to each question booklet, underline any key words or phrases, such as *least, best, outline, describe* and the like. In this way you will tend to answer as requested rather than discover on reviewing your paper that you *listed without describing*, that you selected the *worst* choice rather than the *best* choice, etc.

3) If the examination is of the objective or multiple-choice type – that is, each question will also give a series of possible answers: A, B, C or D, and you are called upon to select the best answer and write the letter next to that answer on your answer paper – it is advisable to start answering each question in turn. There may be anywhere from 50 to 100 such questions in the three or four hours allotted and you can see how much time would be taken if you read through all the questions before beginning to answer any. Furthermore, if you come across a question or group of questions which you know would be difficult to answer, it would undoubtedly affect your handling of all the other questions.

4) If the examination is of the essay type and contains but a few questions, it is a moot point as to whether you should read all the questions before starting to answer any one. Of course, if you are given a choice – say five out of seven and the like – then it is essential to read all the questions so you can eliminate the two that are most difficult. If, however, you are asked to answer all the questions, there may be danger in trying to answer the easiest one first because you may find that you will spend too much time on it. The best technique is to answer the first question, then proceed to the second, etc.

5) Time your answers. Before the exam begins, write down the time it started, then add the time allowed for the examination and write down the time it must be completed, then divide the time available somewhat as follows:
   - If 3-1/2 hours are allowed, that would be 210 minutes. If you have 80 objective-type questions, that would be an average of 2-1/2 minutes per question. Allow yourself no more than 2 minutes per question, or a total of 160 minutes, which will permit about 50 minutes to review.
   - If for the time allotment of 210 minutes there are 7 essay questions to answer, that would average about 30 minutes a question. Give yourself only 25 minutes per question so that you have about 35 minutes to review.

6) The most important instruction is to *read each question* and make sure you know what is wanted. The second most important instruction is to *time yourself properly* so that you answer every question. The third most important instruction is to *answer every question*. Guess if you have to but include something for each question. Remember that you will receive no credit for a blank and will probably receive some credit if you write something in answer to an essay question. If you guess a letter – say "B" for a multiple-choice question – you may have guessed right. If you leave a blank as an answer to a multiple-choice question, the examiners may respect your feelings but it will not add a point to your score. Some exams may penalize you for wrong answers, so in such cases *only*, you may not want to guess unless you have some basis for your answer.

7) Suggestions
   a. Objective-type questions
      1. Examine the question booklet for proper sequence of pages and questions
      2. Read all instructions carefully
      3. Skip any question which seems too difficult; return to it after all other questions have been answered
      4. Apportion your time properly; do not spend too much time on any single question or group of questions

5. Note and underline key words – *all, most, fewest, least, best, worst, same, opposite,* etc.
6. Pay particular attention to negatives
7. Note unusual option, e.g., unduly long, short, complex, different or similar in content to the body of the question
8. Observe the use of "hedging" words – *probably, may, most likely,* etc.
9. Make sure that your answer is put next to the same number as the question
10. Do not second-guess unless you have good reason to believe the second answer is definitely more correct
11. Cross out original answer if you decide another answer is more accurate; do not erase until you are ready to hand your paper in
12. Answer all questions; guess unless instructed otherwise
13. Leave time for review

   b. Essay questions
1. Read each question carefully
2. Determine exactly what is wanted. Underline key words or phrases.
3. Decide on outline or paragraph answer
4. Include many different points and elements unless asked to develop any one or two points or elements
5. Show impartiality by giving pros and cons unless directed to select one side only
6. Make and write down any assumptions you find necessary to answer the questions
7. Watch your English, grammar, punctuation and choice of words
8. Time your answers; don't crowd material

8) Answering the essay question

Most essay questions can be answered by framing the specific response around several key words or ideas. Here are a few such key words or ideas:

M's: manpower, materials, methods, money, management
P's: purpose, program, policy, plan, procedure, practice, problems, pitfalls, personnel, public relations

   a. Six basic steps in handling problems:
1. Preliminary plan and background development
2. Collect information, data and facts
3. Analyze and interpret information, data and facts
4. Analyze and develop solutions as well as make recommendations
5. Prepare report and sell recommendations
6. Install recommendations and follow up effectiveness

   b. Pitfalls to avoid
1. *Taking things for granted* – A statement of the situation does not necessarily imply that each of the elements is necessarily true; for example, a complaint may be invalid and biased so that all that can be taken for granted is that a complaint has been registered

2. *Considering only one side of a situation* – Wherever possible, indicate several alternatives and then point out the reasons you selected the best one
3. *Failing to indicate follow up* – Whenever your answer indicates action on your part, make certain that you will take proper follow-up action to see how successful your recommendations, procedures or actions turn out to be
4. *Taking too long in answering any single question* – Remember to time your answers properly

IX. AFTER THE TEST

Scoring procedures differ in detail among civil service jurisdictions although the general principles are the same. Whether the papers are hand-scored or graded by machine we have described, they are nearly always graded by number. That is, the person who marks the paper knows only the number – never the name – of the applicant. Not until all the papers have been graded will they be matched with names. If other tests, such as training and experience or oral interview ratings have been given, scores will be combined. Different parts of the examination usually have different weights. For example, the written test might count 60 percent of the final grade, and a rating of training and experience 40 percent. In many jurisdictions, veterans will have a certain number of points added to their grades.

After the final grade has been determined, the names are placed in grade order and an eligible list is established. There are various methods for resolving ties between those who get the same final grade – probably the most common is to place first the name of the person whose application was received first. Job offers are made from the eligible list in the order the names appear on it. You will be notified of your grade and your rank as soon as all these computations have been made. This will be done as rapidly as possible.

People who are found to meet the requirements in the announcement are called "eligibles." Their names are put on a list of eligible candidates. An eligible's chances of getting a job depend on how high he stands on this list and how fast agencies are filling jobs from the list.

When a job is to be filled from a list of eligibles, the agency asks for the names of people on the list of eligibles for that job. When the civil service commission receives this request, it sends to the agency the names of the three people highest on this list. Or, if the job to be filled has specialized requirements, the office sends the agency the names of the top three persons who meet these requirements from the general list.

The appointing officer makes a choice from among the three people whose names were sent to him. If the selected person accepts the appointment, the names of the others are put back on the list to be considered for future openings.

That is the rule in hiring from all kinds of eligible lists, whether they are for typist, carpenter, chemist, or something else. For every vacancy, the appointing officer has his choice of any one of the top three eligibles on the list. This explains why the person whose name is on top of the list sometimes does not get an appointment when some of the persons lower on the list do. If the appointing officer chooses the second or third eligible, the No. 1 eligible does not get a job at once, but stays on the list until he is appointed or the list is terminated.

X. HOW TO PASS THE INTERVIEW TEST

The examination for which you applied requires an oral interview test. You have already taken the written test and you are now being called for the interview test – the final part of the formal examination.

You may think that it is not possible to prepare for an interview test and that there are no procedures to follow during an interview. Our purpose is to point out some things you can do in advance that will help you and some good rules to follow and pitfalls to avoid while you are being interviewed.

What is an interview supposed to test?

The written examination is designed to test the technical knowledge and competence of the candidate; the oral is designed to evaluate intangible qualities, not readily measured otherwise, and to establish a list showing the relative fitness of each candidate – as measured against his competitors – for the position sought. Scoring is not on the basis of "right" and "wrong," but on a sliding scale of values ranging from "not passable" to "outstanding." As a matter of fact, it is possible to achieve a relatively low score without a single "incorrect" answer because of evident weakness in the qualities being measured.

Occasionally, an examination may consist entirely of an oral test – either an individual or a group oral. In such cases, information is sought concerning the technical knowledges and abilities of the candidate, since there has been no written examination for this purpose. More commonly, however, an oral test is used to supplement a written examination.

Who conducts interviews?

The composition of oral boards varies among different jurisdictions. In nearly all, a representative of the personnel department serves as chairman. One of the members of the board may be a representative of the department in which the candidate would work. In some cases, "outside experts" are used, and, frequently, a businessman or some other representative of the general public is asked to serve. Labor and management or other special groups may be represented. The aim is to secure the services of experts in the appropriate field.

However the board is composed, it is a good idea (and not at all improper or unethical) to ascertain in advance of the interview who the members are and what groups they represent. When you are introduced to them, you will have some idea of their backgrounds and interests, and at least you will not stutter and stammer over their names.

What should be done before the interview?

While knowledge about the board members is useful and takes some of the surprise element out of the interview, there is other preparation which is more substantive. It *is* possible to prepare for an oral interview – in several ways:

1) Keep a copy of your application and review it carefully before the interview

This may be the only document before the oral board, and the starting point of the interview. Know what education and experience you have listed there, and the sequence and dates of all of it. Sometimes the board will ask you to review the highlights of your experience for them; you should not have to hem and haw doing it.

2) Study the class specification and the examination announcement

Usually, the oral board has one or both of these to guide them. The qualities, characteristics or knowledges required by the position sought are stated in these documents. They offer valuable clues as to the nature of the oral interview. For example, if the job involves supervisory responsibilities, the announcement will usually indicate that knowledge of modern supervisory methods and the qualifications of the candidate as a supervisor will be tested. If so, you can expect such questions, frequently in the form of a hypothetical situation which you are expected to solve. NEVER go into an oral without knowledge of the duties and responsibilities of the job you seek.

3) Think through each qualification required

Try to visualize the kind of questions you would ask if you were a board member. How well could you answer them? Try especially to appraise your own knowledge and background in each area, *measured against the job sought*, and identify any areas in which you are weak. Be critical and realistic – do not flatter yourself.

4) Do some general reading in areas in which you feel you may be weak

For example, if the job involves supervision and your past experience has NOT, some general reading in supervisory methods and practices, particularly in the field of human relations, might be useful. Do NOT study agency procedures or detailed manuals. The oral board will be testing your understanding and capacity, not your memory.

5) Get a good night's sleep and watch your general health and mental attitude

You will want a clear head at the interview. Take care of a cold or any other minor ailment, and of course, no hangovers.

What should be done on the day of the interview?

Now comes the day of the interview itself. Give yourself plenty of time to get there. Plan to arrive somewhat ahead of the scheduled time, particularly if your appointment is in the fore part of the day. If a previous candidate fails to appear, the board might be ready for you a bit early. By early afternoon an oral board is almost invariably behind schedule if there are many candidates, and you may have to wait. Take along a book or magazine to read, or your application to review, but leave any extraneous material in the waiting room when you go in for your interview. In any event, relax and compose yourself.

The matter of dress is important. The board is forming impressions about you – from your experience, your manners, your attitude, and your appearance. Give your personal appearance careful attention. Dress your best, but not your flashiest. Choose conservative, appropriate clothing, and be sure it is immaculate. This is a business interview, and your appearance should indicate that you regard it as such. Besides, being well groomed and properly dressed will help boost your confidence.

Sooner or later, someone will call your name and escort you into the interview room. *This is it.* From here on you are on your own. It is too late for any more preparation. But remember, you asked for this opportunity to prove your fitness, and you are here because your request was granted.

What happens when you go in?

The usual sequence of events will be as follows: The clerk (who is often the board stenographer) will introduce you to the chairman of the oral board, who will introduce you to the other members of the board. Acknowledge the introductions before you sit down. Do not be surprised if you find a microphone facing you or a stenotypist sitting by. Oral interviews are usually recorded in the event of an appeal or other review.

Usually the chairman of the board will open the interview by reviewing the highlights of your education and work experience from your application – primarily for the benefit of the other members of the board, as well as to get the material into the record. Do not interrupt or comment unless there is an error or significant misinterpretation; if that is the case, do not hesitate. But do not quibble about insignificant matters. Also, he will usually ask you some question about your education, experience or your present job – partly to get you to start talking and to establish the interviewing "rapport." He may start the actual questioning, or turn it over to one of the other members. Frequently, each member undertakes the questioning on a particular area, one in which he is perhaps most competent, so you can expect each member to participate in the examination. Because time is limited, you may also expect some rather abrupt switches in the direction the questioning takes, so do not be upset by it. Normally, a board member will not pursue a single line of questioning unless he discovers a particular strength or weakness.

After each member has participated, the chairman will usually ask whether any member has any further questions, then will ask you if you have anything you wish to add. Unless you are expecting this question, it may floor you. Worse, it may start you off on an extended, extemporaneous speech. The board is not usually seeking more information. The question is principally to offer you a last opportunity to present further qualifications or to indicate that you have nothing to add. So, if you feel that a significant qualification or characteristic has been overlooked, it is proper to point it out in a sentence or so. Do not compliment the board on the thoroughness of their examination – they have been sketchy, and you know it. If you wish, merely say, "No thank you, I have nothing further to add." This is a point where you can "talk yourself out" of a good impression or fail to present an important bit of information. Remember, *you close the interview yourself.*

The chairman will then say, "That is all, Mr. _____, thank you." Do not be startled; the interview is over, and quicker than you think. Thank him, gather your belongings and take your leave. Save your sigh of relief for the other side of the door.

How to put your best foot forward

Throughout this entire process, you may feel that the board individually and collectively is trying to pierce your defenses, seek out your hidden weaknesses and embarrass and confuse you. Actually, this is not true. They are obliged to make an appraisal of your qualifications for the job you are seeking, and they want to see you in your best light. Remember, they must interview all candidates and a non-cooperative candidate may become a failure in spite of their best efforts to bring out his qualifications. Here are 15 suggestions that will help you:

1) Be natural – Keep your attitude confident, not cocky

If you are not confident that you can do the job, do not expect the board to be. Do not apologize for your weaknesses, try to bring out your strong points. The board is interested in a positive, not negative, presentation. Cockiness will antagonize any board member and make him wonder if you are covering up a weakness by a false show of strength.

2) Get comfortable, but don't lounge or sprawl

Sit erectly but not stiffly. A careless posture may lead the board to conclude that you are careless in other things, or at least that you are not impressed by the importance of the occasion. Either conclusion is natural, even if incorrect. Do not fuss with your clothing, a pencil or an ashtray. Your hands may occasionally be useful to emphasize a point; do not let them become a point of distraction.

3) Do not wisecrack or make small talk

This is a serious situation, and your attitude should show that you consider it as such. Further, the time of the board is limited – they do not want to waste it, and neither should you.

4) Do not exaggerate your experience or abilities

In the first place, from information in the application or other interviews and sources, the board may know more about you than you think. Secondly, you probably will not get away with it. An experienced board is rather adept at spotting such a situation, so do not take the chance.

5) If you know a board member, do not make a point of it, yet do not hide it

Certainly you are not fooling him, and probably not the other members of the board. Do not try to take advantage of your acquaintanceship – it will probably do you little good.

6) Do not dominate the interview

Let the board do that. They will give you the clues – do not assume that you have to do all the talking. Realize that the board has a number of questions to ask you, and do not try to take up all the interview time by showing off your extensive knowledge of the answer to the first one.

7) Be attentive

You only have 20 minutes or so, and you should keep your attention at its sharpest throughout. When a member is addressing a problem or question to you, give him your undivided attention. Address your reply principally to him, but do not exclude the other board members.

8) Do not interrupt

A board member may be stating a problem for you to analyze. He will ask you a question when the time comes. Let him state the problem, and wait for the question.

9) Make sure you understand the question

Do not try to answer until you are sure what the question is. If it is not clear, restate it in your own words or ask the board member to clarify it for you. However, do not haggle about minor elements.

10) Reply promptly but not hastily

A common entry on oral board rating sheets is "candidate responded readily," or "candidate hesitated in replies." Respond as promptly and quickly as you can, but do not jump to a hasty, ill-considered answer.

11) Do not be peremptory in your answers

A brief answer is proper – but do not fire your answer back. That is a losing game from your point of view. The board member can probably ask questions much faster than you can answer them.

12) Do not try to create the answer you think the board member wants

He is interested in what kind of mind you have and how it works – not in playing games. Furthermore, he can usually spot this practice and will actually grade you down on it.

13) Do not switch sides in your reply merely to agree with a board member

Frequently, a member will take a contrary position merely to draw you out and to see if you are willing and able to defend your point of view. Do not start a debate, yet do not surrender a good position. If a position is worth taking, it is worth defending.

14) Do not be afraid to admit an error in judgment if you are shown to be wrong

The board knows that you are forced to reply without any opportunity for careful consideration. Your answer may be demonstrably wrong. If so, admit it and get on with the interview.

15) Do not dwell at length on your present job

The opening question may relate to your present assignment. Answer the question but do not go into an extended discussion. You are being examined for a *new* job, not your present one. As a matter of fact, try to phrase ALL your answers in terms of the job for which you are being examined.

Basis of Rating

Probably you will forget most of these "do's" and "don'ts" when you walk into the oral interview room. Even remembering them all will not ensure you a passing grade. Perhaps you did not have the qualifications in the first place. But remembering them will help you to put your best foot forward, without treading on the toes of the board members.

Rumor and popular opinion to the contrary notwithstanding, an oral board wants you to make the best appearance possible. They know you are under pressure – but they also want to see how you respond to it as a guide to what your reaction would be under the pressures of the job you seek. They will be influenced by the degree of poise you display, the personal traits you show and the manner in which you respond.

ABOUT THIS BOOK

This book contains tests divided into Examination Sections. Go through each test, answering every question in the margin. We have also attached a sample answer sheet at the back of the book that can be removed and used. At the end of each test look at the answer key and check your answers. On the ones you got wrong, look at the right answer choice and learn. Do not fill in the answers first. Do not memorize the questions and answers, but understand the answer and principles involved. On your test, the questions will likely be different from the samples. Questions are changed and new ones added. If you understand these past questions you should have success with any changes that arise. Tests may consist of several types of questions. We have additional books on each subject should more study be advisable or necessary for you. Finally, the more you study, the better prepared you will be. This book is intended to be the last thing you study before you walk into the examination room. Prior study of relevant texts is also recommended. NLC publishes some of these in our Fundamental Series. Knowledge and good sense are important factors in passing your exam. Good luck also helps. So now study this Passbook, absorb the material contained within and take that knowledge into the examination. Then do your best to pass that exam.

EXAMINATION SECTION

EXAMINATION SECTION
TEST 1

DIRECTIONS: Each question or incomplete statement is followed by several suggested answers or completions. Select the one that BEST answers the question or completes the statement. *PRINT THE LETTER OF THE CORRECT ANSWER IN THE SPACE AT THE RIGHT.*

1. Analysis of a system deals with 1.____
   - A. study of an existing system
   - B. documenting an existing system
   - C. only new systems
   - D. both A and B

2. The primary tool that is used in structured design is known as a 2.____
   - A. data flow diagram
   - B. module
   - C. flow chart
   - D. structure chart

3. Documentation is required at the _____ stage. 3.____
   - A. system analysis
   - B. system design
   - C. system development
   - D. every stage

4. Which one of the following is NOT a factor in the failure of systems development projects? 4.____
   - A. Size of the company
   - B. Inadequate user involvement
   - C. Failure of integration
   - D. Both A and B

5. Which one of the following is considered in system maintenance? 5.____
   - A. System requirements
   - B. Analysis
   - C. Testing
   - D. Remove faults after delivery

6. Which one of the following cannot be used to capture a user's requirements? 6.____
   - A. Interviews
   - B. Questionnaire
   - C. Third-party inquiry
   - D. Observation

7. Cost-Benefit Analysis is performed during the 7.____
   - A. analysis phase
   - B. feasibility study
   - C. design phase
   - D. maintenance phase

8. System development life cycle is divided into _____ stages. 8.____
   - A. five   B. four   C. six   D. seven

9. _____ is the first stage in system development life cycle. 9.____
   - A. Analysis
   - B. Design
   - C. Problem identification
   - D. Development

10. The _____ determines whether a project should go forward or not. 10.____
    - A. feasibility assessment
    - B. system evaluation
    - C. program specification
    - D. both A and B

11. The _____ manages the system development, assigns staff, manages the budget and reporting, and ensures that deadlines are met.
    A. system analyst B. project manager
    C. network engineer D. graphic designer

12. The structure chart that is developed by studying the flow through a system assists the activities of _____ design.
    A. internal control B. database C. output D. file

13. Which one of the following is an INCORRECT statement for the definition of a use case diagram?
    A. It is used to understand requirements
    B. It is an interaction between user and the system
    C. It demonstrates flow of activities
    D. It is used for requirement analysis

14. Which one of the following is NOT a relationship type in use case diagrams?
    A. Include B. Extend C. Aggregation D. Association

15. A(n) _____ diagram is NOT an interaction diagram of the UML.
    A. activity B. sequence C. class D. both A and B

16. Physical components of the system are modeled through a(n) _____ diagram.
    A. component B. class C. activity D. use case

17. In UML, a built-in extensibility mechanism is obtained through
    A. association B. stereotypes C. notations D. comments

18. Software testing that does not require knowledge of the internal code is known as _____ testing.
    A. black box B. gray box C. white box D. regression

19. Total life cycle cost of a software in terms of largest percentage is called _____ cost.
    A. analysis B. coding C. testing D. maintenance

20. Which one of the following is NOT a characteristic of waterfall process model?
    A. Rigid approach B. Sequence of activities
    C. Back-and-forth movement D. Less use these days

21. _____ feasibility determines the availability of support staff and team.
    A. Resource B. Cultural C. Economic D. Schedule

22. Which one of the following is used to represent the schedule of a project?
    A. DFD B. ERD C. GANTT D. CPM

23. _____ is not used in a context level diagram.
    A. Data store B. Data flow C. Process D. Destination

24. In dynamic system development, business requirements are gathered through
    A. JAD
    B. a flip chart
    C. an overhead projector
    D. a board

    24.____

25. A systems analyst determines the use of the system by analyzing the _____ diagram.
    A. use case	B. class	C. activity	D. sequence

    25.____

KEY (CORRECT ANSWERS)

1. D
2. D
3. D
4. A
5. D

6. C
7. B
8. C
9. C
10. A

11. B
12. A
13. C
14. C
15. C

16. A
17. B
18. A
19. D
20. C

21. A
22. C
23. A
24. A
25. A

TEST 2

DIRECTIONS: Each question or incomplete statement is followed by several suggested answers or completions. Select the one that BEST answers the question or completes the statement. *PRINT THE LETTER OF THE CORRECT ANSWER IN THE SPACE AT THE RIGHT.*

1. Data store in DFD represents
   A. disk store
   B. data repository
   C. data
   D. sequential file

   1.____

2. Programs, data files and documentation are an essential part of the _____ system.
   A. conceptual   B. logical   C. physical   D. data

   2.____

3. The _____ phase is very time consuming and crucial.
   A. design   B. analysis   C. development   D. testing

   3.____

4. The _____ phase of the SDLC (Software Development Life Cycle) identifies all of the required information.
   A. system analysis
   B. system design
   C. testing
   D. preliminary investigation

   4.____

5. The _____ provides the documentation of the new system.
   A. system analyst
   B. technical writer
   C. programmer
   D. requirement engineer

   5.____

6. Which one of the following implementation approaches has the LOWEST risk?
   A. Direct   B. Parallel   C. Pilot   D. Phased

   6.____

7. In the system analysis phase, _____ is/are defined.
   A. requirements
   B. program specification
   C. goals
   D. flow of events

   7.____

8. In UML, an optional behavior is specified when _____ relationship is used.
   A. extend   B. include   C. association   D. aggregation

   8.____

9. The _____ is NOT a participant in the requirement definition.
   A. developer
   B. end user
   C. client manager
   D. client engineer

   9.____

10. _____ is an ongoing phase in which the system is evaluated and updated periodically.
    A. Analysis   B. Testing   C. Maintenance   D. Implementation

    10.____

11. _____ is the last step in the system analysis phase.
    A. Collecting data
    B. Proposing changes
    C. Analyzing data
    D. System analysis report

    11.____

12. Which one of the following is a fact-finding technique?
    A. Quality assurance
    B. Sampling of existing documents
    C. Prototyping
    D. Requirement specification

13. Data dictionary in SDLC includes description of
    A. DFD elements
    B. class diagram
    C. ERD
    D. component diagram

14. _____ is the graphical notation that is used in UML.
    A. Stereotype   B. Meta model   C. Model   D. Multiplicity

15. Which one of the following is used in analysis?
    A. Grid table
    B. Check list
    C. Sheet
    D. Interview guidelines

16. DDS is an abbreviation of
    A. Data Digital System
    B. Data Dictionary System
    C. Digital Data Service
    D. Data Defense System

17. Which one of the following is NOT included in DFD?
    A. Processes
    B. Entities
    C. File
    D. Offline storage

18. CASE stands for Computer _____ Engineering.
    A. Aided Software
    B. Analysis and System
    C. Aided System
    D. Analyzed System

19. The first step in application prototyping is
    A. to develop a working model
    B. to identify known requirements
    C. to review prototype
    D. the use of prototype

20. Which one of the following skills is NOT required for the system analyst?
    A. Management
    B. Communication
    C. Technical
    D. Programming

21. In SDLC, a system proposal is developed during the _____ phase.
    A. planning   B. analysis   C. design   D. development

22. Which one of the following provides fast delivery?
    A. Prototyping   B. RAD   C. Spiral   D. Iterative

23. The _____ diagram is a time-oriented diagram.
    A. sequence   B. activity   C. class   D. use case

24. The _____ diagram shows complete or partial view of the structure of a modeled system at a specific time.
    A. class   B. object   C. activity   D. sequence

25. Which one of the following UML diagrams shows static view of the system?   25._____
    A. Use case   B. Collaboration   C. State chart   D. Activity

---

KEY (CORRECT ANSWERS)

1.	B		11.	D
2.	C		12.	B
3.	B		13.	A
4.	D		14.	B
5.	B		15.	B
6.	D		16.	B
7.	B		17.	D
8.	A		18.	A
9.	A		19.	B
10.	C		20.	D

21. B
22. B
23. A
24. B
25. A

TEST 3

DIRECTIONS: Each question or incomplete statement is followed by several suggested answers or completions. Select the one that BEST answers the question or completes the statement. *PRINT THE LETTER OF THE CORRECT ANSWER IN THE SPACE AT THE RIGHT.*

1. Functionality of the system is known as _____ of the system. 1.____
   A. requirement
   B. business need
   C. sponsors
   D. fact

2. The systems analyst determines the system usage through 2.____
   A. actors
   B. use case
   C. package
   D. component

3. _____ occurs in use case to trigger the system. 3.____
   A. Data flow
   B. Process
   C. Event
   D. Data store

4. The _____ system is only an idea that has yet to progress to later stages. 4.____
   A. logical
   B. physical
   C. conceptual
   D. legacy

5. Software testing aims to 5.____
   A. uncover errors
   B. eliminate errors
   C. eliminate need of maintenance
   D. determine productivity of programmers

6. Another name used for black box testing is 6.____
   A. verification
   B. validation
   C. specification-based testing
   D. gray box testing

7. Which of the following diagrams is NOT a UML diagram? 7.____
   A. Broadcast
   B. Component
   C. State chart
   D. Deployment

8. Another term for encapsulation is 8.____
   A. generalization
   B. polymorphism
   C. information hiding
   D. association

9. _____ is not a characteristic of an object. 9.____
   A. Identity
   B. Behavior
   C. Action
   D. State

10. In feasibility study, the _____ feasibility always focuses on the existing computer hardware and software. 10.____
    A. logical
    B. behavior
    C. economic
    D. technical

11. In SDLC, the last step in the development phase is 11.____
    A. documentation
    B. testing the system
    C. acquiring hardware
    D. acquiring software

12. In a DFD, external entities are represented by a(n)
    A. eclipse   B. circle   C. rectangle   D. diamond

13. _____ means using an old system and new system simultaneously to compare the result.
    A. File conversion   B. Parallel operation
    C. Procedure writing   D. Simultaneous processing

14. _____ specification is prepared after the design phase.
    A. System   B. Performance   C. Design   D. Code

15. System _____ is the MOST comprehensive and recent technique to solve computer problems.
    A. analysis   B. data   C. procedure   D. record

16. A data flow diagram is a basic component of the _____ system.
    A. physical   B. logical   C. conceptual   D. real

17. Enhancements, upgrades and bug fixes are done at the _____ phase of SDLC.
    A. development   B. identification
    C. design   D. maintenance and evaluation

18. In a system analyst's job, identification of requirement specifications is similar to _____ a building.
    A. an architect designing   B. a structural engineer designing
    C. a contractor constructing D. the workers who construct

19. It is essential to consult with _____ when drawing requirement specifications.
    A. only managers
    B. only top and middle management
    C. operational managers
    D. top, middle and operational managers and also all who will use the system

20. A feasibility study is carried out by the
    A. system analyst
    B. manager
    C. technical writer
    D. system analyst in consultation with managers of the organization

21. A class is a description of a set of objects that share the same
    A. attributes, behavior and operations
    B. identity, behavior and state
    C. attributes, operations and relationships
    D. relationship, operation and multiplicity

22. A(n) _____ diagram is an interaction diagram that involves time ordering messages.
    A. sequence   B. collaboration   C. activity   D. state

23. _____ measures the strength of association among objects.
    A. Cohesion   B. Coupling
    C. Interaction   D. Collaboration

24. _____ is a combination of data and logic that represents some real-world entities.
    A. Class   B. Attribute   C. Object   D. Relationship

25. A _____ diagram represents the hierarchal relationship between the modules of a computer program.
    A. state chart   B. data flow   C. class   D. activity

KEY (CORRECT ANSWERS)

1.	A		11.	B
2.	B		12.	C
3.	C		13.	B
4.	C		14.	C
5.	A		15.	A
6.	C		16.	B
7.	A		17.	D
8.	C		18.	A
9.	C		19.	D
10.	D		20.	D

21.	C
22.	A
23.	B
24.	C
25.	A

TEST 4

DIRECTIONS: Each question or incomplete statement is followed by several suggested answers or completions. Select the one that BEST answers the question or completes the statement. *PRINT THE LETTER OF THE CORRECT ANSWER IN THE SPACE AT THE RIGHT.*

1. System approval criteria is specified
    A. during the feasibility study
    B. when the final specifications are drawn up
    C. during system study stage
    D. during requirement specification stage

    1.____

2. The PRIMARY objective of system design is to
    A. implement the system
    B. design user interface
    C. find functionality
    D. design the program, database and test plan

    2.____

3. Whenever _____ are changed, the system must be modified.
    A. user requirements   B. test plans
    C. software   D. companies

    3.____

4. What is MOST important when modifying an existing system?
    A. Software tools   B. Hardware
    C. Programming   D. System design at low cost

    4.____

5. Managers cannot design their own system because
    A. this is not their job
    B. they are busy
    C. they don't have required skills for system analysis
    D. the system is novel

    5.____

6. System components can be represented through
    A. DFD   B. PERT   C. GANTT   D. ERD

    6.____

7. Which one of the following cannot be included in phase four of SDLC?
    A. User training   B. Testing
    C. Conducting interviews D. Acquiring hardware/software

    7.____

8. Programmers use _____ to summarize and organize results of problem analysis.
    A. a flow chart   B. an input chart
    C. an output chart   D. HIPO

    8.____

9. Coding and testing are done in a(n) _____ manner.
    A. top-down   B. bottom-up   C. ad hoc   D. cross-sectional

    9.____

10. _____ is the FIRST step in the problem-solving process.
    A. Algorithm planning B. Problem analysis
    C. Evaluation D. Modification

11. Any mistake in system analysis will be exposed during
    A. implementation B. design C. development D. maintenance

12. Which one of the following does NOT belong to the implementation phase?
    A. User training B. File conversion
    C. Program testing D. Designing

13. File conversion is related to system
    A. design B. development C. analysis D. implementation

14. _____ is NOT used in the design phase of the system.
    A. Data flow B. Decision table
    C. Flow chart D. Pie chart

15. Which one of the following is NOT used for system analysis?
    A. Decision table B. Flow charts
    C. Data flow diagrams D. System-test data

16. Initial requirement specification is
    A. not changed until the end of the project
    B. is subject to change continuously
    C. only a rough indication of the requirements
    D. finalized after the feasibility study

17. System test plan is specified when
    A. final specifications are done B. a feasibility study is completed
    C. analysis is done D. design is done

18. The organization chart is a type of _____ chart.
    A. basic B. state C. flow D. hieratical

19. Structure of an organization could be shown through a(n)
    A. state chart B. HIPO
    C. data flow D. organization chart

20. A(n) _____ diagram represents static behavior of the system.
    A. class B. object C. flow chart D. both A and B

21. Which one of the following diagrams is similar to a flow chart?
    A. Sequence B. Use case C. Activity D. Class

22. A(n) _____ diagram is not a structural diagram in UML.
    A. class B. component C. object D. use case

23. A _____ diagram is an example of a behavior diagram. 23._____
    A. collaboration   B. class   C. component   D. deployment

24. The purpose of a(n) _____ diagram is to visualize the organization of 24._____
    objects and their interaction.
    A. collaboration   B. object   C. class   D. activity

25. _____ is used in a class diagram to represent the concurrency of the system. 25._____
    A. Class   B. Activity class
    C. Super class   D. Object

KEY (CORRECT ANSWERS)

1.	B	11.	A
2.	D	12.	C
3.	A	13.	D
4.	D	14.	D
5.	C	15.	D
6.	A	16.	C
7.	C	17.	A
8.	D	18.	D
9.	A	19.	D
10.	B	20.	A

21.	C
22.	D
23.	A
24.	A
25.	B

EXAMINATION SECTION
TEST 1

DIRECTIONS: Each question or incomplete statement is followed by several suggested answers or completions. Select the one that BEST answers the question or completes the statement. *PRINT THE LETTER OF THE CORRECT ANSWER IN THE SPACE AT THE RIGHT.*

1. Knowledge work systems are most typically used by each of the following personnel EXCEPT

    A. middle managers
    B. salespeople
    C. engineers
    D. accountants

2. A media-oriented description of a system's operations is BEST represented by a(n)

    A. systems flowchart
    B. system requirements plan
    C. Gantt chart
    D. program flowchart

3. During preliminary analysis, a feasibility group will study the three fundamental operations of an existing system.
Which of the following is NOT one of these operations?

    A. Output of information
    B. Data processing
    C. Coding
    D. Data preparation and input

4. Normally, the starting point of any systems design is to determine the

    A. output
    B. hardware
    C. throughput
    D. users

5. From its beginnings, the total time required for an entire systems analysis and design process to be completed will MOST likely be

    A. 6-12 months
    B. 12-18 months
    C. 2-3 years
    D. 3-5 years

6. In a data flow diagram, a square like the one shown at the right would be used to represent

    A. input to the system
    B. a terminal
    C. magnetic tape
    D. a display

7. A _____ systems conversion takes place when the old system is switched off and the new one is started up.

    A. day-one   B. direct   C. parallel   D. pilot

8. The MOST common reason for the failure of an information system is

    A. faulty programming
    B. hardware obsolescence
    C. interface complications
    D. faulty problem identification

9. A personnel record in a master file consists of the following fields, containing the indicated number of characters.

Field	Number of Characters
Identication number	5
Social Security number	9
Name	25
Address	35
Sex	2
Code number	1

If the master file contains 2,000 transactions, then approximately how many characters would the file be expected to hold?

A. 56,000   B. 115,500   C. 154,000   D. 231,000

10. Which of the following is NOT one of the primary elements of a data flow diagram?

A. Process
B. External entity
C. Rule number
D. Data store

11. During systems design, each of the following is a consideration involving input EXCEPT

A. media
B. validity checking
C. volume
D. security

12. The MAIN advantage involved with the use of pilot systems conversion is

A. speed of conversion process
B. provides constant backup media
C. makes file conversion unnecessary
D. minimizes problems by confining operations

13. _____ is NOT a type of systems control.

A. Auditing
B. Contingency planning
C. Data security
D. Data control

14. In a _____ type of systems conversion, various capabilities are added to the system over a number of years.

A. graduated   B. pilot   C. phased   D. indirect

15. Which of the following is NOT a standard classification for a system in terms of cost-effectiveness?

A. Risky
B. Safe
C. Pioneering
D. Prudent

16. _____ accounts for the GREATEST expenditure involved in the cost of creating and maintaining a system.

A. Systems design
B. Equipment
C. Evaluation and maintenance
D. Implementation

17. Which of the following is NOT one of the procedures involved in program development? 17._____

    A. Program preparation
    B. Systems audit evaluation
    C. Scheduling
    D. Testing

18. The PRIMARY purpose of the systems analysis phase of the entire analysis and design process is to 18._____

    A. compose an accurate data flow diagram
    B. determine input, output, and processing requirements
    C. determine whether to modify the existing system or convert completely to a new one
    D. consider the people who will be interacting with the new system

19. Which of the following is NOT a major problem associated with systems building? 19._____

    A. Coordination costs
    B. Hardware currency
    C. Requirements analysis
    D. Record keeping

20. Typically, a workable system is the output of the _____ phase of systems analysis and design. 20._____

    A. systems development
    B. systems analysis
    C. systems design
    D. implementation

21. The MOST reliable means of obtaining information about an existing system can be obtained through the use of 21._____

    A. observations
    B. personal interviews
    C. questionnaires
    D. written forms

22. The purpose of a printer spacing chart is to 22._____

    A. represent the exact format of a system's output
    B. assist in data validity checking
    C. coordinate all related fields into a single report
    D. describe the input data needed to produce the system's output

23. The FIRST procedure in a system test plan is usually _____ testing. 23._____

    A. crash proof
    B. system
    C. personnel
    D. unit

24. The cost-benefit analysis of a proposed system is USUALLY performed during the _____ phase of analysis and design. 24._____

    A. systems design
    B. systems analysis
    C. preliminary analysis
    D. implementation

25. The MOST significant output of the systems analysis phase of the entire analysis and design process is the 25._____

    A. detailed system design
    B. system requirements plan
    C. installed and operational system
    D. preliminary plan

KEY (CORRECT ANSWERS)

1.	B	11.	D
2.	A	12.	D
3.	C	13.	A
4.	A	14.	C
5.	C	15.	A
6.	A	16.	D
7.	B	17.	B
8.	D	18.	C
9.	C	19.	B
10.	C	20.	A

21. B
22. A
23. D
24. A
25. B

TEST 2

DIRECTIONS: Each question or incomplete statement is followed by several suggested answers or completions. Select the one that BEST answers the question or completes the statement. *PRINT THE LETTER OF THE CORRECT ANSWER IN THE SPACE AT THE RIGHT.*

1. Systems maintenance involves three important factors that are considered during the design and development phases of a project. Which of the following is NOT one of these three?

    A. Structured programming
    B. System documentation
    C. System auditing
    D. Anticipation of future needs

    1.____

2. In a data flow diagram, an open-ended rectangle like the one shown at the right would be used to represent

    A. an invoice
    B. a punched card
    C. data storage
    D. data preparation

    2.____

3. Systems design reports normally include each of the following EXCEPT a(n)

    A. review of the problems associated with the present system
    B. overview of the proposed system
    C. summation of the major findings of the cost-benefit analysis
    D. list of hardware recommended for the proposed system

    3.____

4. A _____ group is NOT usually involved in a typical systems project team.

    A. vendor
    B. user
    C. management
    D. programming

    4.____

5. The _____ method of systems conversion is typically the riskiest.

    A. parallel   B. pilot   C. day-one   D. direct

    5.____

6. The PRIMARY purpose of a decision table used in systems analysis is to

    A. describe the sequence of operations that must be performed to obtain a computer solution to a problem
    B. represent all the combinations of conditions that must be satisfied before an action can be taken
    C. describe the operations to be performed by the system, with a major emphasis on the media involved, as well as the workstations through which they pass
    D. graphically depict the flow of data and the processes that change or transform data throughout the system

    6.____

7. Which of the following is used to describe a system's necessary input data?

    A. Systems flowchart
    B. CRT layout form
    C. Data flow diagram
    D. Record layout form

    7.____

17

8. The LONGEST phase involved in the systems analysis and design process is the _____ phase.

   A. implementation
   B. systems design
   C. systems development
   D. preliminary analysis

9. The systems development phase of analysis and design normally includes each of the following EXCEPT

   A. purchase of equipment
   B. program testing
   C. user training
   D. program development

10. In cases where it is too expensive to convert a system's old files and applications, a(n) _____ system conversion is commonly used.

    A. parallel   B. pilot   C. direct   D. day-one

11. The PRIMARY purpose of an audit trail is to

    A. trace specific input data to its related output
    B. error-check a new systems program
    C. locate workstations where unauthorized users are at work
    D. check data validity

12. A system requirements plan typically includes each of the following EXCEPT

    A. description of how existing system works
    B. hardware requirements for the new system
    C. information necessary for the new system
    D. major problems of existing system

13. A _____ is typically a member of the programming group of a systems project team.

    A. vendor
    B. user
    C. management
    D. librarian

14. The implementation phase of systems analysis and design does NOT usually include

    A. training
    B. auditing
    C. programming
    D. system conversion

15. The _____ is a document created by the systems project team that takes into account the organizational constraints and the personnel involved in using a new system.

    A. system requirements report
    B. statement of objectives
    C. test plan
    D. request for proposal

16. Which of the following is used as an aid to scheduling system operations?

    A. Gantt chart
    B. Circle graph
    C. Chief programmer
    D. Head node

17. The MAIN disadvantage associated with parallel systems conversion is that 17._____

    A. it usually takes more time than all other approaches
    B. there is costly duplication of personnel efforts and equipment
    C. confusion is involved in constant switch-overs
    D. no backup is provided

18. Transaction processing systems are LEAST likely to be used by 18._____

    A. knowledge professionals
    B. data entry specialists
    C. customers
    D. clerks

19. When a new system is used in its entirety only in one locality or area, _____ is being 19._____
    practiced.

    A. batch processing   B. live data analysis
    C. pilot conversion   D. file conversion

20. Which of the following is NOT a software tool that has been developed to help a systems 20._____
    analyst build better systems in a more timely and cost-effective manner?

    A. CAD tools   B. Project management tools
    C. Prototyping   D. CASE tools

21. Action stubs and conditions entries are components of the 21._____

    A. program flowchart   B. decision table
    C. system flowchart   D. Gantt chart

22. When both an old and a new system are run simultaneously for a period of time to 22._____
    ensure the new system's proper operation, _____ is being practiced.

    A. incremental auditing   B. file conversion
    C. parallel conversion   D. direct switch-over

23. The FIRST operation performed during the implementation phase of analysis and design 23._____
    is usually

    A. file conversion   B. systems evaluation
    C. systems conversion   D. auditing

24. Typically, programming accounts for _____% of the hours spent on systems analysis 24._____
    and design.

    A. 10   B. 20   C. 35   D. 45

25. In a data flow diagram, a circle like the one shown at the right would be used to 25._____
    represent

    A. output from the system
    B. a single file
    C. a manual action
    D. a process that transforms data in some way

KEY (CORRECT ANSWERS)

1. C
2. C
3. D
4. A
5. D

6. B
7. D
8. C
9. C
10. D

11. A
12. B
13. D
14. C
15. B

16. A
17. B
18. A
19. C
20. A

21. B
22. C
23. A
24. B
25. D

EXAMINATION SECTION
TEST 1

DIRECTIONS: Each question or incomplete statement is followed by several suggested answers or completions. Select the one that BEST answers the question or completes the statement. *PRINT THE LETTER OF THE CORRECT ANSWER IN THE SPACE AT THE RIGHT.*

1. The analysis phase of the systems process is divided into

    A. preliminary and detailed
    B. input and output
    C. hardware and software
    D. costs and benefits
    E. people and procedures

1.____

2. Detailed analysis involves

    A. an investigation of the existing system
    B. how an organization collects data
    C. how an organization processes data
    D. how to improve the processing of data
    E. all of the above

2.____

3. When conducting the detailed analysis, the analyst consults with

    A. users
    B. outside vendors
    C. management
    D. other members of the computing services staff
    E. all of the above

3.____

4. Before starting the detailed analysis, the analyst reviews the

    A. organization chart
    C. database design
    E. program specifications
    B. preliminary report
    D. screen lay-out formats

4.____

5. An output from analysis is the

    A. program specifications
    B. module specifications
    C. input data collection screen designs
    D. feasibility study
    E. database design

5.____

6. The FIRST task in detailed analysis is

    A. fact-finding
    B. presentation of analysis to management
    C. review and assignment
    D. interviewing users
    E. none of the above

6.____

21

7. The LAST task in detailed analysis is

   A. fact-finding
   B. presentation of analysis to management
   C. review and assignment
   D. interviewing users
   E. none of the above

8. A tool an analyst can use to assist in scheduling is the

   A. data flow diagram   B. Gantt chart
   C. Warnier-Orr diagram   D. CPM chart
   E. HIPO chart

9. In a Gantt chart, events are listed

   A. as bars
   B. as rectangles
   C. along the left-hand side
   D. along the right-hand side
   E. across the bottom

10. In a Gantt chart personnel assigned to events are listed

    A. as bars
    B. as rectangles
    C. along the left-hand side
    D. along the right-hand side
    E. across the bottom

11. As tasks are completed, the analyst updates the Gantt chart by

    A. filling in hollow horizontal bars
    B. completing a worksheet
    C. reviewing the task assignments
    D. notifying management
    E. none of the above

12. Fact-finding means an analyst needs to

    A. learn as much as possible about the system
    B. interview all company personnel
    C. review the systems study
    D. review the program specifications
    E. talk with hardware vendors

13. Which one of the following is NOT a part of the four W's the analyst must ask?

    A. Who is involved?
    B. What do you do?
    C. While you do it, what are others doing?
    D. Why do you do it the way you do?
    E. When do you do it?

14. Users should be notified of the detailed analysis by 14._____

    A. telephone call
    B. general meeting
    C. a memorandum
    D. a notice in the company newsletter
    E. a meeting at the water fountain

15. During fact-finding, the analyst gathers together 15._____

    A. forms
    B. documents
    C. interviews with key staff members
    D. observations of the system
    E. all of the above

16. Questions posed on a questionnaire should be 16._____

    A. worded using computer jargon
    B. lead the responder to draw conclusions
    C. nonthreatening
    D. vague
    E. general purpose

17. Which type of questionnaire gives respondents a specific set of potential answers? 17._____

    A. Open-ended   B. Multiple choice
    C. Rating   D. Rank
    E. None of the above

18. Which type of questionnaire gives respondents a chance to answer in their own words? 18._____

    A. Open-ended   B. Multiple choice
    C. Rating   D. Rank
    E. None of the above

19. Which type of questionnaire gives respondents a chance to show their satisfaction? 19._____

    A. Open-ended   B. Multiple choice
    C. Rating   D. Rank
    E. None of the above

20. Which type of questionnaire gives respondents a chance to prioritize on a high to low basis? 20._____

    A. Open-ended   B. Multiple choice
    C. Rating   D. Rank
    E. None of the above

KEY (CORRECT ANSWERS)

1. A
2. E
3. E
4. B
5. D

6. C
7. B
8. B
9. C
10. E

11. A
12. A
13. C
14. C
15. E

16. C
17. B
18. A
19. C
20. D

TEST 2

DIRECTIONS: Each question or incomplete statement is followed by several suggested answers or completions. Select the one that BEST answers the question or completes the statement. *PRINT THE LETTER OF THE CORRECT ANSWER IN THE SPACE AT THE RIGHT.*

1. When observing an existing system, an analyst should be   1.____

    A. an observer
    B. a questioner
    C. a part of the system
    D. an answerer
    E. making value judgments

2. When observing a system, it is LIKELY that the system will   2.____

    A. not function
    B. operate 500% faster
    C. operate 50% slower
    D. operate differently than it normally does
    E. none of the above

3. After observing the system, the analyst can draw a diagram of the logical system using which of the following techniques?   3.____

    A. Data flow diagram
    B. Gantt chart
    C. HIPO chart
    D. PERT chart
    E. IPD chart

4. A data flow diagram that shows a system in its MOST general form is called a(n) _____ DFD.   4.____

    A. analysis
    B. context
    C. levelled
    D. decomposed
    E. system

5. A data flow diagram that shows a system in its MOST specific form is called a(n) _____ DFD.   5.____

    A. analysis
    B. context
    C. levelled
    D. decomposed
    E. system

6. To draw a DFD, the analyst should   6.____

    A. identify activities
    B. isolate data flows
    C. look for duplication of data flows
    D. show the relationship between activities
    E. all of the above

7. An alternative that should ALWAYS be considered is   7.____

    A. computerize the process
    B. program the process
    C. do nothing
    D. contract the process to outsiders
    E. all of the above

8. In deciding what to do, the analyst should consider   8._____

   A. costs   B. benefits   C. alternatives
   D. personnel   E. all of the above

9. In deciding what to do, the analyst should consider   9._____

   A. buying a packaged solution
   B. buying a main-frame computer
   C. hiring additional staff
   D. contracting the solution to an outside organization
   E. none of the above

10. The final report of findings produced during analysis is called   10._____

    A. the systems study
    B. the feasibility study
    C. the program study
    D. the programming specifications
    E. none of the above

11. The final report of findings is reviewed by   11._____

    A. management   B. users
    C. computer services staff   D. the analyst
    E. all of the above

12. The final report of findings is approved by   12._____

    A. management   B. users
    C. computer services staff   D. the analyst
    E. all of the above

13. If a recommendation is made to buy software from an outside supplier, the analyst should ask the supplier about   13._____

    A. cost and performance
    B. security and compatability
    C. upgrading and updates
    D. training and support
    E. all of the above

14. Future costs for a system should be   14._____

    A. added together
    B. ignored
    C. discounted
    D. subtracted from current costs
    E. all of the above

15. Besides costs, the analyst needs to calculate   15._____

    A. future needs
    B. benefits
    C. the impact on competitors

D. the impact on users
E. alternative messages

16. Which of the following costs MUST be considered in any alternative? 16.____

    A. System design
    B. System development
    C. Hardware
    D. Software and training
    E. All of the above

17. When collecting documents for an accounts payable system, which is NOT appropriate? 17.____

    A. Invoice
    B. Packing slip
    C. Monthly statement
    D. Check
    E. All are appropriate

18. Who should sign the analysis authorization memorandum? 18.____

    A. The analyst
    B. A manager
    C. A user
    D. A programmer
    E. Any of the above

19. An output from analysis is the 19.____

    A. program specifications
    B. module specifications
    C. input data collection screen designs
    D. analysis documentation
    E. database design

20. During interviews, an analyst functions like a(n) 20.____

    A. newspaper reporter
    B. architect
    C. programmer
    D. supervisor
    E. friend or co-worker

KEY (CORRECT ANSWERS)

1.	A		11.	E
2.	D		12.	A
3.	A		13.	E
4.	B		14.	C
5.	A		15.	B
6.	E		16.	E
7.	C		17.	C
8.	E		18.	B
9.	A		19.	D
10.	B		20.	A

28

EXAMINATION SECTION
TEST 1

DIRECTIONS: Each question or incomplete statement is followed by several suggested answers or completions. Select the one that BEST answers the question or completes the statement. *PRINT THE LETTER OF THE CORRECT ANSWER IN THE SPACE AT THE RIGHT.*

1. In programming, declaring a variable name involves what else other than naming?
   A. Type   B. Length   C. Size   D. Style

   1.____

2. Name of a student is an example of
   A. operation   B. method
   C. attribute   D. none of the above

   2.____

3. Basic strength of a computer is
   A. speed   B. memory   C. accuracy   D. reliability

   3.____

4. *Only girls can become members of the committee. Many of the members of the committee are officers. Some of the officers have been invited for dinner.* Based on the above statements, which is the CORRECT conclusion?
   A. All members of the committee have been invited for the dinner.
   B. Some officers are not girls.
   C. All girls are the members of the committee.
   D. None of the above

   4.____

5. Of the following statements, which of them cannot both be true and both be false?
   I.   All babies cry   II. Some babies cry
   III. No babies cry   IV. Some babies do not cry

   The CORRECT answer is:
   A. I and II   B. I and III   C. III and IV   D. I and IV

   5.____

6. 3, 7, 15, 31, 63, ? What number should come next?
   A. 83   B. 127   C. 122   D. 76

   6.____

7. If 30% of a number is 12.6, find the number?
   A. 45   B. 42   C. 54   D. 60

   7.____

8. 10, 25, 45, 54, 60, 75, 80. The odd one out is
   A. 10   B. 45   C. 54   D. 60

   8.____

9. Complement of an input is produced by which logical function?
   A. AND   B. OR   C. NOT   D. XOR

   9.____

10. *If marks are greater than 70 and less than 85, then the grade is B.*
    This statement is an example of which programming control structure?
    A. Decision B. Loop
    C. Sequence D. None of the above

    10._____

11. In programming, which operator is called the assignment operator?
    A. +   B. =   C. _   D. %

    11._____

12. In programming, which operator is called the modulus operator?
    A. +   B. =   C. %   D. /

    12._____

13. What is the correct order of running a computer program?
    A. Linking, loading, execution, translation
    B. Loading, translation, execution, linking
    C. Execution, translation, linking, loading
    D. Translation, loading, linking, execution

    13._____

14. In the case of structure of programming, which of the following terms means "if none of the other statements are true"?
    A. Else   B. Default   C. While   D. If

    14._____

15. True statements:
    i. All benches are chairs.
    ii. Some chairs are desks.
    iii. All desks are pillars.
    Conclusions:
    I. Some pillars are benches.   II. Some pillars are chairs.
    III. Some desks are benches.   IV. No pillar is a bench.

    The CORRECT answer is:
    A. None of the above
    B. Either I or IV, and III
    C. Either I or IV
    D. Either I or IV, and II
    E. All of the above

    15._____

16. True statements:
    i. Some snakes are reptiles.
    ii. All reptiles are poisonous.
    iii. Some poisonous reptiles are not snakes.
    Conclusions:
    I. Some poisonous reptiles are snakes.   II. All snakes are poisonous.
    III. All reptiles are snakes.   IV. No poisonous reptile is a snake.

    The CORRECT answer is:
    A. None of the above
    B. Either I or IV, and III
    C. Either I or IV, and II
    D. All of the above

    16._____

17. Anna runs faster than Peter.
    Jane runs faster than Anna.
    Peter runs faster than Jane.
    If the first two statements are true, the third statement would be
    A. true   B. false   C. unknown   D. both

18. The sum of the digits of a two-digit number is 10. If the new number formed by reversing the digits is greater than the original number by 36, then what will be the original number?
    A. 37   B. 39   C. 57   D. 28

19. If an inverter is added to the output of an AND gate, what logic function is produced?
    A. AND   B. NAND   C. XOR   D. OR

20. Decimal 7 is represented by which gray code?
    A. 0111   B. 1011   C. 0100   D. 0101

21. According to propositional logic, if p = "A car costs less than $20,000", q = "David will buy a car."
    p → ~q refers to which of the following?
    A. If David will buy a car, the car costs less than $20,000.
    B. David will not buy a car if the car costs less than $20,000.
    C. David will buy a car if the car costs less than $20,000.
    D. None of the above

22. Which Boolean algebra rule is wrong?
    A. 0 + A = A
    B. 0 + A = 1
    C. A + A = A
    D. x • 1 = 1
    E. All of the above

23. The 2's complement of 001011 is
    A. 110101   B. 010101   C. 110100   D. 010100

24. 7, 10, 8, 11, 9, 12. What number should come next?
    A. 12   B. 13   C. 8   D. 10

25. 2, 1, (1/2), (1/4). What number should come next?
    A. (1/16)   B. (1/8)   C. (2/8)   D. 1

KEY (CORRECT ANSWERS)

1.	A		11.	B
2.	C		12.	C
3.	B		13.	D
4.	D		14.	B
5.	B		15.	C
6.	B		16.	C
7.	B		17.	B
8.	C		18.	A
9.	C		19.	B
10.	A		20.	C

21.	B
22.	B
23.	A
24.	D
25.	B

TEST 2

DIRECTIONS: Each question or incomplete statement is followed by several suggested answers or completions. Select the one that BEST answers the question or completes the statement. *PRINT THE LETTER OF THE CORRECT ANSWER IN THE SPACE AT THE RIGHT.*

1. 8, 27, 64, 100, 125, 216, 343. The odd one out is 1.____
   A. 343   B. 8   C. 27   D. 100

2. In programming, what is the operator precedence? 2.____
   A. Arithmetic, comparison, logical
   B. Comparison, arithmetic, logical
   C. Arithmetic, logical, comparison
   D. Logical, arithmetic, comparison

3. Which of the following is NOT a type of programming error? 3.____
   A. Logical   B. Syntax   C. Superficial   D. Runtime

4. Statements: 4.____
   i. No man is good.   ii. Jack is a man.
   Conclusions:
   I. Jack is not good   II. All men are not Jack.

   The CORRECT answer is:
   A. I   B. II
   C. Either I or II   D. Neither I nor II
   E. Both I and II

5. Statements: 5.____
   i. All students are boys.   ii. No boy is dull.
   Conclusions:
   I. There are no girls in the class.   II. No student is dull.

   The CORRECT answer is:
   A. I   B. II
   C. Either I or II   D. Neither I nor II
   E. Both I and II

6. What is the sum of two consecutive even numbers, the difference of whose 6.____
   squares is 84?
   A. 32   B. 36   C. 40   D. 42

7. Choose the odd one out:

   (1) (2) (3) (4)

   A. 1 B. 2 C. 3 D. 4

8. In the Netherlands, almost 200 cyclists die each year on the road.
   Head injury is the main cause of death among cyclists.
   Which of the following statements is true based on the above information?
   A. In the Netherlands, if wearing a helmet was widespread among cyclists, the number of deaths in cyclists could be reduced.
   B. Too many cyclists die each year on the road in the Netherlands.
   C. Most deaths in the Netherlands occur due to cycling.
   D. None of the above

9. According to propositional logic, what is the order of precedence of operators?
   A. ^, v, ↔, →
   B. ~, ^, v, →, ↔
   C. ~, v, ^, ↔, →
   D. →, ~, ^, v, ↔

10. The binary equivalent of the number 50 is
    A. 01101 B. 11010 C. 11100 D. 110010

11. Number 200 can be represented by how many bits?
    A. 1 B. 5 C. 8 D. 10

12. Which of the following is NOT true?
    A. 0 × 0 = 0 B. 1 × 0 = 0 C. 0 × 1 = 1 D. 1 × 1 = 1

13. Get two numbers
    If first number is bigger than second then
    Print first number
    Else
    Print second number
    The above pseudo-code is an example of which control structure?
    A. Loop B. Sequence
    C. Decision D. None of the above

14. A group of variables is called
    A. data structure B. control structure
    C. data object D. linked list

15. The first character of the string variable St is represented by
    A. St[1] B. St[0]
    C. St D. none of the above

16. Statements:
    i. No girl is poor	B. All girls are rich
    Conclusions:
    I. No poor girl is rich	II. No rich girl is poor

    The CORRECT answer is:
    A. I	B. II
    C. Either I or II	D. Neither I nor II
    E. Both I and II

17. Statements:
    i. All fishes are orange in color	ii. Some fishes are heavy
    Conclusions:
    I. All heavy fishes are orange in color
    II. All light fishes are not orange in color

    The CORRECT answer is:
    A. I	B. II
    C. Either I or II	D. Neither I nor II
    E. Both I and II

18. 3, 7, 6, 5, 9, 3, 12, 1, 15. What number should come next?
    A. 18	B. 13	C. 1	D. -1

19. 5184, 1728, 576, 192. What number should come next?
    A. 64	B. 32	C. 120	D. 44

20. $(p \Leftrightarrow r) \Rightarrow (q \Leftrightarrow r)$ is equivalent to
    A. $[(\sim p \lor r) \land (p \lor \sim r)] \lor \sim [(\sim q \lor r) \land (q \lor \sim r)]$
    B. $\sim[(\sim p \lor r) \land (p \lor \sim r)] \lor [(\sim q \lor r) \land (q \lor \sim r)]$
    C. $[(\sim p \lor r) \land (p \lor \sim r)] \land [(\sim q \lor r) \land (q \lor \sim r)]$
    D. $[(\sim p \lor r) \land (p \lor \sim r)] \lor [(\sim q \lor r) \land (q \lor \sim r)]$

21. Which of the following propositions is a tautology?
    A. $(p \lor q) \rightarrow q$	B. $p \lor (q \rightarrow p)$	C. $p \lor (p \rightarrow q)$	D. b & c

22. According to propositional logic, if p = "Mary gets an A in computer science", q = "Mary got 90% marks in computer science."
    $p \leftrightarrow q$ refers to which of the following?
    A. Mary gets an A in computer science if and only if her percentage in computer science is 90%.
    B. Mary might get an A in computer science if her percentage in computer science is 90%
    C. Mary get an A in computer science if her percentage in computer science is 90%.
    D. None of the above

23. What does the following flowchart depict?   23._____

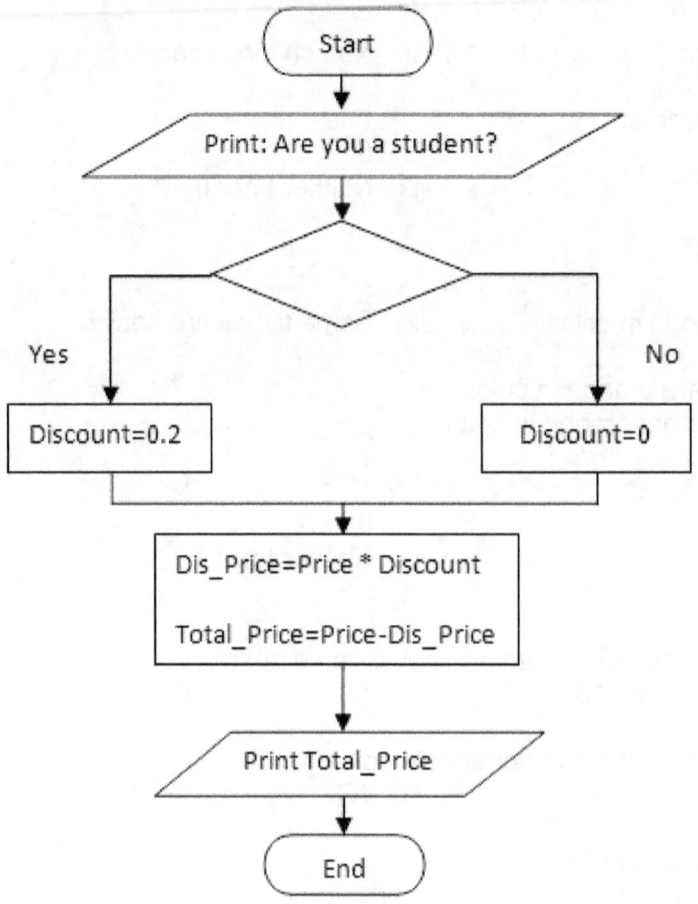

   A. All users get a discount.
   B. If user is a student, only then does he get a discount.
   C. If user is a student, he does not get a discount, while other users get a discount.
   D. None of the above

24. 13, 35, 57, 79, 911. What number should come next?   24._____
    A. 1113   B. 1114   C. 1100   D. 1111

25. Choose the missing shape.   25._____

A. 1   B. 2   C. 3   D. 4

KEY (CORRECT ANSWERS)

1. D
2. A
3. C
4. A
5. E

6. D
7. A
8. A
9. B
10. D

11. C
12. C
13. C
14. A
15. B

16. E
17. A
18. D
19. A
20. B

21. D
22. A
23. B
24. C
25. C

TEST 3

DIRECTIONS: Each question or incomplete statement is followed by several suggested answers or completions. Select the one that BEST answers the question or completes the statement. *PRINT THE LETTER OF THE CORRECT ANSWER IN THE SPACE AT THE RIGHT.*

1. The following flowchart represents which control structure?   1.____

   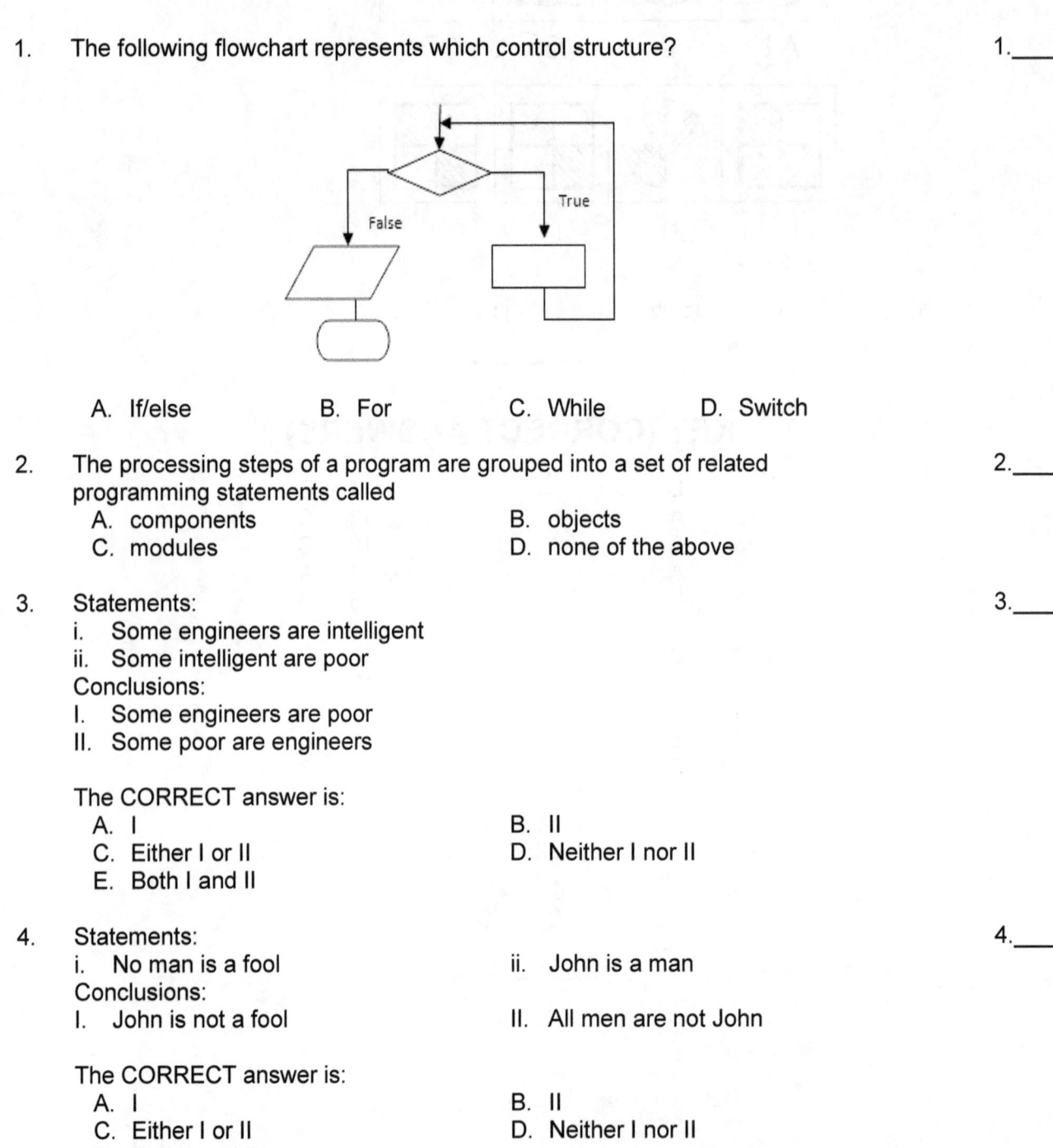

   A. If/else   B. For   C. While   D. Switch

2. The processing steps of a program are grouped into a set of related programming statements called   2.____
   A. components
   B. objects
   C. modules
   D. none of the above

3. Statements: 3.____
   i. Some engineers are intelligent
   ii. Some intelligent are poor
   Conclusions:
   I. Some engineers are poor
   II. Some poor are engineers

   The CORRECT answer is:
   A. I
   B. II
   C. Either I or II
   D. Neither I nor II
   E. Both I and II

4. Statements: 4.____
   i. No man is a fool   ii. John is a man
   Conclusions:
   I. John is not a fool   II. All men are not John

   The CORRECT answer is:
   A. I
   B. II
   C. Either I or II
   D. Neither I nor II
   E. Both I and II

2 (#3)

5. John weighs less than Fred.
   John weighs more than Boomer.
   Of the three dogs, Boomer weighs the least.

   If the first two statements are true, the third statement is
   A. true   B. false   C. uncertain   D. both

   5.____

6. A file contains 10 sheets and none of these sheets is blue. Which of the following statements can be deduced?
   A. None of the 10 sheets contained in the file are blue.
   B. The file contains a blue sheet.
   C. The file contains at least one yellow sheet.
   D. None of the above

   6.____

7. Choose the odd one out:

   (1)   (2)   (3)   (4)

   A. 1   B. 2   C. 3   D. 4

   7.____

8. Which of the following structures requires the statements to be repeated until a condition is met?
   A. Sequence   B. If....Else
   C. For   D. None of the above

   8.____

9. While n is greater than 0
   Increment count
   end
   The above pseudo-code represents which programming structure?
   A. Sequence   B. Loop
   C. Structure   D. None of the above

   9.____

10. Which of the following converts a source code into machine code and turns it into an exe file?
    A. Linker   B. Compiler
    C. Interpreter   D. None of the above

    10.____

11. Which of the following is used to hide data and its functionality?
    A. Structure   B. Loop
    C. Object   D. Selection statement

    11.____

12. Statements:
    i. All apples are golden in color
    ii. No golden colored things are cheap
    Conclusions:
    I. All apples are cheap
    II. Golden colored apples are not cheap

    The CORRECT answer is:
    A. I
    B. II
    C. Either I or II
    D. Neither I nor II
    E. Both I and II

13. Statements:
    i. All cups are glasses
    ii. All glasses are bowls
    iii. No bowl is a plate
    Conclusions:
    I. No cup is a plate
    II. No glass is a plate
    III. Some plates are bowls
    IV. Some cups are not glasses

    The CORRECT answer is:
    A. None of the above
    B. Either I or IV, and III
    C. Either I or IV
    D. Either I or IV, and II
    E. All of the above

14. 331, 482, 551, 263, 383, 362, 284. The odd one out is
    A. 331   B. 383   C. 284   D. 551

15. 3, 5, 7, 12, 17, 19. The odd one out is
    A. 7   B. 17   C. 12   D. 19

16. Ratio of 12 minutes to 1 hour is:
    A. 2:3   B. 1:5   C. 1:6   D. 1:8

17. 10 cats caught 10 rats in 10 seconds. How many cats are required to catch 100 rats in 100 seconds?
    A. 100   B. 50   C. 200   D. 10

18. Four engineers and six technicians can complete a project in 8 days, while three engineers and seven technicians can complete it in 10 days. In how many days will ten technicians complete it?
    A. 40   B. 36   C. 50   D. 45

19. According to propositional logic, if p = "Jane is smart", "q = "Jane is honest", then p v (~p ^ q) refers to which of the following?
    A. Either Jane is smart or honest.
    B. Jane is smart and honest.
    C. Either Jane is smart, or she is not smart but honest.
    D. None of the above

20. In binary number system, the number 102 is equal to 20.____
    A. 1100110   B. 1001100   C. 1110110   D. 1100101

21. In base 8, number 362 is represented as 21.____
    A. 550   B. 552   C. 545   D. 566

22. 396, 462, 572, 427, 671, 264. The odd one out is 22.____
    A. 427   B. 572   C. 671   D. 264

23. A is two years older than B who is twice as old as C. If the total of the ages of A, B and C is 27, then how old is B? 23.____
    A. 10   B. 11   C. 12   D. 13

24. What is 50% of 40% of Rs. 3,450? 24.____
    A. 580   B. 670   C. 690   D. 570

25. What is the minimum number of colors required to fill the spaces in the following diagram without the adjacent sides having the same color? 25.____

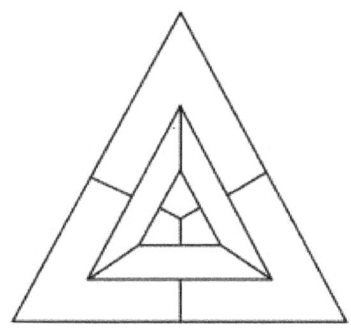

A. 3
C. 6
B. 4
D. Not possible to determine

KEY (CORRECT ANSWERS)

1.	A		11.	A
2.	C		12.	B
3.	E		13.	A
4.	A		14.	D
5.	A		15.	C
6.	A		16.	B
7.	D		17.	D
8.	C		18.	A
9.	B		19.	C
10.	B		20.	A

21. B
22. A
23. A
24. C
25. A

TEST 4

DIRECTIONS: Each question or incomplete statement is followed by several suggested answers or completions. Select the one that BEST answers the question or completes the statement. *PRINT THE LETTER OF THE CORRECT ANSWER IN THE SPACE AT THE RIGHT.*

1. Computer signals that include both measuring and counting are called 1.____
   A. analog
   B. digital
   C. hybrid
   D. none of the above

2. The result of ANDing 5 and 4 is 2.____
   A. 30
   B. 9
   C. 20
   D. none of the above

3. If one wants to trace an organization's purchase orders from creation to final disposition, he should use which of the following? 3.____
   A. Data flow diagram
   B. Internal control flow chart
   C. System flow chart
   D. Program flow chart

4. Statements: 4.____
   i. Some tables are sofas
   ii. All furniture are tables
   Conclusions:
   I. Some furniture are sofas
   II. Some sofas are furniture

   The two statements given should be assumed to be true. Select the conclusion.
   A. I
   B. II
   C. Either I or II
   D. Neither I nor II
   E. Both I and II

5. Statements: 5.____
   i. Many actors are singers.
   ii. All singers are dancers.
   Conclusions:
   I. Some actors are dancers.
   II. No singer is an actor.

   The CORRECT answer is:
   A. I
   B. II
   C. Either I or II
   D. Neither I nor II
   E. Both I and II

6. Anna will not pass both the verbal reasoning test and quantitative reasoning test. This statement refers to which of the following? 6.____
   A. Anna will not pass the verbal reasoning test.
   B. Anna will neither pass quantitative reasoning test nor verbal reasoning test.
   C. Anna will pass either the verbal reasoning test or the numerical reasoning test.
   D. If Anna passes the verbal reasoning test, she will not pass the numerical reasoning test.

7. Which symbol is used at the beginning of the flowchart?

    A. ○   B. ⬭   C. ◇   D. ▭

8. A list of instructions in a proper order to solve a problem is called
    A. sequence   B. algorithm
    C. flowchart   D. none of the above

9. Statements:
    i. Some pearls are stones
    ii. Some stones are diamonds
    iii. No diamond is a gem
    Conclusions:
    I. Some gems are pearls   II. Some gems are diamonds
    III. No gem is a diamond   IV. No gem is a pearl

    The CORRECT answer is:
    A. None of the above   B. Either I or IV, and III
    C. Either I or IV   D. Either I or IV, and II
    E. All of the above

10. 53, 53, 40, 40, 27, 27. What number should come next?
    A. 14   B. 12   C. 13   D. 10

11. 1, 3, 1, 9, 1, 81, 1. What number should come next?
    A. 4   B. 1   C. 343   D. 6561

12. A father is 30 years older than his son. He will be three times as old as his son after 5 years. What is the father's present age?
    A. 30   B. 35   C. 40   D. 45

13. Ahmed is older than Ali
    Maria is older than Ahmed.
    Ali is older than Maria.
    If the first two statements are true, the third statement is
    A. true   B. false   C. unknown D. both

14. All flowers are fruit.
    Some flowers are leaves.
    All leaves are fruit.
    If the first two statements are true, the third statement is
    A. true   B. false   C. unknown D. both

15. The Spring Mall has more stores than the Four Seasons Mall.
    The Four Corners Mall has fewer stores than the Four Seasons Mall.
    The Spring Mall has more stores than the Four Corners Mall.
    If the first two statements are true, the third statement is
    A. true   B. false   C. unknown D. both

3 (#4)

16. Choose the odd one out:

    (1)   (2)   (3)   (4)

    A. 1   B. 2   C. 3   D. 4

17. Fact 1: All cats like to jump.
    Fact 2: Some cats like to run.
    Fact 3: Some cats look like dogs.
    If the first three statements are true, which of the following statements must also be true?
    I. All cats who like to jump look like dogs.
    II. Cats who like to run also like to jump.
    III. Cats who like to jump do not look like dogs.

    The CORRECT answer is:
    A. I only   B. II only
    C. II and III only   D. None of the above

18. Fact 1: All chickens are birds.
    Fact 2: Some chickens are hens.
    Fact 3: Female birds lay eggs.
    If the first three statements are true, which of the following statements must also be true?
    I. All birds lay eggs.
    II. Some hens are birds.
    III. Some chickens are not hens.

    The CORRECT answer is:
    A. I only   B. II only
    C. II and III only   D. None of the above

19. Fact 1: Jake has four watches.
    Fact 2: Two of the watches are black.
    Fact 3: One of the watches is a Rolex.
    If the first three statements are true, which of the following statements must also be true?
    I. Jake has a Rolex.
    II. Jake has three watches.
    III. Jake's favorite color is black.

    The CORRECT answer is:
    A. I only   B. II only
    C. II and III only   D. None of the above

20. Which symbol of a flowchart is used to test a condition?

    A. ○   B. ▱   C. ◇   D. ⬭

21. Which symbol of a flowchart is used for input and output?

    A. ○   B. ▱   C. ◇   D. ▭

22. Which of the following is NOT one of the categories of flowcharting symbols?
    A. Input/output symbols
    B. Processing symbols
    C. Storage symbols
    D. Flow symbols

23. Choose the missing shape.

    A. 1   B. 2   C. 3   D. 4

24. Choose the missing shape.

    A. 1   B. 2   C. 3   D. 4

25. How many minimum numbers of colors will be required to fill a cube without adjacent sides having the same color?
    A. 3
    B. 4
    C. 6
    D. 8

25._____

KEY (CORRECT ANSWERS)

1. C
2. C
3. B
4. E
5. A

6. B
7. B
8. B
9. B
10. A

11. D
12. C
13. B
14. C
15. A

16. A
17. B
18. B
19. A
20. C

21. B
22. C
23. B
24. A
25. A

EXAMINATION SECTION
TEST 1

DIRECTIONS: Each question or incomplete statement is followed by several suggested answers or completions. Select the one the BEST answers the question or completes the statement. *PRINT THE LETTER OF THE CORRECT ANSWER IN THE SPACE AT THE RIGHT.*

1. Which of the following types of firewall techniques is most susceptible to IP spoofing? 1.____

   A. Proxy server
   B. Circuit-level gateway
   C. Packet filter
   D. Application gateway

2. Which of the following is a term for unorganized symbols, words, images, numbers or sound that a computer can transform into something useful? 2.____

   A. Software
   B. Data
   C. Input
   D. Information

3. In relational databases, records are referred to as 3.____

   A. stories
   B. tuples
   C. keys
   D. files

4. Web _____ can be included in HTML-formatted e-mail messages to reveal whether a recipient has received a message, as well as to disclose the recipient's IP address. 4.____

   A. cookies
   B. bots
   C. bugs
   D. tokens

5. Which of the following is NOT typically an element of a GUI? 5.____

   A. Column
   B. Icon
   C. Pointer
   D. Menu

6. Of the three general methods for posing queries to a database, choosing parameters from a menu 6.____

   A. is the least flexible
   B. is the most powerful
   C. requires the user to learn a specialized language
   D. presents the user with a blank record and lets him/her specify fields and values

49

7. Unless the circuitry is part of a workstation's design, LAN computers usually need a(n) _____ to function in the network.

   A. NIC
   B. bus
   C. protocol
   D. EDI

8. A VPN enables a business to

   A. avoid network "tear-downs"
   B. make use of the Internet, rather than build a dedicated network
   C. make a network inherently more secure
   D. work on circuits, rather than packets

9. In a client/server architecture, the component that performs the bulk of the data processing operations is known as the

   A. fat client
   B. portal
   C. server
   D. node

10. The process of translating virtual addresses into real addresses is known as

    A. paging
    B. ghosting
    C. mapping
    D. swapping

11. The first commercially developed operating system was

    A. OS1
    B. Windows
    C. OS360
    D. DOS

12. The relationships between cells in a spreadsheet application are known as

    A. formulas
    B. references
    C. attributes
    D. labels

13. Most contemporary personal computers come with external cache memory that sits between the CPU and the main memory. This cache is known as the _____ cache.

    A. disk
    B. DRAM
    C. Level 1 (L1)
    D. Level 2 (L2)

14. Only _____ language programs can manipulate CPU registers.	14.____
    I. machine
    II. assembly
    III. high-level
    IV. fourth-generation

    A. I and II
    B. II only
    C. I, II and III
    D. IV only

15. In the _____ process, the amplitude of an analog wave is checked at regular intervals in order to enable its encoding into digital form.	15.____

    A. attenuation
    B. sampling
    C. amplification
    D. modulation

16. In the _____ phase of the systems development life cycle, programmers either write software from scratch or purchase software from a vendor.	16.____

    A. implementation
    B. maintenance
    C. needs analysis
    D. development

17. The term "warm boot" refers to	17.____

    A. getting a quick view of stored files
    B. placing files in a more secure location
    C. restarting a computer that is already on
    D. making files more quickly available on a disk

18. In terms of digital security, nonrepudiation can be accomplished through each of the following, EXCEPT	18.____

    A. confirmation services
    B. timestamps
    C. nym servers
    D. digital signatures

19. More advanced microprocessors may begin executing a second instruction before the first has been complete. This is a feature known as	19.____

    A. multitasking
    B. burst mode
    C. pipelining
    D. cascading

20. The main disadvantage associated with ATM network technology is that it   20._____

   A. tends to favor audio and video over traditional data
   B. creates cells of unpredictable size
   C. does not respond well to fluctuations in network traffic
   D. requires large startup costs

21. Computer users make use of hypertext in browser software by clicking the mouse on a   21._____

   A. graphic image
   B. pull-down menu choice
   C. hot spot
   D. button

22. Products using the IEEE 1394 interface may use each of the following names, EXCEPT   22._____

   A. i.link
   B. USB
   C. Fire Wire
   D. Lynx

23. What is the term for the computer's processing circuitry, located within the system's case?   23._____

   A. CPU
   B. RAM
   C. Motherboard
   D. BIOS

24. The primary difficulty in using a LAN to directly connect telephone calls to a server is that   24._____

   A. it would prevent the LAN from working with another remote network
   B. the configuration of the network would change into something that could not strictly be considered a "LAN"
   C. most LAN technologies don't handle voice data very well
   D. the link would require synchronous data

25. Graphical software developers can create virtual environments from two-dimensional images by making use of   25._____

   A. Quicktime VR
   B. MPEG
   C. transcoding
   D. Cinepak

26. In the design of an information system, a(n) _____ is often useful to show all organizations, departments, users, applications, and data that function in the system.   26._____

   A. Gantt chart
   B. data dictionary
   C. schema
   D. entity-relationship diagram

27. Which of the following terms is NOT synonymous with the others?

    A. Bit rate
    B. Vertical frequency
    C. Refresh rate
    D. Frame rate

28. What is the term for the process of adding depth to an image using a volumetric dataset (a set of cross-sectional images)?

    A. Voxelization
    B. Texelization
    C. Interpixellation
    D. Rounding out

29. Assembly language must be translated into _____ before it can run on a computer.

    A. source code
    B. pseudocode
    C. machine language
    D. BASIC

30. Indexing a database field offers the benefit of

    A. establishing an encryption code for selected data items
    B. allowing for the programming of an interface
    C. duplicating information contained within the field for backup purposes
    D. accelerating searches in that field

31. Some computer keyboards have a(n) _____ integrated into them, between the g and h keys.

    A. mini-mouse
    B. trackball
    C. light pen
    D. integrated pointing device

32. Which of the following is a 16-bit standard for denoting characters that can represent most of the world's languages?

    A. ANSI
    B. ASCII
    C. Unicode
    D. ISO Latin-1

33. Mosaic is a _____ browser.

    A. graphical
    B. text-only
    C. markup
    D. plug-in

34. Which of the following can be used to enhance the performance of executing commands on a database?

    A. Connection pools
    B. Two-phase commits
    C. Fixed lengths
    D. Triggers

35. The FIRST step in the photolithographic process is

    A. soft baking
    B. wafer cleaning
    C. barrier layer formation
    D. mask alignment

36. Computer program instructions
    I. are explicit and unequivocal
    II. perform only one task each
    III. are translated into binary code before execution
    IV. are executed in sequence

    A. I and II
    B. I, II and III
    C. III and IV
    D. I, II, III and IV

37. When transferred to a different computer, a(n) _____ language requires very little reprogramming.

    A. high-level
    B. machine
    C. assembly
    D. natural

38. Typically, the operating system kernel is responsible for managing each of the following, EXCEPT

    A. peripherals
    B. program execution
    C. memory
    D. disk

39. The UNIX operating system was the first major program written in the computer language

    A. Ada
    B. C
    C. Java
    D. C++

40. The _____ version of a software product is given to manufacturers to bundle into future versions of their hardware products.   40._____

    A. alpha
    B. maintenance
    C. crippled
    D. RTM

41. MOUS is an acronym that stands for   41._____

    A. Memory Overload/Unusable System
    B. Modulation User Set
    C. Microsoft Office Utility Service
    D. Microsoft Office User Specialist

42. The opposite of "time sharing" in microprocessing is   42._____

    A. multitasking
    B. autosizing
    C. multiprocessing
    D. batch processing

43. A standard compact disc can contain about _____ MB of data.   43._____

    A. 480
    B. 650
    C. 720
    D. 800

44. Which of the following is LEAST similar to the others in its function?   44._____

    A. Extension
    B. Command file
    C. Script
    D. Macro

45. Tools for analyzing data in spreadsheet programs include each of the following, EXCEPT   45._____

    A. conceptual problem-solving
    B. risk modeling
    C. sensitivity analysis
    D. goal seeking

46. Many optical scanners are capable of gray scaling, and typically use from _____ different shades of gray.   46._____

    A. 8 to 32
    B. 16 to 256
    C. 512 to 1024
    D. 300 to 600

47. A language that is designed to specify the layout of a document is known as a(n) _____ language.   47.____

   A. object-oriented
   B. query
   C. assembly
   D. markup

48. A hacker enters the computer system of his credit card company and changes a charge from $1,250.00 to $12.50. This is an example of the computer crime known as   48.____

   A. Van Eck bugging
   B. salami attack
   C. piggybacking
   D. data diddling

49. In the hexadecimal coding system, 1111 equals the   49.____

   A. number two
   B. number four
   C. letter D
   D. letter F

50. A URL may include information about   50.____
   I.   what protocol to use
   II. the IP address
   III. the domain name
   IV. the type of file

   A. I and II
   B. II and III
   C. II, III and IV
   D. I, II, III and IV

KEY (CORRECT ANSWERS)

1. C	11. C	21. D	31. D	41. D
2. B	12. A	22. B	32. C	42. D
3. B	13. D	23. A	33. C	43. B
4. C	14. B	24. C	34. A	44. A
5. A	15. B	25. A	35. B	45. A
6. A	16. D	26. D	36. D	46. B
7. A	17. C	27. A	37. A	47. D
8. B	18. C	28. A	38. A	48. D
9. A	19. C	29. C	39. B	49. D
10. C	20. C	30. D	40. D	50. D

TEST 2

DIRECTIONS: Each question or incomplete statement is followed by several suggested answers or completions. Select the one the BEST answers the question or completes the statement. *PRINT THE LETTER OF THE CORRECT ANSWER IN THE SPACE AT THE RIGHT.*

1. Because of their vertical arrangement, the OSI Reference Model and the TCP/IP protocols are referred to as network protocol 1.____

    A. towers
    B. stacks
    C. dunes
    D. compilers

2. _____ of the operating system are less frequently used, and copied from the disk as needed. 2.____

    A. Nonresident
    B. Peripheral
    C. Application
    D. Unthreaded

3. Presentation programs such as PowerPoint often use the _____ effect to blend slides together while switching from one to the next. 3.____

    A. dithering
    B. transition
    C. slumping
    D. fade-in

4. In a network in which transactions are being recorded, the _____ strategy is designed to ensure that either all the databases on the network are updated or none of them, so that the databases remain synchronized. 4.____

    A. dynaset
    B. two-phase commit
    C. failover
    D. aggregate function

5. Which of the following is an optical storage device? 5.____

    A. CD-ROM
    B. Floppy disk
    C. Hard disk
    D. Cassette tape

6. The capacity of RAM is measured in 6.____

    A. bytes
    B. kilobytes
    C. megabytes
    D. gigabytes

7. The four stages of the CPU's operation cycle, in sequence, are

   A. execute, store, decode, fetch
   B. fetch, execute, translate, store
   C. fetch, decode, execute, store
   D. encode, store, decode, fetch

8. In a database application, a _____ check validation would ensure that a worker's salary did not exceed the maximum of $53,599.

   A. range
   B. completeness
   C. sequence
   D. consistency

9. In a _____ network, all nodes have equivalent capabilities and responsibilities.

   A. peer-to-peer
   B. file server
   C. frame relay
   D. client/server

10. Which of the following is NOT a common technology for the storage of binary information?

    A. Analog
    B. Magnetic
    C. Optical
    D. Electronic

11. Typically, the term "legacy application" is applied to

    A. productivity software
    B. newer, more innovative programs
    C. database management systems
    D. operating systems

12. Which of the following is NOT an example of a database application?

    A. Parts inventory system
    B. Automated teller machine
    C. Mortgage calculator
    D. Flight reservations system

13. A computer component may signal the CPU that it has data available by

    A. shorting the bus
    B. fetching an instruction
    C. flushing the pipeline
    D. sending an interrupt

14. The hexadecimal numbering system uses a base of   14.____

    A. eight
    B. twelve
    C. sixteen
    D. thirty-two

15. POSIX is   15.____

    A. a set of standards to make applications independent of the UNIX operating system
    B. an open-source alternative to the UNIX operating system
    C. a set of standards that makes an operating system look like UNIX to an application
    D. a specialized form of the UNIX operating system for use in medical/ health care applications

16. The type of programming language that most closely mirrors human ways of thinking is _____ language.   16.____

    A. assembly
    B. object-oriented
    C. translator
    D. query

17. The main reason hard disks are used to store data instead of much faster technologies, such as DRAM, is because hard disks are   17.____

    A. capable of reorganizing data from location to location
    B. less prone to read/write errors
    C. more amenable to recovery if something goes wrong
    D. not volatile

18. The final step in producing an executable program is to   18.____

    A. translate pseudocode into source code
    B. translate the source code into object code
    C. translate source code into a language such as C or FORTRAN
    D. transform the object code into machine language

19. What is the term for software that has been written into ROM?   19.____

    A. Warez
    B. Pseudocode
    C. Firmware
    D. Macrocode

20. Variables play an important role in computer programming because they enable programmers to   20.____

    A. maintain strict quality-control standards
    B. make programs backward compatible
    C. avoid repeated iterations
    D. write flexible programs

21. The foremost organization for information systems personnel and managers is the   21._____

    A. Data Processing Management Association
    B. United States Chief Information Officers Council
    C. Information Resources Management Association
    D. Association of Internet Professionals

22. Second-generation graphics systems improved upon first-generation systems by   22._____

    A. adding shading capabilities
    B. supporting texture-mapping
    C. allowing for the movement of objects in 3D space
    D. enabling full-scene antialiasing

23. Suitable standards for testing the quality of a computer program include each of the following, EXCEPT   23._____

    A. semantic errors
    B. logic errors
    C. robustness
    D. reliability

24. Bitmap file formats include each of the following, EXCEPT   24._____

    A. GIF
    B. CGM
    C. PNG
    D. DIB

25. The largest collection of information in a database is the   25._____

    A. file
    B. system
    C. field
    D. record

26. Of the telephone technologies listed below, the oldest is   26._____

    A. FDDI
    B. PSTN
    C. SONET
    D. ISDN

27. The primary difference between a "workstation" and a regular desktop system lies in   27._____

    A. graphics capabilities
    B. the operating system
    C. microprocessing speeds
    D. the number of users

28. In contemporary personal computers, the stripped-down operating system is stored in _____ before a computer is turned on.

    A. RAM
    B. ROM
    C. the hard disk
    D. the CPU

29. When a computer is multitasking, the _____ controls the flow of program tasks through the CPU.

    A. RAM
    B. CPU
    C. disk cache
    D. operating system

30. A digital pulse, viewed on an oscilloscope, appears as a

    A. square wave
    B. short dash
    C. microwave
    D. gamma wave

31. The first operating system developed with preemptive multitasking was

    A. MS-DOS
    B. OS/2
    C. Windows
    D. UNIX

32. Each of the following methods of data compression may involve temporal compression, EXCEPT

    A. JPEG
    B. Content-based
    C. MPEG
    D. P-frame

33. A network manager is considering the implementation of ATM technology. Because the organization uses the network primarily for file transfers, the most appropriate type of ATM service would be _____ bit rate.

    A. available
    B. variable
    C. constant
    D. unspecified

34. Which type of color model is typically used in commercial printing?

    A. CIE
    B. RGB
    C. HGB
    D. CMYK

35. The _____ is an allotted space in which spreadsheet programs allow users to create and edit data and formulas.

    A. register
    B. formula bar
    C. data field
    D. status bar

36. The four-layered protocol that was instrumental in the expansion of the Internet is

    A. OSI
    B. ATM
    C. TCP/IP
    D. UDP/IP

37. The most common top-level domain name suffix used on the World Wide Web is

    A. .gov
    B. .edu
    C. .org
    D. .com

38. The process of synchronizing databases that exist in different localities is known as

    A. replication
    B. distribution
    C. storehousing
    D. backup

39. Productivity software that uses a document-centric approach is made possible by the compound document standards known as

    A. XML and HTML
    B. VAP and AWT
    C. JFS and ISAM
    D. OLE and OpenDoc

40. What is the term for a WAN or LAN that uses TCP/IP protocols and can be accessed only by users from within the organization that owns the network?

    A. Extranet
    B. Intranet
    C. Supranet
    D. Isonet

41. File compression technologies that attempt to eliminate redundant or unnecessary information, such as the technology used with MPEG files, are described as

    A. terse
    B. DCT
    C. lossy
    D. stripped

42. What is the term for a database that is designed to help managers make strategic business decisions?

    A. Data mine
    B. Operational data store
    C. Data mart
    D. Data warehouse

43. Which type of computer virus exploits the automatic command execution capabilities of certain types of application software?

    A. Macro virus
    B. Worm
    C. Trojan horse
    D. Zombie

44. All computers use a _____ to translate between digital code and audio signals.

    A. sound card
    B. SMDI
    C. audio scrubber
    D. Sound Blaster

45. A hard disk's storage capacity can be increased by means of

    A. caching
    B. virtual memory
    C. boot blocking
    D. file compression

46. _____ a standard for describing the location of resources on the World Wide Web.

    A. FTP
    B. URL
    C. XML
    D. HTML

47. Which of the following is a multithreading operating system?

    A. UNIX
    B. MS-DOS
    C. VMS
    D. Linux

48. Probably the easiest method for committing computer crime today is

    A. shoulder surfing
    B. piggybacking
    C. Trojan horses
    D. below-threshold attacks

49. Which of the following types of servers enables users to log on to a host computer and perform tasks as if they're working on the remote computer itself?

    A. Middleware
    B. Telnet
    C. IRC
    D. FTP

50. _____ occurs when a programmer places source code and a compiler or interpreter on a different computer platform, and then creates working object code.

    A. Assembling
    B. Reconfiguring
    C. Replication
    D. Porting

KEY (CORRECT ANSWERS)

1. B	11. C	21. A	31. D	41. C
2. A	12. C	22. A	32. A	42. C
3. B	13. D	23. A	33. D	43. A
4. B	14. C	24. B	34. D	44. A
5. A	15. C	25. A	35. B	45. D
6. A	16. B	26. B	36. C	46. B
7. C	17. D	27. A	37. D	47. D
8. A	18. D	28. B	38. A	48. A
9. A	19. C	29. D	39. D	49. B
10. A	20. D	30. A	40. B	50. D

EXAMINATION SECTION
TEST 1

DIRECTIONS: Each question or incomplete statement is followed by several suggested answers or completions. Select the one that BEST answers the question or completes the statement. *PRINT THE LETTER OF THE CORRECT ANSWER IN THE SPACE AT THE RIGHT.*

1. What is the term for a device that enables a single communications channel to carry data transmissions from many different sources simultaneously?

    A. Compiler
    B. Multitasker
    C. Concentrator
    D. Multiplexer

2. Which of the following represents the earliest stage in the computer language translation process?

    A. Linkage editor
    B. Load module
    C. Compiler
    D. Object code

3. Within data flow diagrams, the transformations that occur within the lowest level are described by

    A. development methodologies
    B. structure charts
    C. selection constructs
    D. process specifications

4. The time or number of operations after which a process in a system repeats itself is expressed in a measure known as

    A. periodicity
    B. synchronicity
    C. loop
    D. iteration

5. What is the term for the single steps or actions in the logic of a program that do NOT depend on the existence of any condition?

    A. Logical construct
    B. Run control
    C. Sequence construct
    D. Rule base

6. Which of the following terms is most different in meaning from the others?

    A. Data file approach
    B. Relational data model
    C. Flat file organization
    D. Traditional file environment

7. Which of the following is a tool for locating data on the Internet that performs key word searches of an actual database of documents, software, and data files available for downloading?

    A. WAIS   B. Archie   C. Acrobat   D. Gopher

8. Typical transaction processing (TPS) systems include all of the following types EXCEPT _____ systems.

    A. finance/accounting
    B. sales/marketing
    C. engineering/design
    D. human resources

65

9. The main weakness of the enterprise analysis approach to systems development is that it

    A. involves little input at the managerial level
    B. is relatively unstructured
    C. produces an enormous amount of data that is expensive to collect and analyze
    D. only generally identifies an organization's informational requirements

10. What is the term for special system software that translates a higher–level language into machine language for execution by the computer?

    A. Compiler   B. Translator   C. Renderer   D. Assembler

11. Compared to private branch exchanges, LANs
    I.   are more expensive to install
    II. have a smaller geographical range
    III. are more inflexible
    IV. require specially trained staff

    The CORRECT answer is

    A. I only   B. I, III
    C. I, II, IV   D. III, IV

12. Each of the following is considered to be a basic component of a database management system EXCEPT a

    A. transform algorithm
    B. data manipulation language
    C. data definition language
    D. data dictionary

13. Which of the following is a technical approach to the study of information systems?

    A. Management science   B. Sociology
    C. Political science   D. Psychology

14. In desktop publishing applications, a user may sometimes elect to alter the standard spacing between two characters. This is a technique known as

    A. weighting   B. kerning   C. pointing   D. leading

15. In systems design, the generic framework used to think about a problem is known as the

    A. schema   B. reference model
    C. prototype   D. operational model

16. What is the term for a small computer that manages communications for the host computer in a network?

    A. Concentrator   B. Multiplexer
    C. Controller   D. Front–end processor

17. Which of the following is a competitive strategy for developing new market niches, where a business can compete in a target area better than its competitors?

    A. Vertical integration   B. Focused differentiation
    C. Multitasking   D. Forward engineering

18. An electronic meeting system (EMS) is considered to be a type of collaborative

    A. executive support system (ESS)
    B. management information system (MIS)
    C. office automation system (OAS)
    D. group decision support system (GDSS)

19. In systems theory, the minimum description required to distinguish a system from its environment is known as a(n)

    A. blip   B. margin   C. mediation   D. boundary

20. The principal advantage of the hierarchical and network database models is

    A. adaptability
    B. architecture simplicity
    C. minimal programming requirements
    D. processing efficiency

21. Which of the following is a character-oriented tool for locating data on the Internet which allows a user to locate textual information through a series of hierarchical menus?

    A. FTP   B. Gopher   C. Lug   D. Archie

22. The principal logical database models include each of the following types EXCEPT

    A. network   B. object-oriented
    C. relational   D. hierarchical

23. Computer programming includes a logic pattern where a stated condition determines which of two or more actions can be taken, depending on the condition. This pattern is known as the

    A. object linkage   B. selection construct
    C. key field   D. iteration construct

24. Which of the following is the tool used by database designers to document a conceptual data model?

    A. Entity-relationship diagram
    B. Partition statement
    C. Gantt chart
    D. Data-flow diagram

25. The phenomenon of _____ refers to the idea that people will avoid new uncertain alternatives and stick with traditional and familiar rules and procedures.   25._____
    A. the Hawthorne effect
    B. bounded rationality
    C. system–oriented reasoning
    D. case–based reasoning

KEY (CORRECT ANSWERS)

1.	D	11.	C
2.	C	12.	A
3.	D	13.	A
4.	A	14.	B
5.	C	15.	B
6.	B	16.	D
7.	B	17.	B
8.	C	18.	D
9.	C	19.	D
10.	A	20.	D

21. B
22. B
23. B
24. A
25. B

TEST 2

DIRECTIONS: Each question or incomplete statement is followed by several suggested answers or completions. Select the one that BEST answers the question or completes the statement. *PRINT THE LETTER OF THE CORRECT ANSWER IN THE SPACE AT THE RIGHT.*

1. In systems theory, the history of a system's structural transformations is referred to as its   1._____

    A. ontology B. entailment
    C. ontogeny D. epistemology

2. Programming language that consists of the 1s and 0s of binary code is referred to as   2._____

    A. machine language B. assemblage
    C. object language   D. pseudocode

3. Generally, the EBCDIC standard can be used to code up to _____ characters in one byte of information.   3._____

    A. 128 B. 256 C. 512 D. 1024

4. In MIS terminology, which of the following offers the best definition of *network*?   4._____

    A. The devices and software that link components and transfer data from one location to another
    B. The media and software governing the storage and organization of data for use
    C. Two or more computers linked to share data or resources such as a printer
    D. Formal rules for accomplishing tasks

5. Which of the following is a type of MIS application used for analysis?   5._____

    A. Database   B. Operations research
    C. Desktop publishing D. Presentation

6. In computer processing, an overload sometimes results when trying to test more rules to reach a solution that the computer is capable of handling. This type of overload is referred to as   6._____

    A. combinatorial explosion B. data crashing
    C. transaction jam   D. conversion error

7. In the normal processing of a workgroup information system, which of the following is an operations procedure, as opposed to a user procedure?   7._____

    A. Maintaining backup
    B. Placing constraints on processing
    C. Initiating access to network
    D. Starting hardware and programs

8. A company's European units want to share information about production schedules and inventory levels to ship excess products from one country to another. The telecommunications technology most appropriate for this is   8._____

    A. teleconferencing B. voice mail
    C. e–mail   D. videoconferencing

69

9. As opposed to systems development, approximately how much of an organization's efforts can be expected to be spent on systems maintenance during the total system life cycle?

   A. 25   B. 45   C. 65   D. 85

10. The most critical, and often most difficult, task of the systems analyst is usually to
    A. define the specific problem that must be solved with an information system
    B. identify the causes of the problem
    C. specify the nature of the solution that will address the problem
    D. define the specific information requirements that must be met by the system solution

11. Which of the following is not a commonly recognized difference between workgroup and enterprise management information systems?
    A. An enterprise MIS is a subfunction of a company.
    B. Workgroup MIS users know and work with each other.
    C. An enterprise MIS uses several different applications.
    D. A workgroup MIS is a peripheral system.

12. The first step in testing the accuracy of a spreadsheet application is usually to
    A. verify the input
    B. stresstest the spreadsheet
    C. check the output
    D. involve others in the process

13. Programs in information systems make use of complete, unambiguous procedures for solving specified problems in a finite number of steps. These procedures are known as
    A. schema   B. protocols
    C. algorithms   D. criteria

14. Weaknesses in a system's _____ controls may permit unauthorized changes in processing.
    A. software   B. computer operations
    C. data file security   D. implementation

15. In the model of case-based reasoning, after a user describes a problem, the system
    A. modifies its solution to better fit the problem
    B. asks the user questions to narrow its search
    C. retrieves a solution
    D. searches a database for a similar problem

16. The particular form that information technology takes in a specific organization to achieve selected goals or functions is referred to as the organization's
    A. information configuration
    B. knowledge base
    C. operability
    D. information architecture

17. Which of the following applications is most likely to require real-time response from a telecommunications network?

    A. Intercomputer data exchange
    B. Administrative message switching
    C. Process control
    D. On-line text retrieval

18. The main DISADVANTAGE associated with the use of application software packages to solve organizational problems is that

    A. the initial costs of purchase are often prohibitive
    B. they often involve the added costs of customization and additional programming
    C. maintenance and support will usually have to come from within the purchasing organization
    D. the new program usually requires intensive training

19. Which of the following is a disadvantage associated with distributed data processing?

    A. Drains on system power
    B. Reliance on high-end telecommunications technology
    C. Increased vulnerability of storage location
    D. Reduced responsiveness to local users

20. In the current environment of systems development, end-user computing contributes most effectively to the _____ aspects of the process.

    A. problem identification and systems study
    B. installation and maintenance
    C. systems study and installation
    D. programming and detail design

21. Which of the following steps in the machine cycle of a computer occurs during the execution cycle (e-cycle)?

    A. Instruction fetched
    B. Data sent from main memory to storage register
    C. Instruction decoded
    D. Instruction placed into instruction register

22. Of the following, which offers the least accurate definition of *information* as it applies to the study of MIS?

    A. Data placed within a context
    B. The amount of uncertainty that is reduced when a message is received
    C. A thing or things that are known to have occurred, to exist, or to be true
    D. Knowledge derived from data

23. Programming languages in which each source code statement generates multiple statements at the machine-language level are described as

    A. incremental   B. high-level
    C. first-generation   D. hierarchical

24. Which of the following types of visual representations is used as an overview, to depict an entire system as a single process with its major inputs and outputs?   24.____

    A. Context diagram   B. Decision tree
    C. Data flow diagram   D. Nomograph

25. Once an organization has developed a business telecommunications plan, it must determine the initial scope of the project, taking several factors into account. The first and most important of these factors is   25.____

    A. security   B. connectivity
    C. distance   D. multiple access

KEY (CORRECT ANSWERS)

1.	C		11.	A
2.	A		12.	C
3.	B		13.	C
4.	C		14.	A
5.	B		15.	D
6.	A		16.	D
7.	D		17.	D
8.	C		18.	B
9.	C		19.	B
10.	D		20.	D

21. B
22. C
23. B
24. A
25. C

TEST 3

DIRECTIONS: Each question or incomplete statement is followed by several suggested answers or completions. Select the one that BEST answers the question or completes the statement. *PRINT THE LETTER OF THE CORRECT ANSWER IN THE SPACE AT THE RIGHT.*

1. Which of the following is a commonly used term for the programming environment of an expert system?

    A. Model B. Ada C. Schema D. AI shell

2. In the language of dataflow diagrams, the external entity that absorbs a dataflow is known as a

    A. store B. sink C. cache D. source

3. Which of the following is most clearly a fault tolerant technology?

    A. Random access memory
    B. On–line transaction processing
    C. Secondary storage
    D. Mobile data networks

4. Each of the following is a type of input control used with applications EXCEPT

    A. data conversion B. run control totals
    C. edit checks D. batch control totals

5. In a typical organization, approximately what percentage of total system maintenance time is spent making user enhancements, improving documentation, and recoding system components?

    A. 20 B. 40 C. 60 D. 80

6. Which of the following is NOT considered to be an operations control used with information systems?

    A. Error detection circuitry
    B. Control of equipment maintenance
    C. Regulated access to data centers
    D. Control of archival storage

7. Which of the following styles of systems development is most often used for information systems at the workgroup level?

    A. Traditional life cycle
    B. Life cycle for licensed programs
    C. Prototyping
    D. Outsourcing

8. Which of the following systems exists at the management level of an organization?

    A. Decision support system (DSS)
    B. Executive support system (ESS)
    C. Office automation system (OAS)
    D. Expert system

9. What is the term for a special language translator that translates each source code statement into machine code and executes it one at a time?

   A. Adapter
   B. Assembler
   C. Compiler
   D. Interpreter

10. Which of the following is NOT perceived to be a difference between a decision support system and a management information system?

    A. In an MIS, systems analysis is aimed at identifying information requirements.
    B. The philosophy of a DSS is to provide integrated tools, data, and models to users.
    C. The design process of an MIS is never really considered to be finished.
    D. The design of a DSS is an interative process.

11. Which of the following is a programming language that resembles machine language but substitutes mnemonics for numeric codes?

    A. Pseudocode
    B. BASIC
    C. C
    D. Assembly language

12. Each of the following is a rule of thumb for handling type in desktop publishing applications EXCEPT

    A. use small capitals for acronyms
    B. use sans serif typefaces when presenting a lot of text
    C. generally limit the different number of typefaces in a document to two
    D. use distinctly different typefaces together in the same document

13. Typically, a microcomputer is classified as a desktop or portable machine that has up to

    A. 1 gigabyte of secondary storage space
    B. 5 gigabytes of secondary storage space
    C. 64 megabytes of RAM
    D. 1 gigabyte of RAM

14. Which of the following is NOT considered to be a basic component of a decision support system?

    A. Electronic meeting system
    B. Database
    C. DSS software system
    D. Model base

15. Information systems that monitor the elementary activities and transactions of the organization are said to be functioning at the _____ level.

    A. tactical
    B. operational
    C. strategic
    D. managerial

16. Which of the following applications would be most likely to use the sequential method of file organization in a database?   16.____

    A. Personnel evaluations
    B. Inventory
    C. Asset turnover calculations
    D. Payroll

17. Each of the following is a reason for the increased vulnerability of computerized systems to external threats EXCEPT   17.____

    A. invisible appearance of procedures
    B. inability to replicate manually
    C. wider overall impact than manual systems
    D. multiple points of access

18. Membership functions are nonspecific terms that are used to solve problems in applications of   18.____

    A. decision support   B. expert systems
    C. neural networks   D. fuzzy logic

19. Rules or standards used to rank alternatives in order of desirability are known as   19.____

    A. norms   B. algorithms
    C. parameters   D. criteria

20. In most organizations, the database administration group performs each of the following functions EXCEPT   20.____

    A. developing security procedures
    B. performing data quality audits
    C. maintaining database management software
    D. defining and organizing database structure and content

21. What is the term for on-line data that appears in the form of fixed-format reports for management executives?   21.____

    A. Browsers   B. Briefing books
    C. Modules   D. Web pages

22. Which of the following is a likely application of the optimization models of a decision-support system?   22.____

    A. Forecasting sales
    B. Determining the proper product mix within a given market
    C. Predicting the actions of competitors
    D. Goal seeking

23. In database management, a group of related fields is known as a(n)   23.____

    A. domain   B. register   C. record   D. file

24. Storage of _____ is NOT a function of a computer's primary storage.
    A. operating system programs
    B. data being used by the program
    C. all or part of the program being executed
    D. long–term data in a nonvolatile space

25. Which of the following is equal to 1 billion bytes of information?
    A. Nanobyte   B. Gigabyte   C. Terabyte   D. Megabyte

KEY (CORRECT ANSWERS)

1.	D	11.	D
2.	B	12.	B
3.	B	13.	C
4.	B	14.	A
5.	C	15.	B
6.	A	16.	D
7.	B	17.	C
8.	A	18.	D
9.	D	19.	D
10.	C	20.	B

21. B
22. B
23. C
24. D
25. B

EXAMINATION SECTION
TEST 1

DIRECTIONS: Each question or incomplete statement is followed by several suggested answers or completions. Select the one that BEST answers the question or completes the statement. *PRINT THE LETTER OF THE CORRECT ANSWER IN THE SPACE AT THE RIGHT.*

1. The stage in a system's life cycle in which logical and physical specifications are produced is called 1.____

    A. implementation
    B. design
    C. conception
    D. documentation

2. Which of the following is a network topology that links a number of computers by a single circuit with all messages broadcast to the entire network? 2.____

    A. Daisy–chain
    B. Broadband
    C. Bus
    D. Ring

3. Of the following statements about information as a resource, which is generally FALSE? 3.____

    A. It has value and lends itself to the process of management.
    B. It can be overabundant and overused.
    C. Its usefulness tends to decrease with time.
    D. It can be consumed and expended in the same way as many capital resources.

4. What is the term for the extra bit built into EBCDIC and ASCII codes that is used as a check bit to insure accuracy? 4.____

    A. Parity   B. Auditor   C. Damper   D. Buffer

5. In the systems development process, which of the following is typically performed FIRST? 5.____

    A. Conversion
    B. Programming
    C. Production
    D. Testing

6. Which of the following is a term for a device used to store and retrieve large numbers of optical disks? 6.____

    A. Warehouse   B. Vault   C. Clearing   D. Jukebox

7. Each of the following can generally be said to be an element of the changing contemporary business environment EXCEPT 7.____

    A. global work groups
    B. stable environment
    C. location independence
    D. time–based competition

8. Of the following methods of changing from one information system to another, which is generally considered to be the safest? 8.____

    A. Pilot study
    B. Direct cutover
    C. Phased approach
    D. Parallel strategy

9. Which of the following is NOT typically a characteristic of a management information system?

   A. Extensive analytical capability
   B. Known and stable information requirements
   C. Internal rather than external orientation
   D. Generally reporting–and control–oriented

10. In information systems terminology, a person, place, or thing about which information must be kept is referred to as a(n)

   A. element
   B. entity
   C. assemblage
   D. pixel

11. Which of the following are considered to be moral dimensions that are emblematic of the information age?
   I. Accountability and control
   II. Property rights
   III. Quality of life
   IV. Information rights and obligations
   The CORRECT answer is:

   A. I, II
   B. I, II, III
   C. I, III, IV
   D. I, II, III, IV

12. In order to be classified as a *mainframe,* a computer must typically have at LEAST

   A. 1 remote access server
   B. 50 megabytes of RAM
   C. 1 gigabyte of RAM
   D. 5 gigabytes of secondary storage space

13. For most organizations, the FIRST step in developing a telecommunications plan should be to

   A. identify critical areas where telecommunications currently has an impact
   B. identify the organization's long–range business plan
   C. identify critical areas where telecommunications may have a future impact
   D. audit existing telecommunications functions

14. What is the term for a change in a data signal, from positive to negative or vice–versa, that is used as a measure of transmission speed?

   A. Baud
   B. Switch
   C. Byte
   D. Bit

15. Currently, in service industries such as finance, insurance, and real estate, information technology generally constitutes about _____ % of invested capital.

   A. 10
   B. 30
   C. 50
   D. 70

16. Which of the following signifies the emerging standard language for relational database management systems?

   A. SGML
   B. HTML
   C. Perl
   D. SQL

17. Over time, organizations have developed an ethical framework for handling system-related issues. Generally, the first step in any organization's ethical analysis should be to identify

    A. the higher-order values involved
    B. the potential consequences of any decision
    C. reasonable options
    D. the stakeholders

17.____

18. Telephone lines that are continously available for transmission by a lessee are described as

    A. validated   B. denuded
    C. formalized   D. dedicated

18.____

19. In a typical telecommunications system, a message that originates from the host computer will then pass through a

    A. front-end processor   B. modem
    C. controller   D. multiplexer

19.____

20. The table or list that relates record keys to physical locations on direct access files is called the

    A. key   B. index   C. card file   D. criterion

20.____

21. Which of the following offers the best definition of *data* as it applies to information systems?

    A. Things that are known to have occurred, to exist, or to be true
    B. Productions of exact copies of documents by electronic scanning and transmission
    C. Information not previously known to people within an organization
    D. Raw facts that have not been organized and arranged into understandable and usable form

21.____

22. A logical unit of a program that performs one or a small number of functions is known as a(n)

    A. module   B. element   C. loop   D. packet

22.____

23. Which of the following is a fourth-generation computer language?

    A. FORTRAN   B. dBASE   C. C   D. Ada

23.____

24. The logical description of an entire database, listing all the data elements and the relationships among them, is known as the

    A. value chain   B. schema
    C. matrix   D. shell

24.____

25. Systems theory defines a system as an entity that is generally greater than the sum of its parts. Which of the following terms describes this condition?

    A. Synchronicity   B. Collectivism
    C. Interdependence   D. Synergy

25.____

KEY (CORRECT ANSWERS)

1.	B		11.	D
2.	C		12.	B
3.	D		13.	D
4.	A		14.	A
5.	D		15.	D
6.	D		16.	D
7.	B		17.	A
8.	D		18.	D
9.	A		19.	A
10.	B		20.	B

21. D
22. A
23. B
24. B
25. D

TEST 2

DIRECTIONS: Each question or incomplete statement is followed by several suggested answers or completions. Select the one that BEST answers the question or completes the statement. *PRINT THE LETTER OF THE CORRECT ANSWER IN THE SPACE AT THE RIGHT.*

1. Of the types of organizational change that are enabled by information technology, which involves the highest levels of risk and reward? 1.____

    A. Paradigm shift
    B. Automation
    C. Business reengineering
    D. Rationalization of procedures

2. Most local–area networks (LANS) are _____ networks. 2.____

    A. token ring   B. ring   C. star   D. bus

3. Which of the following is an input device which translates images into digital form for processing? 3.____

    A. Surveyor   B. Pen   C. Compiler   D. Scanner

4. In a system, the appearance of an additional pattern or sequence of states is referred to as 4.____

    A. autonomy   B. differentiation
    C. bifurcation   D. variation

5. Which of the following is NOT considered to be an information output? 5.____

    A. Storage   B. Expert–system advice
    C. Query response   D. Report

6. Which of the following is a direct access storage device (DASD)? 6.____

    A. Punch card   B. Sequential tape
    C. Printed page   D. Magnetic disk

7. Which of the following is most likely to be an output from a knowledge work system (KWS)? 7.____

    A. Special report   B. Model
    C. Summary report   D. Query response

8. A system resting on accepted and fixed definitions of data and procedures, operating with predefined rules, is described in systems terminology as 8.____

    A. formal   B. computer–based
    C. fixed   D. expert

9. Which of the following is a characteristic of operational data? They 9.____

    A. are stored on a single platform
    B. contain recent as well as historical data
    C. are organized around major business informational subjects
    D. are generally used by isolated legacy systems

10. Which of the following signifies a telecommunications network that requires its own dedicated channels and encompasses a limited physical distance?

    A. WAN   B. KWS   C. LAN   D. ISDN

11. Which of the following terms is used for the capture or collection of raw data from within the organization, or from its external environment, for processing in an information system?

    A. Feedback   B. Tracking   C. Entry   D. Input

12. What is the term for the high–speed storage of frequently used instructions and data?

    A. Cache   B. Index   C. Reserve   D. Packet

13. Which of the following represents the largest unit of data?

    A. Byte   B. Record   C. Field   D. File

14. In most organizations, the entire system–building effort is driven by

    A. user information requirements
    B. existing hardware
    C. user training requirements
    D. availability of packaged applications

15. Which of the following terms is used to describe a process of change governed by probabilities at each step?

    A. Adiabatic   B. Stochastic
    C. Multifinal   D. Probabilistic

16. In object–oriented programming, a specific class of objects often receives the features of a more general class. This process is referred to as

    A. aliasing   B. inheritance
    C. summation   D. incrementation

17. In a typical organization, the strategic planning of an MIS would be the responsibility of the

    A. steering committee
    B. project teams
    C. operations personnel and end users
    D. chief information officer

18. Which of the following is a specialized computer that supervises communications traffic between the CPU and the peripheral devices in a telecommunications system?

    A. Controller   B. Concentrator
    C. Connector   D. Compiler

19. Of the following steps in the machine cycle of a computer, which occurs FIRST? 19.____

    A. Transmission of data from main memory to storage register
    B. Placement of instruction in instruction register
    C. ALU performance
    D. Placement of instruction in address register

20. Which of the following is a process of recoding information which reduces the number of different characters in a message while increasing the different number of characters to be recognized? 20.____

    A. The black box method   B. Daisy chaining
    C. Aliasing   D. Chunking

21. Of the following methodologies for establishing organizational MIS requirements, which is most explicitly oriented toward deploying information systems as a competitive weapon? 21.____

    A. Critical success factors (CSF)
    B. Strategic cube and value chain
    C. Business sytems planning (BSP)
    D. Strategy set transformation

22. Which of the following is a type of MIS application used for tracking and monitoring? 22.____

    A. Database
    B. Decision Support System (DSS)
    C. Spreadsheet
    D. Desktop publishing

23. An organization's information requirements are often analyzed by looking at the entire organization in terms of units, functions, processes, and data elements. What is the term most frequently used for such an examination? 23.____

    A. Semantic networking   B. Decision support
    C. Enterprise analysis   D. Run control

24. Which of the following would most likely be classifed as an *information worker*? 24.____

    A. Engineer   B. Scientist
    C. Data processor   D. Architect

25. In an organization that uses a decision support system to make stock investment decisions, which of the following would be classified as memory aids to the system? 25.____

    A. Graphs   B. Databases
    C. Menus   D. Training documents

KEY (CORRECT ANSWERS)

1. A
2. D
3. D
4. C
5. A

6. D
7. B
8. A
9. D
10. C

11. D
12. A
13. D
14. A
15. B

16. B
17. D
18. A
19. B
20. D

21. B
22. A
23. C
24. C
25. B

TEST 3

DIRECTIONS: Each question or incomplete statement is followed by several suggested answers or completions. Select the one that BEST answers the question or completes the statement. *PRINT THE LETTER OF THE CORRECT ANSWER IN THE SPACE AT THE RIGHT.*

1. In the _____ process, the components of a system and their relationship to each other are laid out as they would appear to users.

    A. external integration
    B. logical design
    C. file serving
    D. hierarchical

    1.____

2. Over the past two decades, technological trends have raised ethical issues in society, especially in the area of privacy. Which of the following trends has LEAST directly impacted the issue of privacy?

    A. Advances in data storage techniques and declining storage costs
    B. Advances in telecommunications infrastructure
    C. The doubling of computer power every 18 months
    D. Advances in data mining techniques for large databases

    2.____

3. Which of the following systems exists at the strategic level of an organization?

    A. Expert system
    B. Decision support system (DSS)
    C. Value chain
    D. Executive support system (ESS)

    3.____

4. Which of the following is equal to one-billionth of a second?

    A. Millisecond
    B. Picosecond
    C. Nanosecond
    D. Microsecond

    4.____

5. A small section of a program that can be easily stored in primary storage and quickly accessed from secondary storage is a(n)

    A. sector   B. module   C. page   D. applet

    5.____

6. Which of the following statements about hierarchical and network database systems is TRUE?
   They

    A. do support English-language inquiries for information
    B. involve easily changeable access pathways
    C. are difficult to install
    D. are relatively inefficient processors

    6.____

7. Which of the following is a programming language that is portable across different brands of soft hardware, and is used for both military and nonmilitary applications?

    A. FORTRAN   B. Pascal   C. Ada   D. C

    7.____

8. Which of the following would be LEAST likely to be an output of an office automation system (OAS)?

    A. Memo   B. Schedule   C. List   D. Mail

    8.____

85

9. At a minimum, an information system must consist of all of the following EXCEPT

   A. computers   B. data   C. people   D. procedures

10. What is the term for the strategy used to search through the rule base in an expert system?

    A. Index server   B. Key field
    C. Register   D. Inference engine

11. Which of the following communications media has the greatest frequency range?

    A. Wireless (electromagnetic)
    B. Fiber optics
    C. Wireless (PCS)
    D. Microwave

12. Models of decision–making in which decisions are shaped by the organization's standard operation procedures are described as

    A. systems–oriented   B. indexed
    C. bureaucratic   D. sequential

13. The first element involved in a standard dataflow diagram is a(n)

    A. dataflow   B. external entity
    C. data store   D. process

14. A system that seeks a set of related goals is described as

    A. purposive   B. closed   C. fixed   D. driven

15. Weaknesses in a system's _____ controls may affect the entire system of general controls, which may not be properly executed or enforced.

    A. administrative   B. software
    C. implementation   D. computer operations

16. Current and historical data from operational systems is often consolidated for management reporting and analysis into a database with reporting and query tools. This type of database is usually referred to as a(n)

    A. warehouse   B. redundancy
    C. controller   D. library

17. A project manager at an organization plans to compose letters outlining details of an upcoming trade show to be addressed individually to several dozen employees. The most appropriate type of application for this purpose is

    A. simple word processing   B. desktop publishing
    C. a mail merge   D. an automated document

18. In the process of systems analysis, which of the following procedures is typically performed FIRST?

    A. Defining a problem that can be solved by a newly designed system
    B. Examining existing documents
    C. Identifying the primary owners and users of data in the organization
    D. Identifying the information requirements that must be met by a system solution

19. Each of the following is a method for performing a data quality audit EXCEPT surveying

    A. data dictionaries
    B. entire data files
    C. end users for perceptions of data quality
    D. samples from data files

20. Which of the following signifies semiconductor memory chips that contain program instructions?

    A. RAM   B. ROM   C. CPU   D. ALU

21. The Fair Information Practices Principles set forth in 1973 include:
    I. Individuals have rights of access, inspection, review, and amendment to systems that contain information about them
    II. Managers of systems are responsible and can be held liable for the damages done by systems, for the reliability, and for their security
    III. Managers do not have the right of access to any form of interorganizational correspondence if individuals do not wish to grant such access
    IV. Governments have the right to intervene in the information relationships among private parties

    The CORRECT answer is:

    A. I, II
    C. I, II, IV
    B. II, III
    D. II, III, IV

22. In information systems terminology, a group of records of the same type is known as a

    A. class   B. field   C. batch   D. file

23. In systems theory, communication which travels through informal rather than formal channels is known as

    A. noise
    B. back channel communication
    C. cross-talk
    D. the grapevine

24. In order to be useful as a resource, information must satisfy each of the following conditions EXCEPT it must

    A. be accurate
    B. be available when needed
    C. reinforce beliefs
    D. relate to the business or matters at hand

25. In most contemporary organizations, the role of an MIS department can be described as 25.____
    A. performing key design and analysis functions, before and after a systems design has been implemented
    B. designing, installing, testing, and maintaining all organizational computer–based information and communications systems
    C. providing and perfecting all information and communications needs at the organization's management level
    D. coordinating corporate MIS efforts and providing an overall computational infrastructure

KEY (CORRECT ANSWERS)

1.	B	11.	C
2.	C	12.	C
3.	D	13.	B
4.	C	14.	A
5.	C	15.	A
6.	C	16.	A
7.	C	17.	C
8.	C	18.	C
9.	A	19.	A
10.	D	20.	B

21. C
22. D
23. B
24. C
25. D

EXAMINATION SECTION
TEST 1

DIRECTIONS: Each question or incomplete statement is followed by several suggested answers or completions. Select the one that BEST answers the question or completes the statement. *PRINT THE LETTER OF THE CORRECT ANSWER IN THE SPACE AT THE RIGHT.*

1. _____ is commonly used to report on project performance.
    A. Earned Value Management
    B. WBS
    C. Quality Management Plan
    D. RBS

1._____

2. Which of the following is NOT a process associated with communications management?
    A. Distribute information
    B. Manage stakeholder expectations
    C. Plan communication
    D. Survey questionnaire

2._____

3. As a project manager, you are expected to make relevant information available to project stakeholders as planned. Which process does this relate to?
    A. Distribute information
    B. Manage stakeholder expectations
    C. Plan communication
    D. Report performance

3._____

4. Report performance involves all of the following EXCEPT
    A. collecting and distributing performance data
    B. collecting and distributing progress measurements
    C. collecting stakeholder information needs
    D. collecting and distributing forecasts

4._____

5. Of the following examples listed, which is a sign of feedback from the receiver?
    A. No written response from the receiver
    B. An acknowledgement or additional questions from the receiver
    C. Encoding the message by the receiver
    D. Decoding the message by the receiver

5._____

6. As a project manager you are expected to create a scope statement. Once you have the statement, you find it to be useful in all the following ways EXCEPT
    A. describing the purpose of the project
    B. describing the objectives of the project
    C. distributing information
    D. explaining the business problems the project is expected to solve

6._____

7. What are project deliverables?
   A. Tangible products that the project is expected to deliver
   B. Prioritized list of deliverables
   C. Project scope statement
   D. Project documents

8. As a project manager, you are arranging criteria for project completion criteria. You could organize it using all of the following EXCEPT
   A. functional department
   B. milestones
   C. tasks of projects
   D. project phase

9. Which of the following is not a task under "Developing human resource plan"?
   A. Documenting organizational relationships
   B. Looking for the availability of required human resources
   C. Identification and documentation of project roles and responsibilities
   D. Creating a staffing plan

10. If you are a project manager who is keen in managing a project team, you would undertake any of the following EXCEPT
    A. creating a staffing plan
    B. evaluating individual team member performance
    C. providing feedback
    D. resolving conflicts

11. Nurturing the team is a vital role of a project manager. If you have to do so, what would you avoid?
    A. Guide the team members as required
    B. Provide mentoring throughout the project
    C. Remove the team member who is found to be less skilled
    D. On-the-job training

12. War room creation is an example of
    A. co-location
    B. management skills
    C. rewards and recognitions
    D. establishing ground rules

13. The team member roles and responsibilities could be documented using all of the following EXCEPT
    A. functional chart
    B. text-oriented format
    C. hierarchical type organizational chart
    D. matrix-based responsibility chart

14. _____ is NOT an example of constraints placed upon the project by current organizational policies.
    A. Hiring freeze
    B. Reduced training funds
    C. Organizational chart templates
    D. Rewards and Increments Freeze

15. As a project manager, you have decided to have a virtual team. What kind of limitation would this create with regards to team development?
    A. Rewards and recognition
    B. Establishing ground rules
    C. Team building
    D. Co-location

16. Unplanned training means
    A. team building using virtual team arrangement
    B. competencies developed as a result of project performance appraisals
    C. on-the-job training
    D. training that is done without any planning in advance

17. Resource break down structure is an example of
    A. functional chart
    B. text-oriented format
    C. hierarchical type organizational chart
    D. matrix-based responsibility chart

18. A project manager would consider the following as inputs to define scope EXCEPT
    A. requirements document
    B. project Charter
    C. product management plan
    D. organizational process charts

19. Aldo is a project manager and has to terminate a project earlier than planned. The level and extent of completion should be documented. Under which is this done?
    A. Verify scope
    B. Create scope
    C. Control scope
    D. Define scope

20. Sam, an IT project manager, is having difficulty in getting resources for his project, and hence has to depend highly on department heads. Which type of organization is Sam most likely working with?
    A. Functional
    B. Tight matrix
    C. Weak matrix
    D. Projectized

Questions 21-25.

Len is a project manager of an infrastructure project manager of a well-known company. He is involved in various processes of scope management. Look at the following chart and align the different processes to various tasks listed. Choose the appropriate answer for each process and list them under corresponding tasks.

	Processes	Corresponding tasks	List of tasks
21.	Define scope	21._____	A. Monitoring project scope and project status
22.	Control scope	22._____	B. Defining and documenting stakeholder needs
23.	Collect requirements	23._____	C. Formalizing acceptance of the complete project deliverables
24.	Verify scope	24._____	D. Breaking down the project into smaller, more manageable tasks
25.	Create WBS	25._____	E. Developing a detailed description of the project and its ultimate product

---

KEY (CORRECT ANSWERS)

1. A
2. D
3. A
4. C
5. B

6. C
7. A
8. C
9. B
10. A

11. C
12. A
13. A
14. C
15. D

16. B
17. C
18. C
19. A
20. A

21. E
22. A
23. B
24. C
25. D

TEST 2

DIRECTIONS: Each question or incomplete statement is followed by several suggested answers or completions. Select the one that BEST answers the question or completes the statement. *PRINT THE LETTER OF THE CORRECT ANSWER IN THE SPACE AT THE RIGHT.*

1. In which of the following processes would risk be identified?
    A. Risk identification
    B. Risk monitoring and control
    C. Qualitative risk analysis
    D. Risk identification, monitoring and control

    1._____

2. Jack has prepared a risk management plan for his project and also identified risks in his project. Which of the following processes should Jack do next?
    A. Plan risk responses
    B. Perform qualitative analysis
    C. Perform quantitative analysis
    D. Monitor and control risk

    2._____

3. Which of the following is NOT a step in risk management?
    A. Perform qualitative analysis
    B. Monitor and control risk
    C. Risk identification
    D. Risk breakdown structure

    3._____

4. Sue is a project manager for an IT project at a corporate office. She is engaged in the process of identifying risks. To do so, she collects inputs from experts from the field through a questionnaire. What is this technique called?
    A. Interview
    B. Documentation review
    C. Delphi technique
    D. Register risk

    4._____

5. Positive risks may be responded by which of the following:
    I. Exploit   II. Accept   III. Mitigate   IV. Share

    A. I and III
    B. All of the above
    C. I, II and IV
    D. I, II and III

    5._____

6. Risk _____ is a response to negative risks.
    A. identification
    B. mitigation
    C. response plan
    D. management plan

    6._____

7. Which of the following statements is NOT true about risk management?
   A. Risk register documents all the risks in detail
   B. Risks always have negative impacts and not positive
   C. Risk mitigation is a response to negative risks
   D. Risk register documents the risks in detail

8. _____ is the document that lists all the risks in a hierarchical fashion.
   A. Risk breakdown structure
   B. Lists of risks
   C. Risk management plan
   D. Monte Carlo diagram

9. Nicole is a project manager of a reforestation project. In one of the project reviews, she realizes that a risk has occurred. Which document should Nicole refer to take an appropriate action?
   A. Risk response plan
   B. Risk register
   C. Risk management plan
   D. Risk breakdown structure

10. As a project manager, you have invited experts for an effective brainstorming session to identify risks involved in the project. What is the ideal group size?
    A. 3   B. 6   C. 4   D. 5

11. Of the following personnel, who is NOT involved in project risk identification activities?
    A. Clerical staff
    B. Subject matter experts
    C. Other project managers
    D. Risk management experts

12. _____ is one of the tools/techniques used in risk identification.
    A. Risk tracker
    B. Checklist analysis
    C. Risk register
    D. Project scope

13. Jim is a project manager in a bank. He is collecting input for the risk identification process. What input would he be collecting to identify risks?
    I. Project scope statement
    II. Enterprise environmental factors
    III. Project management plan
    IV. Diagramming techniques

    A. I and IV only
    B. III and IV only
    C. All of the above
    D. I, II and III only

14. Which of the following could a project manager collect from a risk tracker?
    I. Root causes of risk and updated risk categories
    II. List of identified risks
    III. Risk register
    IV. List of potential responses

    A. I and IV only
    B. III and IV only
    C. I, II and IV
    D. II only

15. The risk management plan should describe the entire risk management process, including auditing of the process, and should also define _____.
    A. reporting
    B. environmental factors
    C. organizational process assets
    D. project management plan

16. What do risk categories define?
    A. How to communicate risk activities and their results
    B. Types and sources of risks
    C. How risk management will be done on the process
    D. When and how the risk management activities appear in the project schedule

17. Which of the following is not a method of risk identification?
    A. Diagramming
    B. Interviewing
    C. SWOT
    D. RBS

18. Shauna is conducting a qualitative risk analysis for her project. What is she required to do?
    A. Apply a numerical rating to each risk
    B. Assess the probability and impact of each identified risk
    C. Assign each major risk to a risk owner
    D. Outline a course of action for each major risk identified

19. Which of the following is not a criterion to close a risk?
    A. Risk is no longer valid
    B. Risk event has occurred
    C. Risk activities are recorded regularly
    D. Risk closure at the direction of a project manager

20. As a project manager, you establish a risk contingency budget. Which of the following is not a purpose of establishing a risk contingency budget?
    A. To be reviewed as a standing agenda item for project team meetings
    B. To prepare in advance to manage the risks successfully
    C. To have some reserve funds
    D. To avoid going over the budget allotted

21. Which of the following statements is NOT correct in terms of designing a risk management?
    A. Risk is inherent to project work
    B. In any organization, projects will have common risks
    C. Some risks may occur more than once in the life a project
    D. Risks identified will definitely occur

22. All identified potential risk events that are viewed to be relevant to the project are to be recorded using the
    A. risk register
    B. risk management matrix
    C. risk report
    D. SOW

23. _____ is/are an example of a business risk.
    A. Poorly understood requirements
    B. A merger
    C. Introduction of new technology to the organization
    D. Work outside the project scope

24. Personnel turnover in a project is a
    A. Business risk
    B. Not a risk at all
    C. Technology risk
    D. Project risk

25. Which of the following is not an example of mitigation?
    A. Set expectations
    B. Involve customer in early planning process
    C. Provide training for personnel
    D. Hiring a backup person for a key team member

KEY (CORRECT ANSWERS)

1. D
2. B
3. D
4. C
5. C

6. B
7. B
8. A
9. A
10. A

11. A
12. B
13. D
14. C
15. A

16. B
17. D
18. B
19. C
20. A

21. D
22. B
23. B
24. D
25. D

TEST 3

DIRECTIONS: Each question or incomplete statement is followed by several suggested answers of completions. Select the one that best answers the question or complete the statement. *PRINT THE LETTER OF THE CORRECT ANSWER IN THE SPACE AT THE RIGHT.*

1. Project cost management deals with all the following EXCEPT:
   A. Estimating costs
   B. Budgeting
   C. Controlling costs
   D. Communicating costs

   1.____

2. Which of the following is not a process associated with project cost management?
   A. Control costs
   B. Maintain reserves
   C. Estimate costs
   D. Determine budget

   2.____

3. _____ is not a key deliverable of project cost processes.
   A. Cost performance baseline
   B. Activity cost estimates
   C. Results of estimates
   D. Work performance measurements

   3.____

4. As a project manager, you are calculating depreciation for an object. You are doing this by depreciating the same amount from the cost each year.
   What kind of depreciation technique are you applying?
   A. Sum of year depreciation
   B. Double-declining balance
   C. Multiple depreciation
   D. Straight line depreciation

   4.____

5. Which of the following is not a characteristic of analogous estimating?
   A. It is a top-down approach
   B. It is a form of an expert judgment
   C. It makes less time when compared to bottom-up estimation
   D. It is more accurate when compared to bottom-up estimation

   5.____

6. CPI = EV/AC. If CPI is less than 1, the project
   A. is over the budget
   B. is within the budget
   C. would be left over with unused budget
   D. efficiency is less

   6.____

7. Which of the following is not a tool used for estimating cost?
   A. Cost of quality
   B. Expert judgment
   C. Two point estimates
   D. Three point estimates

   7.____

8. What are the traditional project management triple constraints?
   A. Time, cost, resources
   B. Scope, cost, resources
   C. Scope, time, cost
   D. Resources, scope, budget

   8.____

9. Sam, an IT project manager, is having difficulty getting resources for his project, and hence has to depend highly on department heads.
   Which type of organization is Sam most likely working with?
   A. Functional
   B. Tight Matrix
   C. Weak Matrix
   D. Projectized

9._____

10. After-project costs are called _____.
    A. cost of quality
    B. extra costs
    C. life cycle costs
    D. over budget costs

10._____

11. Critical chain is a tool and technique for _____.
    A. developing schedule process
    B. defining critical path
    C. sequencing activities process
    D. estimating activity duration

11._____

12. The following are outputs for sequencing activities:
    A. Project schedule network diagram, Milestone list
    B. Project document updates, Project schedule network diagram
    C. Project schedule, Project document updates
    D. Schedule data, Schedule baseline

12._____

13. The schedule performance index is a measure of:
    A. Difference between earned value and planned value
    B. Ratio between earned value and planned value
    C. Difference between earned value and estimate at completion
    D. Ratio between estimate at completion and earned value

13._____

14. Which of the following is not an input, output or tools and technique for control schedule process?
    A. Project schedule, work performance measurements and variance analysis
    B. Project management plan, project document updates and schedule compression
    C. Work performance information, schedule baseline and schedule data
    D. Project schedule, change requests and resource leveling

14._____

15. Contracts, resource calendar, risk register and forecasts are all termed as
    A. inputs to administer procurements process
    B. outputs from close procurements process
    C. project documents
    D. tools and techniques of conduct procurement process

15._____

16. Fast tracking can be best described as
    A. one of the schedule compression techniques
    B. adding resources to activities on critical path
    C. shared or critical resources available only at specific times
    D. performing activities in parallel to shorten project duration

16._____

17. Which of the following contract types places the highest risk on the seller?
    A. Cost plus fixed fee
    B. Firm fixed price
    C. Cost plus incentive fee
    D. Time and material

18. Using the Power/Interest grid, a stakeholder with low power and having high interest on the project should be
    A. monitored
    B. managed closely
    C. kept satisfied
    D. kept informed

19. Stakeholder classification information is found in which of the following documents?
    A. Communications management plan
    B. Stakeholder register
    C. Stakeholder management strategy document
    D. Human resource plan

20. Thomas is a project manager of a well-reputed organization. One of your senior managers approaches you to explain constraints on labor utilization followed by a request to delay a couple of your projects. What is the best way to approach this situation?
    A. Agree with the senior manager and delay a couple of your projects
    B. Perform an impact analysis of the requested change
    C. Report the situation to the senior management and make a complaint against the senior manager
    D. Disagree with the senior manager and continue with the progress of the projects managed by you

21. Project management is defined as
    A. completion of a project
    B. gaining trust of the people involved in the project
    C. completing a WBS
    D. the application of specific knowledge, skills and tools

22. The most common form of dependency is
    A. Start to Start
    B. Finish to Start
    C. Finish to Finish
    D. Start to Finish

23. Kelly is a project manager who is in phase of project evaluation. Which of the following has to be considered during project evaluation phase?
    I. Give feedback to team members
    II. Learn from experiences
    III. Monitor
    IV. Celebrate

The correct answer(s) is/are:
A. I only
B. I, IV and III
C. III only
D. I, II and IV

24. Which of the following are very vital for the implementation of the project, and also must be repeated over and over during project's life.
    I. Correct
    II. Monitor
    III. Estimate time and cost
    IV. Analyze

    The correct answer(s) is/are:
    A. I, II and III
    B. III only
    C. I, III and IV
    D. I, II and IV

25. What is the average amount of time is to be allocated to project planning?
    A. 10%
    B. 25%
    C. 22%
    D. 2%

KEY (CORRECT ANSWERS)

1. D
2. B
3. C
4. C
5. D

6. A
7. C
8. C
9. A
10. C

11. A
12. B
13. B
14. C
15. C

16. D
17. B
18. D
19. B
20. B

21. D
22. B
23. D
24. D
25. A

TEST 4

DIRECTIONS: Each question or incomplete statement is followed by several suggested answers of completions. Select the one that best answers the question or complete the statement. *PRINT THE LETTER OF THE CORRECT ANSWER IN THE SPACE AT THE RIGHT.*

1. Imagine you are assigned a project for which you do not have the required competency and experience to manage. What is the best plan of action?
   A. Make sure that you disclose any areas of improvement that need to be immediately addressed with the project sponsor before accepting the assignment
   B. Do not inform anyone about the gaps and learn as much as you can before any critical activity is due for delivery
   C. Consider the opportunity as a stepping stone for your career development and accept it
   D. Tell your boss that you cannot manage as you do not have the relevant experience and decline it

2. You are the project manager of a new project and are involved in selecting a vendor for acquiring products required for the project. Your close friend is running a company that is also very competitive and a reputed one along with other vendors who are competing for the bid. How can you handle this situation?
   A. Do not participate in the vendor selection process as this may be considered a conflict of interest
   B. Provide information to help your friend get the contract as you are the project manager of the project
   C. Do not inform anyone about your personal contact and be involved in the vendor selection process as normal
   D. Discuss with your project sponsor the possibility of a conflict of interest and leave the decision to him on the next steps

3. You have provided good guidance to your team members and this has resulted in successful execution of all of the phases involved. There was a particular phase that has been identified as very critical and the presence of a technical expert helped achieve this success. In the senior management review meeting you were credited with the success of the project, with specific mention of that particular phase. What do you do in this situation?
   A. Accept the appreciation and feel proud about the success of the project
   B. Do not mention anything about the technical expert role as you were the project manager for this project
   C. Give credit to the technical expert and let the senior management know how the presence of the technical expert helped the team to be successful
   D. Accept the appreciation from the senior management and thank the technical expert in private for achieving this success

4. As a project manager you are preparing status reports for a meeting with the stakeholders. One of your team members has come out with an issue that will cause some delay in the project timeline. You have a plan that can be implemented to make sure that this issue can be managed without causing any delay in the timeline, but you currently do not have the time to update the project plan. How will you handle this situation?
    A. Present the status of the project as *on-track* without discussing anything about this issue as you will have time to prepare before the next meeting
    B. Cancel the meeting as you do not have the time to update the details to be provided to the stakeholders
    C. Present the status of the project *as-is* without minimizing the effect of the delay and discuss details of the planned approach to solve this issue
    D. Fire your team that is responsible for causing this delay as it has created a bad impression of you amongst the stakeholders

5. John is an Associate Director in a pharmaceutical company managing its internal projects. He has presented whitepapers on project execution methodologies and is highly respected within the organization. He also regularly conducts workshops & lectures in coordination with PMO. What kind of power does John possess?
    A. Referent power
    B. Coercive power
    C. Reward power
    D. Expert power

6. You are a project manager working for a non-profit organization. You had been assigned a project that is in the initial stage and involves development of an eco-system in a large community. You are reviewing the deliverables and templates from similar projects that are available in the company lessons learnt knowledge base. Which item will be of much importance to you?
    A. Project Information Management System
    B. Enterprise Environmental Factors
    C. Organization Process Assets
    D. Standard Templates

7. A project that you were managing is nearing completion. As part of the deliverables you are required to complete lessons-learned documentation of the project. What is the primary purpose of creating lessons-learned documentation?
    A. Provide information of project success
    B. Help identify all the failures
    C. Provide information on minimizing negative impacts and maximizing positive events for future projects of similar nature
    D. Comply with the organization's objectives

8. You are managing project teams that work from different locations and there has been issues with the teams' ability to effectively perform. This has resulted in delay in timeline. Which kind of team development technique would be most effective in this situation?
    A. Mediation
    B. Training
    C. Co-location
    D. Rewards

9. The project sponsor has requested that you create a project charter for a new project that you will manage next month. Which document will you utilize to create the project charter that will justify the need for the project?
    A. Project SOW
    B. Business Need
    C. Business Case
    D. Cost-benefit Analysis

10. An audit is being performed by a team for the project you are managing. The team reports that the standards utilized need to be analyzed as several processes that are not relevant to the current project.
What is the process that the team is currently involved?
    A. Quality planning
    B. Quality control
    C. Quality assurance
    D. Benchmark creation

11. The change control board of your organization has approved changes that were submitted and the project team is executing them.
What would this process be considered?
    A. Executing the change request
    B. Implementing a corrective action
    C. Gold-plating
    D. Approving the change request

12. Which is the primary technique that is carried out to ensure that a contract award is executed correctly or not?
    A. Litigation
    B. Contract negotiation
    C. Inspections
    D. Procurement audit

13. In the final stages of completing a project, you and your team are involved in creating the project report that will be presented to the stakeholders. Which of the following information is not appropriate to be included in the final report?
    A. Recommendations from your team
    B. Project success factors
    C. WBS dictionary
    D. Details of the process improvements

14. At the completion of a project, your team has completed the lessons-learned documentation and archived in the database. Who should have access to these documents?
    A. Project team members
    B. Operations department
    C. All of the company's members
    D. Functional managers

15. You are project manager for a large project that is in the final stages of completion and you need to formally provide information on the major milestone achieved. You are also in need of immediate feedback from the stakeholders. Which is the best communication method to meet this requirement?
    A. E-mail
    B. Web publishing
    C. Meeting
    D. Videoconferencing

16. Which document will formally authorize a project manager to start the project?
    A. Project SOW
    B. Project Charter
    C. Business Case
    D. Stakeholder Register

17. Which of the following documents would be utilized to ascertain the project's investment worthiness?
    A. Project Charter
    B. Business Case
    C. Business Need
    D. Procurement documents

18. Which of the following conflict resolution is considered as Lose-lose solution?
    A. Problem-solving
    B. Forcing
    C. Compromising
    D. Withdrawing

19. McGregor's Theory states that all workers fit into one of the two groups. Which of the following theories believes that people are willing to work on their own and need less supervision?
    A. Theory X
    B. Theory Y
    C. Maslow's Hierarchy
    D. Expectancy

20. The major cause for conflicts on a project are schedule, project priorities and _____.
    A. cost
    B. resources
    C. personality
    D. management

21. The project manager is responsible for
    A. the success of the project
    B. achieving the project objectives
    C. authorizing the project
    D. performing the project work

22. Which of the following actions correspond to reducing the consequences of future problems?
    A. Corrective action
    B. Preventive action
    C. Defect repair
    D. Change request

23. As a project manager for a large-scale project, you are in the process of procuring materials required for the project. Which of the following documents will you not be responsible for?
    A. Procurement documents
    B. Procurement statements of work
    C. Source selection criteria
    D. Proposals

24. During which process group will the detailed requirements be gathered?
    A. Initiating
    B. Planning
    C. Executing
    D. Closing

25. The values that illustrate PMIs code of ethics and professional conduct are
    A. respect, honesty, responsibility and honorability
    B. honesty, cultural diversity, integrity and responsibility
    C. fairness, responsibility, honesty and respect
    D. honorability, fairness, respect and responsibility

KEY (CORRECT ANSWERS)

1. A
2. D
3. C
4. C
5. D

6. C
7. C
8. C
9. C
10. C

11. A
12. D
13. C
14. C
15. D

16. B
17. B
18. C
19. B
20. B

21. B
22. B
23. D
24. B
25. C

EXAMINATION SECTION
TEST 1

DIRECTIONS: Each question or incomplete statement is followed by several suggested answers or completions. Select the one that BEST answers the question or completes the statement. *PRINT THE LETTER OF THE CORRECT ANSWER IN THE SPACE AT THE RIGHT.*

1. A database management system is

    A. hardware that monitors user log-ons and log-offs
    B. software that merges data into one pool
    C. firmware that allows high level languages to be used
    D. ROM used to store data
    E. RAM used to store data

    1.____

2. A database manager

    A. is a software package
    B. is a collection of related files
    C. permits data to be easily retrieved and manipulated
    D. permits data to be easily stored
    E. all of the above

    2.____

3. A specific advantage of a database management system is

    A. consolidation of files
    B. program dependence
    C. making programming harder
    D. restricting data flexibility
    E. all of the above

    3.____

4. Which of the following is NOT an advantage of a database management system?

    A. Easing program maintenance
    B. Restricting data flexibility
    C. Providing data security
    D. Restricting data accessibility
    E. All of the above are advantages

    4.____

5. One of the advantages of a database management system is

    A. standardization of program names
    B. standardization of paragraph names
    C. standardization of screen formats
    D. standardization of data names
    E. all are advantages of a database management system

    5.____

6. A database management system promotes

    A. data distribution   B. program distribution
    C. data security   D. special situation values
    E. access distribution

    6.____

107

7. Which of the following is NOT a type of database?

    A. Network
    B. Flat file
    C. Relational
    D. Hierarchical
    E. All are types of databases

8. In a hierarchical database management system,

    A. one data set is subservient to another
    B. a data set can be subservient to two or more other data sets
    C. data sets can be viewed as two-dimensional tables
    D. child data sets govern two or more parent data sets
    E. child data sets govern a single parent data set

9. In a network database management system,

    A. one data set is subservient to another
    B. a data set can be subservient to two or more other data sets
    C. data sets can be viewed as two-dimensional tables
    D. child data sets govern two or more parent data sets
    E. child data sets govern a single parent data set

10. In a relational database management system,

    A. one data set is subservient to another
    B. a data set can be subservient to two or more other data sets
    C. data sets can be viewed as two-dimensional tables
    D. child data sets govern two or more parent data sets
    E. child data sets govern a single parent data set

11. In a hierarchical database management system, a parent data set can govern how many other data sets?

    A. 1 B. 2 C. 3
    D. 4 E. All of the above

12. In a hierarchical database management system, a child data set is subservient to how many parent data sets?

    A. 1 B. 2 C. 3
    D. 4 E. All of the above

13. In a network database management system, a child data set is subservient to how many parent data sets?

    A. 1 B. 2 C. 3
    D. 4 E. All of the above

14. In a network database management system, a parent data set can govern how many other data sets?

    A. 1 B. 2 C. 3
    D. 4 E. All of the above

15. Which of the following database management systems is classified as relational?   15.____

    A. SQL   B. IMAGE   C. DDL   D. DML   E. IMS

16. Which of the following database management systems is classified as network?   16.____

    A. SQL   B. IMAGE   C. DDL   D. DML   E. IMS

17. Which of the following database management systems is classified as hierarchical?   17.____

    A. SQL   B. IMAGE   C. DDL   D. DML   E. IMS

18. In a relational database management system, a record is called a(n)   18.____

    A. relation   B. attribute   C. tuple
    D. join   E. none of the above

19. In a relational database management system, a file is called a(n)   19.____

    A. relation   B. attribute   C. tuple
    D. join   E. none of the above

20. In a relational database management system, a field is called a(n)   20.____

    A. relation   B. domain   C. tuple
    D. join   E. none of the above

KEY (CORRECT ANSWERS)

1. B   11. E
2. E   12. A
3. A   13. E
4. B   14. E
5. D   15. A

6. C   16. B
7. B   17. E
8. A   18. C
9. B   19. A
10. C   20. B

TEST 2

DIRECTIONS: Each question or incomplete statement is followed by several suggested answers or completions. Select the one that BEST answers the question or completes the statement. *PRINT THE LETTER OF THE CORRECT ANSWER IN THE SPACE AT THE RIGHT.*

1. Which of the following is NOT a basic operation for a relational database management system?

    A. Delete a table
    B. Create a table
    C. Join a table
    D. Union a table
    E. Delete a tuple

2. A database management system that contains its own language for manipulating the database management system is called

    A. self-contained
    B. host language
    C. network
    D. QUERY
    E. relational

3. A database management system that uses a high level language like COBOL to manipulate the database management system is called

    A. self-contained
    B. host language
    C. network
    D. QUERY
    E. relational

4. Which of the following is a language designed for novice users to locate and retrieve data?

    A. IMS   B. DDL   C. QUERY   D. COBOL   E. Pascal

5. Which of the following is NOT a common database management system utility routine?

    A. Initialization
    B. Copying
    C. Capacity changes
    D. Transaction logging
    E. None of the above

6. Generally given credit for development of relational database management systems is

    A. Grace Hopper
    B. Ada Lovelace
    C. Blaise Pascal
    D. Edgar Codd
    E. Warnier Orr

7. Relational database management systems were developed in the

    A. 1950's   B. 1960's   C. 1970's   D. 1980's   E. 1940's

8. Relational database management system can be found on _____ computers.

    A. personal
    B. main frame
    C. mini
    D. hobby
    E. all types of

9. Which of the following relational operations means to combine relations?

    A. Copy
    B. Print
    C. Create
    D. Join
    E. Add an attribute

10. We define a database management system with a

    A. DML B. COBOL program C. schema or DDL
    D. IMS E. QUERY

11. We can read, store, or modify data in a database management system with a(n)

    A. DML B. COBOL program C. schema or DDL
    D. IMS E. QUERY

12. A novice user can interrogate a database management system with

    A. DML B. COBOL program C. schema or DDL
    D. IMS E. QUERY

13. A commonly used database management system is

    A. DML B. COBOL program C. schema or DDL
    D. IMS E. QUERY

14. Which of the following is NOT an example of a database management system control system?

    A. Transaction logging B. Checking access rights
    C. Back down D. Back up
    E. All are control systems

15. Which of the following database management system control system records all changes made to the database management system?

    A. Transaction logging B. Checking access rights
    C. Back down D. Back up
    E. All are control systems

16. Which of the following database management system control systems tests for read or write capability?

    A. Transaction logging B. Checking access rights
    C. Back down D. Back up
    E. All are control systems

17. Which of the following database management system control systems copies the database management system to another disk or tape?

    A. Transaction logging B. Checking access rights
    C. Back down D. Back up
    E. All are control systems

18. IMAGE is a

    A. network database management system
    B. operation on Hewlett Packard computers
    C. system that has an Inquiry language called QUERY
    D. host language system
    E. All of the above

19. IBM's IMS

    A. is a network database management system
    B. operates on Hewlett Packard computers
    C. has an Inquiry language called QUERY
    D. is a host language system
    E. is none of the above

20. Burroughs DMS-II

    A. is a network database management system
    B. operates on Hewlett Packard computers
    C. has an Inquiry language called QUERY
    D. is a host language system
    E. is all of the above

KEY (CORRECT ANSWERS)

1.	D	11.	B
2.	A	12.	E
3.	B	13.	D
4.	C	14.	C
5.	E	15.	A
6.	D	16.	B
7.	C	17.	D
8.	E	18.	E
9.	D	19.	E
10.	C	20.	A

EXAMINATION SECTION
TEST 1

DIRECTIONS: Each question or incomplete statement is followed by several suggested answers or completions. Select the one that BEST answers the question or completes the statement. *PRINT THE LETTER OF THE CORRECT ANSWER IN THE SPACE AT THE RIGHT.*

1. Which of the following is NOT a characteristic of a relational database   1.____

    A. It is a two-dimensional table.
    B. Each row is distinct.
    C. The key fields are created by a programmer.
    D. Each column has a distinct name.
    E. The order of columns is immaterial.

2. Each row of a relational database is called a   2.____

    A. table   B. row   C. column
    D. tuple   E. none of the above

3. Each column of a relational database is called a   3.____

    A. table   B. row   C. column
    D. tuple   E. attribute

4. The _____ is NOT a component of a database application system.   4.____

    A. hardware   B. programs
    C. data   D. procedures
    E. decision support system

5. The structure of the entire database is called a   5.____

    A. DBMS   B. schema
    C. application mechanism D. DBA
    E. hierarchy

6. Which of the following is the national query language?   6.____

    A. IDMS   B. dBase III Plus
    C. SQL   D. DB2
    E. none of the above

7. Metadata is a term MOST closely associated with the _____ of a data base management system.   7.____

    A. forms generator
    B. data dictionary
    C. database programming language
    D. query languages
    E. data models

8. The _____ is responsible for the development, operation, maintenance, and administration of the database.   8.____

    A. DDL   B. DBM   C. DBA   D. DL/1   E. DBTG

113

9. In a local area network, the common database is located in the microcomputer 9.___

    A. subdirectory
    B. LAN
    C. file server
    D. Distributed Transaction Manager (DTM)
    E. Device Media Control Locator (DMCL)

10. The _____ data model is also called the *tree* model. 10.___

    A. hierarchical   B. relational   C. network
    D. inverted   E. none of the above

11. A group of one or more attributes (columns in a relation) that uniquely identifies a record in a file is called a 11.___

    A. descriptor   B. indicator   C. key
    D. field   E. pointer

12. The *lock manager* is responsible for 12.___

    A. securing the DBMS from unauthorized users
    B. securing the DBMS from disasters such as fire or flood
    C. preventing undesirable results from occurring during concurrent processing
    D. rollback and recovery procedures
    E. all of the above

13. The MOST common computer programming language used with database management systems is 13.___

    A. PL/1   B. Fortran   C. Basic
    D. QBE   E. COBOL

14. Which of the following is NOT a microcomputer database management system? 14.___

    A. Rbase   B. dBase   C. Oracle
    D. DB2   E. None of the above

15. Which of the following symbols is NOT used with data flow diagrams? 15.___

A. (circle)　　B. (square)　　C. (curved arrow)

D. (diamond)　　E. (open rectangle)

16. The *father* of the relational database model is 16.____

    A. Codd   B. Martin   C. Djikstra
    D. Kroenke   E. Boyce

17. The process of grouping together fields in a database to form a well-structured relation is called 17.____

    A. dependency   B. data modeling
    C. normalization   D. logical database design
    E. relational design

18. A relationship between fields in a database is called 18.____

    A. relational dependency
    B. functional dependency
    C. first normal form
    D. logical database design
    E. domain/key normal form

19. The notation used for describing a one-to-many relationship between data is 19.____

    A. 1:M   B. 1:!   C. M:1
    D. 1:N   E. none of the above

20. The data in a database is the property of the 20.____

    A. users
    B. database administrator
    C. manufacturer of the database software
    D. government
    E. none of the above

21. The data dictionary lists the 21.____

    A. standard names for data items in the database
    B. files in a database system
    C. relationships between data in a database
    D. all of the above
    E. none of the above

22. The process of recreating a database system from start is called 22.____

    A. recovery   B. rollback   C. rebuilding
    D. back-up   E. reduplication

23. The process of correcting an error or group of errors is called 23.____

    A. recovery   B. rollback   C. data validation
    D. back-up   E. re-initiation

24. *Deadlock* occurs when

   A. multiple users *log on* with identical passwords
   B. users cannot decide on who owns the data in the database system
   C. one group of users will not let other users have access to data
   D. two users are waiting for data that each other has locked
   E. database software does not operate properly on certain hardware

25. The PRIMARY responsibility of the database administrator (DBA) is to

   A. maintain the data dictionary
   B. meet with end users to determine their needs from the database management system
   C. safeguard the database and optimize the benefits users derive from it
   D. develop database applications
   E. specify the software to be used for the database management system

---

KEY (CORRECT ANSWERS)

1.	C	11.	C
2.	D	12.	C
3.	E	13.	E
4.	E	14.	E
5.	B	15.	D
6.	C	16.	A
7.	B	17.	C
8.	C	18.	B
9.	C	19.	D
10.	A	20.	A

21.	D
22.	A
23.	B
24.	D
25.	C

TEST 2

DIRECTIONS: Each question or incomplete statement is followed by several suggested answers or completions. Select the one that BEST answers the question or completes the statement. *PRINT THE LETTER OF THE CORRECT ANSWER IN THE SPACE AT THE RIGHT.*

1. The database administrator (DBA) must TYPICALLY address _____ problems. 1.____

    A. technical
    B. psychological
    C. organizational political
    D. managerial
    E. all of the above

2. The PRIMARY goal of normalization in a database is to 2.____

    A. reduce data redundancy
    B. maintain database security
    C. reduce data integrity
    D. reduce storage requirements
    E. reduce data entry volume

3. Which of the following is NOT typical of a microcomputer database management system? They 3.____

    A. use simpler administration than of mainframe database systems
    B. are primarily single-user systems
    C. are developed by end users
    D. handle up to five different applications
    E. use the hierarchial or network data model

4. The _____ data model requires the MOST maintenance by a professional database staff. 4.____

    A. relational   B. network   C. hierarchial
    D. tree   E. none of the above

5. Concatenation is 5.____

    A. the joining of two fields (attributes) to uniquely identify a record in a field
    B. the splitting of one field into two separate parts
    C. a method of changing the definition of a field
    D. a type of relationship between two files
    E. a type of random access

6. A general language used to communicate with the database management system is 6.____
    A. DDL   B. CODASYL   C. DBTG   D. DAD   E. QBE

7. A mathematical formula for calculating a disk address for a key field is called   7.___

   A. linear projection
   B. location numeration
   C. hierarchial sequential access method
   D. indexing
   E. hashing

8. The transferring of data from a personal computer to a mainframe computer is called   8.___

   A. downloading   B. uploading   C. modeming
   D. handshaking   E. none of the above

9. The initial one-time cost of starting up a database management system is called   9.___

   A. software maintenance
   B. software development
   C. computer system overhead
   D. DBMS installation
   E. training

10. Which of the following is NOT a benefit that is derived from having a well-designed database management system?   10.___

    A. Improved security of data
    B. Better information provided to users
    C. Reduced administration resources
    D. More accurate information
    E. Reduced maintenance and program development costs

11. In many companies, user departments are charged for using the database management system.   11.___
    Resource utilization billing charges the area user based upon

    A. a fixed amount per period
    B. a fixed amount, dependent on the type of application being used
    C. time, transactions processed, computer resources
    D. a fixed amount per user
    E. the number of transactions processed

12. _____ is NOT a function of the database administrator(DBA).   12.___

    A. Training
    B. Data dictionary management
    C. Database loading
    D. Entering data and querying database for users
    E. Database security

13. The process of evaluating the proper hardware environment for the database management system is called   13.___

    A. tuning   B. performance monitoring
    C. sizing   D. feature evaluation
    E. feature implementation

14. A data model is the 14.____

    A. method for organizing a database
    B. physical structure of the database
    C. language used to query the database
    D. database management system software
    E. conceptual view of the database

15. The data model which is GENERALLY considered to be the *slowest* in performance is 15.____
    the _____ model.

    A. network   B. hierarchial   C. inverted
    D. relational   E. all of the above

16. Which data model provides the link in which data is related together within the data 16.____
    itself?

    A. Network   B. Hierarchial   C. Plex
    D. Tree   E. Relational

Questions 17-20.

DIRECTIONS: Use the following relational database to answer Questions 17 through 20.

23	SIMMONS	1B	.324
31	WILSON	OF	.309
19	FARMER	P	.144

17. How many *tuples* are depicted? 17.____

    A. One   B. Two   C. Three
    D. Four   E. None of the above

18. How many *tables* are depicted? 18.____

    A. One   B. Two   C. Three
    D. Four   E. None of the above

19. How many *data elements* are depicted? 19.____

    A. One   B. Two   C. Three
    D. Four   E. None of the above

20. How many *attributes* are depicted? 20.____

    A. One   B. Two   C. Three
    D. Four   E. None of the above

21. A database administrator (DBA) is analogous to a 21.____

    A. salesperson   B. accountant   C. vice president
    D. auditor   E. controller

22. _____ is the preferred method of recovering a database system from a system failure.   22._____

    A. Reprocessing
    B. Rollback
    C. Rollforward
    D. Rollback/rollforward
    E. Restoring from backup tapes or disks

23. A set of possible values for a data field that defines a range of valid data entries for that field is called a   23._____

    A. derived range
    B. validation check
    C. domain
    D. enumerated range
    E. condition name

24. The _____ database operation produces a new relationship by combining two existing relations.   24._____

    A. extract
    B. join
    C. combine
    D. selection
    E. all of the above

25. Which of the following is a selection criteria for a data model?   25._____

    A. Vendor support
    B. Security
    C. Performance
    D. User interface
    E. All of the above

KEY (CORRECT ANSWERS)

1. E
2. A
3. E
4. B
5. A

6. A
7. E
8. B
9. D
10. C

11. C
12. D
13. C
14. A
15. D

16. E
17. C
18. A
19. E
20. D

21. E
22. D
23. C
24. B
25. E

EXAMINATION SECTION
TEST 1

DIRECTIONS: Each question or incomplete statement is followed by several suggested answers or completions. Select the one that BEST answers the question or completes the statement. *PRINT THE LETTER OF THE CORRECT ANSWER IN THE SPACE AT THE RIGHT.*

1. A database uses _____ to identify information.

    A. record numbers
    B. register addresses
    C. field names
    D. directories

    1.____

2. _____ could be added to a database in order to increase the number of search and access points available to a user.

    A. Subject discriptors
    B. Partitions
    C. Term authority lists
    D. Call programs

    2.____

3. The central idea behind the management of a database is

    A. procedural and nonprocedural interfaces
    B. minimal redundancy and minimal storage space
    C. physical data independence
    D. the separation of data description and data manipulation

    3.____

4. Which of the following is NOT a type of query language operator used in database searches?

    A. Object-oriented
    B. Logical
    C. Relational
    D. Mathematical

    4.____

5. When accessing a record in an indexed file, which of the following steps would be performed FIRST?

    A. Accessing the index
    B. Disk access to the record or bucket
    C. Data transfer from disk to main program memory
    D. Relative address conversion to absolute address

    5.____

6. A database management system (DBMS) that employs a hierarchy, but may relate each lower-level data element to more than one parent element, is classified specifically as a(n) _____ DBMS.

    A. object-oriented
    B. network
    C. relational
    D. aggregational

    6.____

7. A value-added field might be added to a database in order to

    A. standardize field formats
    B. estimate the disk capacity for a full database
    C. provide indexing consistency
    D. improve retrieval

    7.____

8. Each of the following disks is a type of direct-access disk-storage system EXCEPT

   A. magnetic disk
   B. floppy
   C. moving-capstan
   D. fixed-head

9. In determining an appropriate file organization, three principal factors must be considered.
   Which of the following is NOT one of these factors?

   A. Volatility
   B. Conversion
   C. Activity
   D. Size

10. A _____ file is used to update or modify data in a master file.

    A. descriptor
    B. transaction
    C. secondary
    D. conversion

11. Which of the following steps in designing and using a database would be performed FIRST?

    A. Selecting a name for the file
    B. Deciding the form into which information should be stored
    C. Data definition
    D. Defining the type of data to be stored in each field

12. Each of the following is an advantage associated with the use of a DBMS over a flat-file system EXCEPT

    A. fewer storage requirements
    B. better data integrity
    C. lower software costs
    D. lower operating costs

13. Memory storage space that is not directly addressable by processor instructions, but by specialized I/O instructions, is called

    A. allocated memory
    B. secondary storage
    C. internal storage
    D. main memory

14. Which of the following is NOT a disadvantage associated with sequential file processing?

    A. Master files must be sorted into key field sequence.
    B. Files are only current immediately after an update.
    C. Files are difficult to design.
    D. Transaction files must be stored in the same key.

15. When data is updated in some, but not all, of the files in which it appears, _____ has occurred.

    A. data confusion
    B. data dependence
    C. cross-keying
    D. data redundancy

16. The MOST common medium for direct-access storage is

    A. optical disk
    B. magnetic tape
    C. hard card
    D. magnetic disk

17. The purpose of *hashing* is to

    A. discover an unpartitioned sector onto which data may be written
    B. determine a schedule by which batch-processed data may be submitted to the computer
    C. create a buffer delay between data entry and output during interactive processing
    D. convert the key field value for a record to the address of the record on a file

18. What is the term for the description of a specific set of data corresponding to a model of an enterprise, which is obtained by using a particular data description language?

    A. Schema
    B. Descriptor
    C. Object instance
    D. Conceptualization

19. In a sequential file, records are arranged in sequence according to one or more

    A. query languages
    B. column numbers
    C. key fields
    D. hash marks

20. Which of the following is NOT a mathematical query language operator used in database searches?

    A. +
    B. >=
    C. ^
    D. /

21. In _____ file organization, the cost per each transaction processed remains about the same as the percent of records accessed on a file increases.

    A. sequential
    B. hashed
    C. indexed sequential
    D. random

22. For more complex data types, such as those used in multimedia applications, what type of DBMS would be MOST useful?

    A. Hierarchical
    B. Relational
    C. Object-oriented
    D. Network

23. When determining how many generations of a file to retain in a database, the PRIMARY factor is usually

    A. hardware capabilities
    B. storage space
    C. whether files are keyed or indexed
    D. probability of need to access old data for recovery purposes

24. When data is transferred from a user program to secondary storage, it first passes through

    A. program private memory
    B. file system buffers
    C. I/O buffers
    D. program code

25. In order to maintain files in a database, each of the following operations is typically required EXCEPT

    A. balancing index trees
    B. altering the file system's directory
    C. changing field widths
    D. adding fields to records

KEY (CORRECT ANSWERS)

1. C
2. A
3. D
4. A
5. A

6. B
7. D
8. C
9. B
10. B

11. B
12. C
13. B
14. C
15. A

16. D
17. D
18. A
19. C
20. B

21. D
22. C
23. D
24. D
25. B

TEST 2

DIRECTIONS: Each question or incomplete statement is followed by several suggested answers or completions. Select the one that BEST answers the question or completes the statement. *PRINT THE LETTER OF THE CORRECT ANSWER IN THE SPACE AT THE RIGHT.*

1. An installation has two tape drives and one disk drive. An application program requires access to three sequential files: an old master file, a transaction file, and an updated master file.
   Typically, the _____ file should be stored on the disk.

   A. old master
   B. transaction
   C. updated master
   D. both versions of the master

   1._____

2. The purpose of *record blocking* is to

   A. allow multiple records to be brought into main memory in a single access to secondary storage
   B. create the illusion of a *virtual device* for the program until the spooler copies a record to the real device
   C. allocate more free buffer space to a file prior to run-unit determination
   D. offload responsibilities for building data paths from the CPU

   2._____

3. Entries in a database's secondary key tables (index files), which tell the computer where a data is stored on the disk, are

   A. logical records   B. data addresses
   C. physical records   D. secondary keys

   3._____

4. Of the types of file organization below, which involves the LOWEST volatility?

   A. Direct   B. Sequential
   C. Master-keyed   D. Indexed

   4._____

5. Typically each of the following elements is defined during the *data definition* process EXCEPT

   A. field types   B. field names
   C. number of columns   D. width of fields

   5._____

6. A database's master index contains

   A. the key values for an indexed sequential file
   B. the machine code for every field in a given set of records
   C. the logical record for every randomly-accessed file
   D. each field's physical location on a disk pack

   6._____

7. Which of the following types of information would MOST likely be stored in a logic field?

   A. Calendar month/day/year
   B. A patient or customer's mailing address
   C. Numbers that may later be involved in some mathematical calculations
   D. The designation of an employee's status is hourly or salaried

   7._____

125

8. When determining how frequently a sequential master file should be updated, each of the following factors should be considered EXCEPT

   A. activity ratio
   B. rate of data change
   C. storage space
   D. urgency for current data

9. Which of the following programs is a file manager, rather than a DBMS?

   A. Q&A   B. FoxPro   C. Approach   D. Paradox

10. Which of the following is NOT an advantage associated with the use of indexed file processing?

    A. No need for hashing algorithm
    B. Random access is faster than direct processing
    C. Can function with applications required for both sequential and direct processing
    D. Access to specific records faster than sequential processing

11. Of the query language operators listed below, which is mathematical?

    A. AND   B. SUB   C. <   D. SQRT(N)

12. A collection of records may sometimes be structured as a file on secondary storage, rather than as a data structure in main memory.
    Which of the following is NOT a possible reason for this?

    A. Permanence of storage
    B. Security concerns
    C. Size of collection
    D. Selective access requirements

13. What is the term for the disk rotation time needed for the physical record to pass under read/write heads?

    A. Transaction time
    B. Latency time
    C. Head displacement time
    D. Transfer time

14. The subset of a database schema required by a particular application program is referred to as a(n)

    A. root
    B. user's view
    C. logical structure
    D. node

15. Which of the following steps in designing and using a database would be performed LAST?

    A. Defining the type of data that will be stored in each field
    B. Assigning field names
    C. Data definition
    D. Defining the width of alphanumeric and numeric fields

16. What type of database structure organizes data in the form of two-dimensional tables?

    A. Relational
    B. Network
    C. Logical
    D. Hierarchical

17. What is the term for the specific modules that are capable of reading and writing buffer contents on devices?

    A. Spoolers
    B. Device handlers
    C. I/O managers
    D. Memory allocators

18. Each of the following is a disadvantage associated with the use of a DBMS EXCEPT

    A. extensive conversion costs
    B. possible wide distribution of data losses and damage
    C. reduced data security
    D. start-up costs

19. _____ decisions about a database begin after a feasibility study and continue to be refined throughout the design and creation process.

    A. Procedural
    B. Structural
    C. Conversion
    D. Content

20. Each of the following is an advantage associated with direct file processing EXCEPT

    A. ability to update several files at the same time
    B. no need for separate transaction files
    C. files do not have to be sorted into key field sequence
    D. fewer storage space required than for sequential processing

21. The core of any file management system accesses secondary storage through

    A. the I/O manager
    B. file system buffers
    C. relative addressing
    D. key access

22. Each of the following is a responsibility typically belonging to a file system EXCEPT

    A. maintaining directories
    B. interfacing the CPU with a secondary storage device
    C. establishing paths for data flow between main memory and secondary storage
    D. buffering data for delivery to the CPU or secondary devices

23. In a hierarchical database, there are several phone numbers belonging to a single address.
    This is an example of

    A. vector data aggregate
    B. data dependence
    C. data confusion
    D. data redundancy

24. A DBMS might access the data dictionary for each of the following purposes EXCEPT

    A. change the description of a data field
    B. to determine if a data element already exists before adding
    C. request and deliver information from the database to the user
    D. determine what application programs can access what data elements

25. _____ would MOST likely be stored in a memo field.   25.____
    A. A revisable listing of symptoms specific to a particular ailment
    B. The designation of a patient's gender (male/female)
    C. A patient's billing number
    D. The date of a patient's last visit

KEY (CORRECT ANSWERS)

1.	B	11.	D
2.	A	12.	B
3.	A	13.	B
4.	B	14.	B
5.	C	15.	D
6.	A	16.	A
7.	D	17.	B
8.	C	18.	C
9.	A	19.	B
10.	B	20.	D

21. A
22. B
23. A
24. C
25. A

READING COMPREHENSION
UNDERSTANDING AND INTERPRETING WRITTEN MATERIAL

EXAMINATION SECTION
TEST 1

DIRECTIONS: Each question or incomplete statement is followed by several suggested answers or completions. Select the one that BEST answers the question or completes the statement. *PRINT THE LETTER OF THE CORRECT ANSWER IN THE SPACE AT THE RIGHT.*

Questions 1-7.

DIRECTIONS: Questions 1 through 7 are to be answered SOLELY on the basis of the following passage.

The first step in establishing a programming development schedule is to rate the programs to be developed or to be maintained on the basis of complexity, size, and input-output complexity. The most experienced programmer should rate the program complexity based on the system flow chart. The same person should do all of the rating so that all programs are rated in the same manner. If possible, the same person who rates the complexity should estimate the program size based on the number of pages of coding. This rating can easily be checked, after coding has been completed, against the number of pages of coding actually produced. If there is consistent error in the estimates for program size, all future estimates should be corrected for this error or the estimating method reviewed.

The input-output rating is a mechanical count of the number of input and output units or tapes which the program uses. The objective is to measure the number of distinct files which the program must control.

After the ratings have been completed, the man-days required for each of the tasks can be calculated. Good judgment or, if available, a table of past experience is used to translate the ratings into man-days, the units in which the schedule is expressed. The calculations should keep the values for each task completely separate so that a later evaluation can be made by program, programmer, and function.

After the values have been calculated, it is a simple matter to establish a development schedule. This can be a simple bar chart which assigns work to specific programmers, a complex computer program using the *PERT* technique of critical path scheduling, or other useful type of document.

1. The rating and estimating of the programs should be performed by   1.____
    A. the person who will do the programming
    B. a programmer trainee
    C. the most experienced programmer
    D. the operations supervisor

2. The measurement used to express the programming schedule is the number of

    A. distinct files controlled by the programmer
    B. man-days
    C. pages of coding
    D. programmers

3. A mechanical count of the number of input and output units or tapes should be considered as a(n)

    A. input-output rating
    B. measure of the number of man-days required
    C. rating of complexity
    D. estimate of the number of pages of coding

4. Programming development scheduling methods are for

    A. new programs only
    B. programs to be developed and maintained
    C. large and complicated programs only
    D. maintenance programs only

5. If there is a consistent error in the estimates for program size, all estimates should be

    A. adjusted for future programs
    B. eliminated for all programs
    C. replaced by rating of complexity
    D. replaced by input-output rating

6. It is intimated that

    A. the calculations should keep the valuations for each task completely separated
    B. it is a simple matter to establish a development schedule
    C. the man-days required for each of the tasks can be calculated
    D. a later evaluation will be made

7. Complexity of programs can be checked

    A. before coding has been completed
    B. after future estimates have been corrected for error
    C. as a first step in establishing a complex computer program
    D. with reference to the number of pages of coding produced

Questions 8-13.

DIRECTIONS: Questions 8 through 13 are to be answered SOLELY on the basis of the following passage.

The purposes of program testing are to determine that the program has been coded correctly, that the coding matches the logical design, and that the logical design matches the basic requirements of the job as set down in the specifications. Program errors fall into the following categories: errors in logic, clerical errors, misidentification of the computer components' functions, misinterpretation of the requirements of the job, and system analysis errors.

The number of errors in a program will average one for each 125 instructions, assuming that the programmer has been reasonably careful in his coding system. The number of permutations and combinations of conditions in a program may reach into the billions before each possibility has been thoroughly checked out. It is, therefore, a practical impossibility to check out each and every possible combination of conditions—the effort would take years, even in the simplest program. As a result, it is quite possible for errors to remain latent for a number of years, suddenly appearing when a particular combination is reached which had not previously occurred.

Latent program errors will remain in operating programs, and their occurrence should be minimized by complete and thorough testing. The fact that the program is operative and reaches end-of-job satisfactorily does not mean that all of the exception conditions and their permutations and combinations have been tested. Quite the contrary, many programs reach end-of-job after very few tests, since the *straight-line* part of the program is often simplest. However, the exceptions programmed to deal with a minimal percentage of the input account for a large percentage of the instructions. It is, therefore, quite possible to reach the end-of-job halt with only 10% of the program checked out.

8. One of the MAIN points of this passage is that

   A. it is impossible to do a good job of programming
   B. reaching end-of-job means only 10% of the program is checked out
   C. standard testing procedures should require testing of every possible combination of conditions
   D. elimination of all errors can never be assured, but the occurrence of errors can be minimized by thorough testing

9. Latent program errors GENERALLY

   A. evade detection for some time
   B. are detected in the last test run
   C. test the number of permutations and combinations in a program
   D. allow the program to go to end-of-job

10. Which one of the following statements pertaining to errors in a program is CORRECT?

    A. If the program has run to a normal completion, then all program errors have been eliminated.
    B. Program errors, if not caught in testing, will surely be detected in the first hundred runs of the program.
    C. It is practically impossible to verify that the typical program is free of errors.
    D. A program that is coded correctly is free of errors.

11. Among other things, program testing is designed to

    A. assure that the documentation is correct
    B. assure that the coding is correct
    C. determine the program running time
    D. measure programmer's performance

12. The difficulty in detecting errors in programs is due to   12._____

    A. the extremely large number of conditions that exist in a program
    B. poor analysis of work errors
    C. very sophisticated and clever programming
    D. reaching the end-of-job halt with only 10% of the program checked out

13. If the program being tested finally reaches the end-of-job halt, it means that   13._____

    A. one path through the program has been successfully tested
    B. less than 10% of the program has been tested
    C. the program has been coded correctly
    D. the logical design is correct

Questions 14-20.

DIRECTIONS: Questions 14 through 20 are to be answered SOLELY on the basis of the following passage.

　　Systems analysis represents a major link in the chain of translations from the problem to its machine solution. After the problem and its requirements for solution have been stated in clear terms, the systems analyst defines the broad outlines of the machine solution. He must know the overall capabilities of the equipment, and he must be familiar with the application. The ultimate output of the analysis is a detailed job specification containing all the tools necessary to produce a series of computer programs. The purpose of the specifications is to document and describe the system by defining the problem and the proposed solution, explain system outputs and functions, state system requirements for programmers, and to avoid misunderstandings among involved departments. The specification serves as a link between the analysis of the problem and the next function, programming. Systems analysis relies on creativity rather than rote analysis to develop effective computer systems. But this creativity must be channeled and documented effectively if lasting value is to be obtained.

14. According to the above paragraph, the systems analyst MUST be familiar with   14._____

    A. programming and the machine solution
    B. the machine solution and the next function
    C. the application and programming
    D. the application and the equipment capabilities

15. According to the above paragraph, the time that systems analysis MUST be performed is   15._____

    A. *after* the problem analysis
    B. *after* programming
    C. *before* problem definition
    D. *before* problem analysis

16. According to the above paragraph, the MAIN task performed by the systems analyst is to   16._____

    A. write the program
    B. analyze the problem
    C. define the overall capacities of the equipment
    D. define the machine solution of the problem

17. According to the above paragraph, the document produced by the systems analyst as his main output does NOT normally include

    A. an explanation of system outputs
    B. system requirements for programmers
    C. a statement of the problem
    D. performance standards

17._____

18. According to the above paragraph, the systems analysis function is

    A. relatively straightforward, requiring little creative effort
    B. extremely complex, making standard procedures impossible
    C. primarily a rote memory procedure
    D. a creative effort

18._____

19. According to the above paragraph, the specification

    A. is a major link in the sequence from problem to machine solution
    B. states the problem and its requirements for solution
    C. is chiefly concerned with the overall capabilities of the equipment
    D. represents the ultimate product of systems analysis

19._____

20. According to the above paragraph, the sequential function after the analysis of the program is

    A. documentation   B. application
    C. definition   D. programming

20._____

Questions 21-25.

DIRECTIONS: Questions 21 through 25 are to be answered SOLELY on the basis of the following passage.

Currently, memory represents one of the main limitations on computer performance and, as a result, is one of the areas where technological improvements will prove most fruitful.

Historically, the main problem of computer memories has been a very unfavorable cost-to-speed ratio. Memory devices which have great speed cost disproportionately more than those with less speed. This problem has forced computer designers to use minimum amounts of rapid access memory and to rely mainly on slower, large capacity storage. This practice has resulted in a *memory tree,* where a hierarchy of memory devices provides various increments of storage at different costs and speeds for various purposes.

To achieve better speed/cost ratios, designers are increasingly turning to memory media other than the traditional ferrite cores. These cores now account for over 90% of the memory market. Plated wire and semiconductors are the media most likely to supplant ferrite cores. Semiconductors are expected to rapidly displace cores, starting with higher speed memories. Their costs are dropping sharply and are expected to drop as much as five-fold by the middle of this decade, while their speeds are at least doubling.

Despite the increasing use of competing technologies, ferrite cores will probably still dominate the extended random access storage area. Since the largest increment of storage is associated with ferrite core memory devices, their share of the internal memory market was well over 50% by 1980. The only factor militating against this is the possibility that the largest manufacturers of computers may abandon the extended internal storage concept.

Memory developments likely to happen later in this decade include the progressive replacement of magnetic drums by magnetic disks. The latter were themselves displaced near the end of the seventies by electro optical units, followed by magnetic bubble storage. It also may prove possible to show the feasibility of associative processors. Under this concept, which is still experimental, data access would be considerably speeded through use of Contents-Addressable-Memories (CAM).

21. According to the above passage, a hierarchy of memory devices which provides various increments of storage at different costs and speeds has been used by designers because

    A. one of the larger manufacturers of computers might abandon the extended internal storage concept
    B. of the very unfavorable cost-to-speed ratio of computer memories
    C. magnetic disks have progressively replaced magnetic drums in the mid-seventies
    D. data access is expected to be appreciably speeded up through the use of Content-Addressable-Memories

22. According to the above passage, which of the following memory developments is MOST likely to have occurred by 1980?

    A. Designers will turn to memories other than core for 90% of their needs.
    B. Cores and semiconductors will largely replace plated wire memories.
    C. Cores and semiconductors will largely be replaced by electro optical and magnetic bubble storage.
    D. Ferrite core will continue to dominate the internal memory market.

23. According to the above passage, the speed/cost ratio for semiconductors is

    A. becoming more favorable
    B. the same as the speed/cost ratio for plated wire
    C. remaining constant
    D. less favorable than the speed/cost ratio for ferrite core

24. According to the information in the passage, development of improved memory technology is IMPORTANT because

    A. it demonstrates the feasibility of associative processors
    B. memory represents one of the chief limitations on computer performance today
    C. semiconductors are expected to largely replace core which now represents about half of the memory market
    D. data can now be speeded through the use of CAM

25. Three types of memory media which are discussed in the above passage are

    A. core, plated wire, semiconductors
    B. high speed buffer, magnetic disks, rotating magnetic storage
    C. ferrite cores, magnetic drums, remote data terminals
    D. high speed buffers, magnetic disks, magnetic drums

KEY (CORRECT ANSWERS)

1. C
2. B
3. A
4. B
5. A

6. D
7. D
8. D
9. A
10. C

11. B
12. A
13. A
14. D
15. A

16. D
17. D
18. D
19. D
20. D

21. B
22. D
23. A
24. B
25. A

TEST 2

DIRECTIONS: Each question or incomplete statement is followed by several suggested answers or completions. Select the one that BEST answers the question or completes the statement. *PRINT THE LETTER OF THE CORRECT ANSWER IN THE SPACE AT THE RIGHT.*

Questions 1-5.

DIRECTIONS: Questions 1 through 5 are to be answered SOLELY on the basis of the following paragraph.

Work standards presuppose an ability to measure work. Measurement in office management is needed for several reasons. First, it is necessary to evaluate the overall efficiency of the office itself. It is then essential to measure the efficiency of each particular section or unit and that of the individual worker. To plan and control the work of sections and units, one must have measurement. A program of measurement goes hand in hand with a program of standards. One can have measurement without standards, but one cannot have work standards without measurement. Providing data on amount of work done and time expended, measurement does not deal with the amount of energy expended by an individual although, in many cases, such energy may be in direct proportion to work output. Usually from two-thirds to three-fourths of all work can be measured. However, less than two-thirds of all work is actually measured because measurement difficulties are encountered when office work is non-repetitive and irregular, or when it is primarily mental rather than manual. These obstacles are often used as excuses for non-measurement far more frequently than is justified.

1. According to the above paragraph, an office manager cannot set work standards unless he can   1.____

   A. plan the amount of work to be done
   B. control the amount of work that is done
   C. estimate accurately the quantity of work done
   D. delegate the amount of work to be done to efficient workers

2. According to the above paragraph, the type of office work that would be MOST difficult to measure would be   2.____

   A. checking warrants for accuracy of information
   B. recording payroll changes
   C. processing applications
   D. making up a new system of giving out supplies

3. According to the above paragraph, the ACTUAL amount of work that is measured is _____ of all work.   3.____

   A. less than two-thirds
   B. two-thirds to three-fourths
   C. less than three-sixths
   D. more than three-fourths

4. Which of the following would be MOST difficult to determine by using measurement techniques?   4.____

   A. The amount of work that is accomplished during a certain period of time
   B. The amount of work that should be planned for a period of time
   C. How much time is needed to do a certain task
   D. The amount of incentive a person must have to do his job

5. The one of the following which is the MOST suitable title for the above paragraph is

   A. HOW MEASUREMENT OF OFFICE EFFICIENCY DEPENDS ON WORK STANDARDS
   B. USING MEASUREMENT FOR OFFICE MANAGEMENT AND EFFICIENCY
   C. WORK STANDARDS AND THE EFFICIENCY OF THE OFFICE WORKER
   D. MANAGING THE OFFICE USING MEASURED WORK STANDARDS

Questions 6-9.

DIRECTIONS: Questions 6 through 9 are to be answered SOLELY on the basis of the following passage.

    Work measurement concerns accomplishment or productivity. It has to do with results; it does not deal with the amount of energy used up, although in many cases this may be in direct proportion to the work output. Work measurement not only helps a manager to distribute work loads fairly, but it also enables him to define work success in actual units, evaluate employee performance, and determine where corrective help is needed. Work measurement is accomplished by measuring the amount produced, measuring the time spent to produce it, and relating the two. To illustrate, it is common to speak of so many orders processed within a given time. The number of orders processed becomes meaningful when related to the amount of time taken.

    Much of the work in an office can be measured fairly accurately and inexpensively. The extent of work measurement possible in any given case will depend upon the particular type of office tasks performed, but usually from two-thirds to three-fourths of all work in an office can be measured. It is true that difficulty in work measurement is encountered, for example, when the office work is irregular and not repeated often, or when the work is primarily mental rather than manual. These are problems, but they are used as excuses for doing no work measurement far more frequently than is justified.

6. According to the above passage, which of the following BEST illustrates the type of information obtained as a result of work measurement?

   A. Clerk takes one hour to file 150 folders
   B. Typist types five letters
   C. Stenographer works harder typing from shorthand notes than she does typing from a typed draft
   D. Clerk keeps track of employees' time by computing sick leave, annual leave, and overtime leave

7. The above passage does NOT indicate that work measurement can be used to help a supervisor to determine

   A. *why* an employee is performing poorly on the job
   B. *who* are the fast and slow workers in the unit
   C. *how* the work in the unit should be divided up
   D. *how* long it should take to perform a certain task

8. According to the above passage, the kind of work that would be MOST difficult to measure would be such work as

    A. sorting mail
    B. designing a form for a new procedure
    C. photocopying various materials
    D. answering inquiries with form letters

9. The excuses mentioned in the above passage for failure to perform work measurement can be BEST summarized as the

    A. repetitive nature of office work
    B. costs involved in carrying out accurate work measurement
    C. inability to properly use the results obtained from work measurement
    D. difficulty involved in measuring certain types of work

Questions 10-13.

DIRECTIONS: Questions 10 through 13 are to be answered SOLELY on the basis of the following passage.

Job analysis combined with performance appraisal is an excellent method of determining training needs of individuals. The steps in this method are to determine the specific duties of the job, to evaluate the adequacy with which the employee performs each of these duties, and finally to determine what significant improvements can be made by training.

The list of duties can be obtained in a number of ways: asking the employee, asking the supervisor, observing the employee, etc. Adequacy of performance can be estimated by the employee, but the supervisor's evaluation must also be obtained. This evaluation will usually be based on observation.

What does the supervisor observe? The employee, while he is working; the employee's work relationships; the ease, speed, and sureness of the employee's actions; the way he applies himself to the job; the accuracy and amount of completed work, its conformity with established procedures and standards; the appearance of the work; the soundness of judgment it shows; and, finally, signs of good or poor communication, understanding, and cooperation among employees.

Such observation is a normal and inseparable part of the everyday job of supervision. Systematically recorded, evaluated, and summarized, it highlights both general and individual training needs.

10. According to the above passage, job analysis may be used by the supervisor in

    A. increasing his own understanding of tasks performed in his unit
    B. increasing efficiency of communication within the organization
    C. assisting personnel experts in the classification of positions
    D. determining in which areas an employee needs more instruction

11. According to the above passage, the FIRST step in determining the training needs of employees is to

    A. locate the significant improvements that can be made by training
    B. determine the specific duties required in a job
    C. evaluate the employee's performance
    D. motivate the employee to want to improve himself

12. On the basis of the above passage, which of the following is the BEST way for a supervisor to determine the adequacy of employee performance? 12.____

    A. Check the accuracy and amount of completed work
    B. Ask the training officer
    C. Observe all aspects of the employee's work
    D. Obtain the employee's own estimate

13. Which of the following is NOT mentioned by the above passage as a factor to be taken into consideration in judging the adequacy of employee performance? 13.____

    A. Accuracy of completed work
    B. Appearance of completed work
    C. Cooperation among employees
    D. Attitude of the employee toward his supervisor

Questions 14-15.

DIRECTIONS: Questions 14 and 15 are to be answered SOLELY on the basis of the following paragraph.

The fundamental characteristic of the type of remote control which management needs to bridge the gap between itself and actual operations is the more effective use of records and reports — more specifically, the gathering and interpretation of the facts contained in records and reports. Facts, for management purposes, are those data (narrative and quantitative) which express in simple terms the current standing of the agency's program, work, and resources in relation to the plans and policies formulated by management. They are those facts or measures (1) which permit management to compare current status with past performance and with its forecasts for the immediate future, and (2) which provide management with a reliable basis for long-range forecasting.

14. For management purposes, facts are, according to the above paragraph, 14.____

    A. forecasts which can be compared to current status
    B. data which can be used for certain control purposes
    C. a fundamental characteristic of a type of remote control
    D. the data contained in records and reports

15. An inference which can be drawn from this statement is that 15.____

    A. management which has a reliable basis for long-range forecasting has at its disposal a type of remote control which is needed to bridge the gap between itself and actual operations
    B. data which do not express in simple terms the current standing of the agency's program, work, and resources in relationship to the plans and policies formulated by management may still be facts for management purposes
    C. data which express relationships among the agency's program, work, and resources are management facts
    D. the gap between management and actual operations can only be bridged by characteristics which are fundamentally a type of remote control

Questions 16-17.

DIRECTIONS: Questions 16 and 17 are to be answered SOLELY on the basis of the following passage.

Two approaches are available in developing criteria for the evaluation of plans. One approach, designated Approach A, is a review and analysis of characteristics that differentiate successful plans from unsuccessful plans. These criteria are descriptive in nature and serve as a checklist against which the plan under consideration may be judged. These characteristics have been observed by many different students of planning, and there is considerable agreement concerning the characteristics necessary for a plan to be successful.

A second approach to the development of criteria for judging plans, designated Approach B, is the determination of the degree to which the plan under consideration is economic. The word *economic* is used here in its broadest sense; i.e., effective in its utilization of resources. In order to determine the economic worth of a plan, it is necessary to use a technique that permits the description of any plan in economic terms and to utilize this technique to the extent that it becomes a *way of thinking* about plans.

16. According to Approach B, the MOST successful plan is *generally* one which 16.____

    A. costs least to implement
    B. gives most value for resources expended
    C. uses the least expensive resources
    D. utilizes the greatest number of resources

17. According to Approach A, a successful plan is one which is 17.____

    A. descriptive in nature
    B. lowest in cost
    C. similar to other successful plans
    D. agreed upon by many students of planning

Questions 18-20.

DIRECTIONS: Questions 18 through 20 are to be answered SOLELY on the basis of the following passage.

The primary purpose of control reports is to supply information intended to serve as the basis for corrective action if needed. At the same time, the significance of control reports must be kept in proper perspective. Control reports are only a part of the planning-management information system. Control information includes nonfinancial as well as financial data that measure performance and isolate variances from standard. Control information also provides feedback so that planning information may be updated and corrected. Whenever possible, control reports should be designed so that they provide feedback for the planning process as well as provide information of immediate value to the control process.

Since the culmination of the control process is the taking of necessary corrective action to bring performance in line with standards, it follows that control information must be directed to the person who is organizationally responsible for taking the required action. Usually the same information, though in a somewhat abbreviated form, is given to the responsible manager's superior. A district sales manager needs a complete daily record of the performance of each of his salesmen; yet, the report forwarded to the regional sales manager summarizes only the performance of each sales district in his region. In preparing reports for higher echelons of management, summary statements and recommendations for action should appear on the first page; substantiating data, usually the information presented to the person directly responsible for the operation, may be included if needed.

18. A control report serves its primary purpose as part of the process which leads DIRECTLY to

    A. better planning for future action
    B. increasing the performance of district salesmen
    C. the establishment of proper performance standards
    D. taking corrective action when performance is poor

19. The one of the following which would be the BEST description of a control report is that a control report is a form of

    A. planning
    B. communication
    C. direction
    D. organization

20. If control reports are to be effective, the one of the following which is LEAST essential to the effectiveness of control reporting is a system of

    A. communication
    B. standards
    C. authority
    D. work simplification

Questions 21-23.

DIRECTIONS: Questions 21 through 23 are to be answered SOLELY on the basis of the following passage.

The need for the best in management techniques has given rise to the expression *scientific management*. Within reasonable limits, management can be scientific, but it will probably be many decades before it becomes truly scientific either in the factory or in the office. As long as it is impossible to measure accurately individual performance and to equate human behavior, so long will it be impossible to develop completely scientific techniques of office management. There is a likelihood, of course, that management might be reduced to a science when it is applied to inanimate objects which facilitate operations such as machinery, office equipment and furnishings, and forms. The limiting factor, therefore, is the human element.

21. The above passage is concerned PRIMARILY with the

    A. value of scientific office management
    B. methods for the development of scientific office management
    C. need for the best office management techniques
    D. possibility of reducing office management to a science

22. According to the above passage, the realization of truly scientific office management is dependent upon the

    A. expression of management techniques
    B. development of accurate personnel measurement techniques

C. passage of many decades, most probably
D. elimination of individual differences in human behavior

23. According to the above passage, the scientific management of inanimate objects   23._____

    A. occurs automatically because there is no human factor
    B. cannot occur in a factory, but can occur in an office
    C. could be achieved without the concurrent achievement of truly scientific office management
    D. is not a necessary component of truly scientific office management

Questions 24-25.

DIRECTIONS: Questions 24 and 25 are to be answered SOLELY on the basis of the following paragraph.

Your role as human resources utilization experts is to submit your techniques to operating administrators, for the program must, in reality, be theirs, not yours. We, in personnel, have been guilty of encouraging operating executives to believe that these important matters affecting their employees are personnel department matters, not management matters. We should hardly be surprised, as a consequence, to find these executives playing down the role of personnel and finding personnel routines a nuisance, for these are not in the mainstream of managing the enterprise – or so we have encouraged them to believe.

24. The BEST of the following interpretations of the above paragraph is that   24._____

    A. personnel people have been guilty of *passing the buck* on personnel functions
    B. operating officials have difficulty understanding personnel techniques
    C. personnel employees have tended to usurp some functions rightfully belonging to management
    D. matters affecting employees should be handled by the personnel department

25. The BEST of the following interpretations of the above paragraph is that   25._____

    A. personnel departments have aided and abetted the formulation of negative attitudes on the part of management
    B. personnel people are labor relations experts and should carry out these duties
    C. personnel activities are not really the responsibility of management
    D. management is now being encouraged by personnel experts to assume some responsibility for personnel functions

KEY (CORRECT ANSWERS)

1. C
2. D
3. A
4. D
5. B

6. A
7. A
8. B
9. D
10. D

11. B
12. C
13. D
14. B
15. C

16. B
17. C
18. D
19. B
20. D

21. D
22. B
23. C
24. C
25. A

TEST 3

DIRECTIONS: Each question or incomplete statement is followed by several suggested answers or completions. Select the one that BEST answers the question or completes the statement. *PRINT THE LETTER OF THE CORRECT ANSWER IN THE SPACE AT THE RIGHT.*

Questions 1-3

DIRECTIONS: Questions 1 through 3 are to be answered SOLELY on the basis of the following paragraph.

   Prior to revising its child care program, a department feels that it is necessary to get some information from the mothers served by the existing program in order to determine where changes are required. A questionnaire is to be constructed to obtain this information.

1. Of the following points which can be taken into consideration in the construction of the questionnaire, the one which is of LEAST importance is

   A. that the data are to be put into punch cards
   B. the aspects of the program which seem to be in need of change
   C. the type of person who will fill out the questionnaire
   D. testing the questionnaire for ambiguity in advance of general distribution
   E. setting up a control group so that answers received can be compared to a standard

2. To discuss this questionnaire with all mothers who have been asked to answer it, before they actually fill it out, is

   A. *desirable;* the mothers may be able to offer valuable suggestions for changes in the form of the questionnaire
   B. *undesirable;* it is of some value but consumes too much valuable time
   C. *desirable;* cooperation and uniform interpretation will tend to be achieved
   D. *undesirable;* it may cause the answers to be biased
   E. *desirable;* the group will tend to support the program

3. Of the following items included in the questionnaire, the one which will be of LEAST assistance for comparing attitudes toward the program among different kinds of persons is

   A. name   B. address   C. age
   D. place of birth   E. education

Questions 4-6.

DIRECTIONS: Questions 4 through 6 are to be answered SOLELY on the basis of the following paragraph.

   The supervisor of a large clerical and statistical division has assigned to one of the units under his supervision the preparation of a special statistical report required by the department head. The unit head accepted the assignment without comment but soon ran into considerable difficulty because no one in his unit had had any statistical training.

4. If a result of this lack of training is that the report is not completed on time, although everyone has done all that could be expected, the responsibility for the failure rests with

   A. the department head   B. the supervisor
   C. the unit head   D. the employees in the unit
   E. no one

5. This incident indicates that the supervisory staff has insufficient knowledge of employee

   A. capabilities
   B. reaction to increased demands
   C. on-the-job training needs
   D. work habits
   E. ability to perform ordinary assignments

6. After working on the report for two days, the unit head notifies the supervisor that he will not be able to get the report out in the required time. He states that his staff will be completely trained in another day or two and that after that preparing the report will be a simple matter. At this stage, the supervisor decides to have the statistical unit prepare the report. This action on the part of the supervisor is

   A. *undesirable;* the unit head should be given an incentive to continue with his training program which may produce good results
   B. *desirable;* it is the most effective way in which the supervisor can show his displeasure with the unit head's failure
   C. *undesirable;* it may adversely affect the morale of the unit
   D. *desirable;* it will generally result in a better report completed in a shorter time
   E. *undesirable;* the time spent on training the unit will be completely wasted

Questions 7-9.

DIRECTIONS: Questions 7 through 9 are to be answered SOLELY on the basis of the following paragraph.

The regressive uses of discipline are ubiquitous. Administrative architects who seek the optimum balance between structure and morale must accordingly look toward the identification and isolation of disciplinary elements. The whole range of disciplinary sanctions, from the reprimand to the dismissal, presents opportunities for reciprocity and accommodation of institutional interests. When rightly seized upon, these opportunities may provide the moment and the means for fruitful exercise of leadership and collaboration.

7. The one of the following ways of reworking the ideas presented in the above paragraph in order to be BEST suited for presentation in an in-service training course in supervision is:

   A. When one of your men does something wrong, talk it over with him. Tell him what he should have done. This is a chance for you to show the man that you are on his side and that you would welcome him on your side.
   B. It is not necessary to reprimand or to dismiss an employee because he needs disciplining. The alert foreman will lead and collaborate with his subordinates, making discipline unnecessary.
   C. A good way to lead the men you supervise is to take those opportunities which present themselves to use the whole range of disciplinary sanctions from reprimand to dismissal as a means for enforcing collaboration.
   D. Chances to punish a man in your squad should be welcomed as opportunities to show that you are a *good guy* who does not bear a grudge.
   E. Before you talk to a man or have him report to the office for something he has done wrong, attempt to lead him and get him to work with you. Tell him that his actions were wrong, that you expect him not to repeat the same wrong act, and that you will take a firmer stand if the act is repeated.

8. Of the following, the PRINCIPAL point made in the paragraph above is that   8.____

   A. discipline is frequently used improperly
   B. it is possible to isolate the factors entering into a disciplinary situation
   C. identification of the disciplinary elements is desirable
   D. disciplinary situations may be used to the advantage of the organization
   E. obtaining the best relationship between organizational form and spirit depends upon the ability to label disciplinary elements

9. The MOST novel idea presented in the above paragraph is that   9.____

   A. discipline is rarely necessary
   B. discipline may be a joint action of man and supervisor
   C. there are disciplinary elements which may be identified
   D. a range of disciplinary sanctions exists
   E. it is desirable to seek for balance between structure and morale.

Questions 10-11.

DIRECTIONS: Questions 10 and 11 are to be answered SOLELY on the basis of the following paragraph.

People must be selected to do the tasks involved and must be placed on a payroll in jobs fairly priced. Each of these people must be assigned those tasks which he can perform best; the work of each must be appraised, and good and poor work singled out appropriately. Skill in performing assigned tasks must be developed, and the total work situation must be conducive to sustained high performance. Finally, employees must be separated from the work force either voluntarily or involuntarily because of inefficient or unsatisfactory performance or because of curtailment of organizational activities.

10. A personnel function which is NOT included in the above description is   10.____

    A. classification   B. training   C. placement
    D. severance   E. service rating

11. The underlying implied purpose of the policy enunciated in the above paragraph is   11.____

    A. to plan for the curtailment of the organizational program when it becomes necessary
    B. to single out appropriate skill in performing assigned tasks
    C. to develop and maintain a high level of performance by employees
    D. that training employees in relation to the total work situation is essential if good and poor work are to be singled out
    E. that equal money for equal work results in a total work situation which insures proper appraisal

Questions 12-16.

DIRECTIONS: Questions 12 through 16 are to be answered SOLELY on the basis of the following sections which appeared in a report on the work production of two bureaus of a department. Throughout the report, assume that each month has 4 weeks.

Each of the two bureaus maintains a chronological file. In Bureau A, every 9 months on the average, this material fills a standard legal size file cabinet sufficient for 12,000 work units. In Bureau B, the same type of cabinet is filled in 18 months. Each bureau maintains three complete years of information plus a current file. When the current file cabinet is filled, the cabinet containing the oldest material is emptied, the contents disposed of, and the cabinet used for current material. The similarity of these operations makes it possible to consolidate these files with little effort.

Study of the practice of using typists as filing clerks for periods when there is no typing work showed (1) Bureau A has for the past 6 months completed a total of 1500 filing work units a week using on the average 200 man-hours of trained file clerk time and 20 man-hours of typist time, (2) Bureau B has in the same period completed a total of 2000 filing work units a week using on the average 125 man-hours of trained file clerk time and 60 hours of typist time. This includes all work in chronological files. Assuming that all clerks work at the same speed and that all typists work at the same speed, this indicates that work other than filing should be found for typists or that they should be given some training in the filing procedures used.... It should be noted that Bureau A has not been producing the 1,600 units of technical (not filing) work per 30 day period required by Schedule K, but is at present 200 units behind. The Bureau should be allowed 3 working days to get on schedule.

12. What percentage (approximate) of the total number of filing work units completed in both units consists of the work involved in the maintenance of the chronological files?

   A. 5%   B. 10%   C. 15%   D. 20%   E. 25%

12.____

13. If the two chronological files are consolidated, the number of months which should be allowed for filling a cabinet is

   A. 2   B. 4   C. 6   D. 8   E. 14

13.____

14. The MAXIMUM number of file cabinets which can be released for other uses as a result of the consolidation recommended is

   A. 0
   B. 1
   C. 2
   D. 3
   E. not determinable on the basis of the data given

14.____

15. If all the filing work for both units is consolidated without any diminution in the amount to be done and all filing work is done by trained file clerks, the number of clerks required (35-hour work week) is

   A. 4   B. 5   C. 6   D. 7   E. 8

15.____

16. In order to comply with the recommendation with respect to Schedule K, the present work production of Bureau A must be increased by

   A. 50%   B. 100%
   C. 150%   D. 200%
   E. an amount which is not determinable on the basis of the data given

16.____

Questions 17-18.

DIRECTIONS: Questions 17 and 18 are to be answered SOLELY on the basis of the following paragraph.

Production planning is mainly a process of synthesis. As a basis for the positive act of bringing complex production elements properly together, however, analysis is necessary, especially if improvement is to be made in an existing organization. The necessary analysis requires customary means of orientation and preliminary fact gathering with emphasis, however, on the recognition of administrative goals and of the relationship among work steps.

17. The entire process described is PRIMARILY one of

   A. taking apart, examining, and recombining
   B. deciding what changes are necessary, making the changes and checking on their value
   C. fact finding so as to provide the necessary orientation
   D. discovering just where the emphasis in production should be placed and then modifying the existing procedure so that it is placed properly
   E. recognizing administrative goals and the relationship among work steps

18. In production planning, according to the above paragraph, analysis is used PRIMARILY as

   A. a means of making important changes in an organization
   B. the customary means of orientation and preliminary fact finding
   C. a development of the relationship among work steps
   D. a means for holding the entire process intact by providing a logical basis
   E. a method to obtain the facts upon which a theory can be built

Questions 19-21.

DIRECTIONS: Questions 19 through 21 are to be answered SOLELY on the basis of the following paragraph.

Public administration is policy-making. But it is not autonomous, exclusive, or isolated policy-making. It is policy-making on a field where mighty forces contend, forces engendered in and by society. It is policy-making subject to still other and various policy makers. Public administration is one of a number of basic political processes by which these people achieve and control government.

19. From the point of view expressed in the above paragraph, public administration is

   A. becoming a technical field with completely objective processes
   B. the primary force in modern society
   C. a technical field which should be divorced from the actual decision-making function
   D. basically anti-democratic
   E. intimately related to politics

20. According to the above paragraph, public administration is NOT entirely   20._____

    A. a force generated in and by society
    B. subject at times to controlling influences
    C. a social process
    D. policy-making relating to administrative practices
    E. related to policy-making at lower levels

21. The above paragraph asserts that public administration   21._____

    A. develops the basic and controlling policies
    B. is the result of policies made by many different forces
    C. should attempt to break through its isolated policymaking and engage on a broader field
    D. is a means of directing government
    E. is subject to the political processes by which acts are controlled

Questions 22-24.

DIRECTIONS: Questions 22 through 24 are to be answered SOLELY on the basis of the following paragraph.

In order to understand completely the source of an employee's insecurity on his job, it is necessary to understand how he came to be, who he is, and what kind of a person he is away from his job. This would necessitate an understanding of those personal assets and liabilities which the employee brings to the job situation. These arise from his individual characteristics and his past experiences and established patterns of interpersonal relations. This whole area is of tremendous scope, encompassing everything included within the study of psychiatry and interpersonal relations. Therefore, it has been impracticable to consider it in detail. Attention has been focused on the relatively circumscribed area of the actual occupational situation. The factors considered – those which the employee brings to the job situation and which arise from his individual characteristics and his past experience and established patterns of interpersonal relations – are: intellectual level or capacity, specific aptitudes, education, work experience, health, social and economic background, patterns of interpersonal relations and resultant personality characteristics.

22. According to the above paragraph, the one of the following fields of study which would be of LEAST importance in the study of the problem is the   22._____

    A. relationships existing among employees
    B. causes of employee insecurity in the job situation
    C. conflict, if it exists, between intellectual level and work experience
    D. distribution of intellectual achievement
    E. relationship between employee characteristics and the established pattern of interpersonal relations in the work situation

23. According to the above paragraph, in order to make a thoroughgoing and comprehensive study of the sources of employee insecurity, the field of study should include   23._____

    A. only such circumscribed areas as are involved in extra-occupational situations
    B. a study of the dominant mores of the period
    C. all branches of the science of psychology

D. a determination of the characteristics, such as intellectual capacity, which an employee should bring to the job situation
E. employee personality characteristics arising from previous relationships with other people

24. It is implied by the above paragraph that it would be of GREATEST advantage to bring to this problem a comprehensive knowledge of   24.____

    A. all established patterns of interpersonal relations
    B. the milieu in which the employee group is located
    C. what assets and liabilities are presented in the job situation
    D. methods of focusing attention on relatively circumscribed regions
    E. the sources of an employee's insecurity on his job

Questions 25-26.

DIRECTIONS: Questions 25 and 26 are to be answered SOLELY on the basis of the following paragraph.

If, during a study, some hundreds of values of a variable (such as annual number of latenesses for each employee in a department) have been noted merely in the arbitrary order in which they happen to occur, the mind cannot properly grasp the significance of the record; the observations must be ranked or classified in some way before the characteristics of the series can be comprehended, and those comparisons, on which arguments as to causation depend, can be made with other series. A dichotomous classification is too crude; if the values are merely classified according to whether they exceed or fall short of some fixed value, a large part of the information given by the original record is lost. Numerical measurements lend themselves with peculiar readiness to a manifold classification.

25. According to the above paragraph, if the values of a variable which are gathered during a study are classified in a few subdivisions, the MOST likely result will be   25.____

    A. an inability to grasp the significance of the record
    B. an inability to relate the series with other series
    C. a loss of much of the information in the original data
    D. a loss of the readiness with which numerical measurements lend themselves to a manifold classification
    E. that the order in which they happen to occur will be arbitrary

26. The above paragraph advocates, with respect to numerical data, the use of   26.____

    A. arbitrary order
    B. comparisons with other series
    C. a two value classification
    D. a many value classification
    E. all values of a variable

Question 27.

DIRECTIONS: Question 27 is to be answered SOLELY on the basis of the following paragraph.

A more significant manifestation of the concern of the community with the general welfare is the collection and dissemination of statistics. This statement may cause the reader to smile, for statistics seem to be drab and prosaic things. The great growth of statistics, however, is one of the most remarkable characteristics of the age. Never before has a community kept track from month to month, and in some cases from week to week, of how many people are born, how many die and from what causes, how many are sick, how much is being produced, how much is being sold, how many people are at work, how many people are unemployed, how long they have been out of work, what prices people pay, how much income they receive and from what sources, how much they owe, what they intend to buy. These elaborate attempts of the country to keep informed about what is happening mean that the community is concerned with how its members are faring and with the conditions under which they live. For this reason, the present age may take pride in its numerous and regular statistical reports and in the rapid increase in the number of these reports. No other age has evidenced such a keen interest in the conditions of the people.

27. The writer implies that statistics are   27._____

    A. too scientific for general use
    B. too elaborate and too drab
    C. related to the improvement of living conditions
    D. frequently misinterpreted
    E. a product of the machine age

KEY (CORRECT ANSWERS)

1.	E	11.	C
2.	C	12.	C
3.	A	13.	C
4.	B	14.	B
5.	A	15.	D
6.	D	16.	E
7.	A	17.	A
8.	D	18.	E
9.	B	19.	E
10.	A	20.	D

21.	D
22.	D
23.	E
24.	B
25.	C
26.	D
27.	C

PREPARING WRITTEN MATERIAL
EXAMINATION SECTION
TEST 1

DIRECTIONS: Each of the sentences in this test may be classified under one of the following four categories:
- A. Faulty because of incorrect grammar or word usage
- B. Faulty because of incorrect punctuation
- C. Faulty because of incorrect capitalization or incorrect spelling
- D. Correct

Examine each sentence carefully to determine under which of the above four options it is best classified. Then, in the space to the right, print the capital letter preceding the option which is the BEST of the four suggested above. (Note that each faulty sentence contains but one type of error. Consider a sentence to be correct if it contains none of the types of errors mentioned, even though there may be other correct ways of expressing the same thought.)

1. He sent the notice to the clerk who you hired yesterday. 1.____

2. It must be admitted, however that you were not informed of this change. 2.____

3. Only the employee who have served in this grade for at least two years are eligible for promotion. 3.____

4. The work was divided equally between she and Mary. 4.____

5. He thought that you were not available at that time. 5.____

6. When the messenger returns; please give him this package. 6.____

7. The new secretary prepared, typed, addressed, and delivered, the notices. 7.____

8. Walking into the room, his desk can be seen at the rear. 8.____

9. Although John has worked here longer than She, he produces a smaller amount of work. 9.____

10. She said she could of typed this report yesterday. 10.____

11. Neither one of these procedures are adequate for the efficient performance of this task. 11.____

12. The typewriter is the tool of the typist; the cash register, the tool of the cashier. 12.____

13. "The assignment must be completed as soon as possible" said the supervisor. 13.____

14. As you know, office handbooks are issued to all new Employees. 14.____

15. Writing a speech is sometimes easier than to deliver it before an audience. 15.____

16. Mr. Brown our accountant, will audit the accounts next week. 16.____

17. Give the assignment to whomever is able to do it most efficiently. 17.____

18. The supervisor expected either your or I to file these reports. 18.____

KEY (CORRECT ANSWERS)

1.	A	11.	A
2.	B	12.	C
3.	D	13.	B
4.	A	14.	C
5.	D	15.	A
6.	B	16.	B
7.	B	17.	A
8.	A	18.	A
9.	C		
10.	A		

TEST 2

DIRECTIONS: Each of the sentences in this test may be classified under one of the following four categories:
- A. Faulty because of incorrect grammar or word usage
- B. Faulty because of incorrect punctuation
- C. Faulty because of incorrect capitalization or incorrect spelling
- D. Correct

Examine each sentence carefully to determine under which of the above four options it is best classified. Then, in the space to the right, print the capital letter preceding the option which is the BEST of the four suggested above. (Note that each faulty sentence contains but one type of error. Consider a sentence to be correct if it contains none of the types of errors mentioned, even though there may be other correct ways of expressing the same thought.)

1. The fire apparently started in the storeroom, which is usually locked. 1.____
2. On approaching the victim, two bruises were noticed by this officer. 2.____
3. The officer, who was there examined the report with great care. 3.____
4. Each employee in the office had a seperate desk. 4.____
5. All employees including members of the clerical staff, were invited to the lecture. 5.____
6. The suggested Procedure is similar to the one now in use. 6.____
7. No one was more pleased with the new procedure than the chauffeur. 7.____
8. He tried to persaude her to change the procedure. 8.____
9. The total of the expenses charged to petty cash were high. 9.____
10. An understanding between him and I was finally reached. 10.____

KEY (CORRECT ANSWERS)

1.	D	6.	C
2.	A	7.	D
3.	B	8.	C
4.	C	9.	A
5.	B	10.	A

TEST 3

DIRECTIONS: Each of the sentences in this test may be classified under one of the following four categories:
  A. Faulty because of incorrect grammar or word usage
  B. Faulty because of incorrect punctuation
  C. Faulty because of incorrect capitalization or incorrect spelling
  D. Correct

Examine each sentence carefully to determine under which of the above four options it is best classified. Then, in the space to the right, print the capital letter preceding the option which is the BEST of the four suggested above. (Note that each faulty sentence contains but one type of error. Consider a sentence to be correct if it contains none of the types of errors mentioned, even though there may be other correct ways of expressing the same thought.)

1. They told both he and I that the prisoner had escaped. 1.____

2. Any superior officer, who, disregards the just complaint of his subordinates, is remiss in the performance of his duty. 2.____

3. Only those members of the national organization who resided in the Middle West attended the conference in Chicago. 3.____

4. We told him to give the national organization assignment to whoever was available. 4.____

5. Please do not disappoint and embarass us by not appearing in court. 5.____

6. Although the office's speech proved to be entertaining, the topic was not relevent to the main theme of the conference. 6.____

7. In February all new officers attended a training course in which they were learned in their principal duties and the fundamental operating procedure of the department. 7.____

8. I personally seen inmate Jones threaten inmates Smith and Green with bodily harm if they refused to participate in the plot. 8.____

9. To the layman, who on a chance visit to the prison observes everything functioning smoothly, the maintenance of prison discipline may seem to be a relatively easily realizable objective. 9.____

10. The prisoners in cell block fourty were forbidden to sit on the cell cots during the recreation hour. 10.____

KEY (CORRECT ANSWERS)

1.	A	6.	C
2.	B	7.	A
3.	C	8.	A
4.	D	9.	D
5.	C	10.	C

TEST 4

DIRECTIONS: Each of the sentences in this test may be classified under one of the following four categories:
   A. Faulty because of incorrect grammar or word usage
   B. Faulty because of incorrect punctuation
   C. Faulty because of incorrect capitalization or incorrect spelling
   D. Correct

Examine each sentence carefully to determine under which of the above four options it is best classified. Then, in the space to the right, print the capital letter preceding the option which is the BEST of the four suggested above. (Note that each faulty sentence contains but one type of error. Consider a sentence to be correct if it contains none of the types of errors mentioned, even though there may be other correct ways of expressing the same thought.)

1. I cannot encourage you any.   1._____
2. You always look well in those sort of clothes.   2._____
3. Shall we go to the park?   3._____
4. The man whome he introduced was Mr. Carey.   4._____
5. She saw the letter laying here this morning.   5._____
6. It should rain before the Afternoon is over.   6._____
7. They have already went home.   7._____
8. That Jackson will be elected is evident.   8._____
9. He does not hardly approve of us.   9._____
10. It was he, who won the prize.   10._____

KEY (CORRECT ANSWERS)

1.	A	6.	C
2.	A	7.	A
3.	D	8.	D
4.	C	9.	A
5.	A	10.	B

TEST 5

DIRECTIONS: Each of the sentences in this test may be classified under one of the following four categories:
- A. Faulty because of incorrect grammar or word usage
- B. Faulty because of incorrect punctuation
- C. Faulty because of incorrect capitalization or incorrect spelling
- D. Correct

Examine each sentence carefully to determine under which of the above four options it is best classified. Then, in the space to the right, print the capital letter preceding the option which is the BEST of the four suggested above. (Note that each faulty sentence contains but one type of error. Consider a sentence to be correct if it contains none of the types of errors mentioned, even though there may be other correct ways of expressing the same thought.)

1. Shall we go to the park. 1.____
2. They are, alike, in this particular way. 2.____
3. They gave the poor man sume food when he knocked on the door. 3.____
4. I regret the loss caused by the error. 4.____
5. The students' will have a new teacher. 5.____
6. They sweared to bring out all the facts. 6.____
7. He decided to open a branch store on 33rd street. 7.____
8. His speed is equal and more than that of a racehorse. 8.____
9. He felt very warm on that Summer day. 9.____
10. He was assisted by his friend, who lives in the next house. 10.____

KEY (CORRECT ANSWERS)

1.	B	6.	A
2.	B	7.	C
3.	C	8.	A
4.	D	9.	C
5.	B	10.	D

TEST 6

DIRECTIONS: Each of the sentences in this test may be classified under one of the following four categories:
   A. Faulty because of incorrect grammar or word usage
   B. Faulty because of incorrect punctuation
   C. Faulty because of incorrect capitalization or incorrect spelling
   D. Correct

Examine each sentence carefully to determine under which of the above four options it is best classified. Then, in the space to the right, print the capital letter preceding the option which is the BEST of the four suggested above. (Note that each faulty sentence contains but one type of error. Consider a sentence to be correct if it contains none of the types of errors mentioned, even though there may be other correct ways of expressing the same thought.)

1. The climate of New York is colder than California.   1._____
2. I shall wait for you on the corner.   2._____
3. Did we see the boy who, we think, is the leader.   3._____
4. Being a modest person, John seldom talks about his invention.   4._____
5. The gang is called the smith street bos.   5._____
6. He seen the man break into the store.   6._____
7. We expected to lay still there for quite a while.   7._____
8. He is considered to be the Leader of his organization.   8._____
9. Although I recieved an invitation, I won't go.   9._____
10. The letter must be here some place.   10._____

KEY (CORRECT ANSWERS)

1.	A	6.	A
2.	D	7.	A
3.	B	8.	C
4.	D	9.	C
5.	C	10.	A

TEST 7

DIRECTIONS: Each of the sentences in this test may be classified under one of the following four categories:
- A. Faulty because of incorrect grammar or word usage
- B. Faulty because of incorrect punctuation
- C. Faulty because of incorrect capitalization or incorrect spelling
- D. Correct

Examine each sentence carefully to determine under which of the above four options it is best classified. Then, in the space to the right, print the capital letter preceding the option which is the BEST of the four suggested above. (Note that each faulty sentence contains but one type of error. Consider a sentence to be correct if it contains none of the types of errors mentioned, even though there may be other correct ways of expressing the same thought.)

1. I though it to be he. 1._____
2. We expect to remain here for a long time. 2._____
3. The committee was agreed. 3._____
4. Two-thirds of the building are finished. 4._____
5. The water was froze. 5._____
6. Everyone of the salesmen must supply their own car. 6._____
7. Who is the author of Gone With the Wind? 7._____
8. He marched on and declaring that he would never surrender. 8._____
9. Who shall I say called? 9._____
10. Everyone has left but they. 10._____

KEY (CORRECT ANSWERS)

1.	A	6.	A
2.	D	7.	B
3.	D	8.	A
4.	A	9.	D
5.	A	10.	D

TEST 8

DIRECTIONS: Each of the sentences in this test may be classified under one of the following four categories:
- A. Faulty because of incorrect grammar or word usage
- B. Faulty because of incorrect punctuation
- C. Faulty because of incorrect capitalization or incorrect spelling
- D. Correct

Examine each sentence carefully to determine under which of the above four options it is best classified. Then, in the space to the right, print the capital letter preceding the option which is the BEST of the four suggested above. (Note that each faulty sentence contains but one type of error. Consider a sentence to be correct if it contains none of the types of errors mentioned, even though there may be other correct ways of expressing the same thought.)

1. Who did we give the order to?   1.____
2. Send your order in immediately.   2.____
3. I believe I paid the Bill.   3.____
4. I have not met but one person.   4.____
5. Why aren't Tom, and Fred, going to the dance?   5.____
6. What reason is there for him not going?   6.____
7. The seige of Malta was a tremendous event.   7.____
8. I was there yesterday I assure you   8.____
9. Your ukulele is better than mine.   9.____
10. No one was there only Mary.   10.____

KEY (CORRECT ANSWERS)

1.	A	6.	A
2.	D	7.	C
3.	C	8.	B
4.	A	9.	C
5.	B	10.	A

TEST 9

DIRECTIONS: In each of the following groups of sentences, one of the four sentences is faulty in grammar, punctuation, or capitalization. Select the INCORRECT sentence in each case.

1. A. If you had stood at home and done your homework, you would not have failed in arithmetic.
    B. Her affected manner annoyed every member of the audience.
    C. How will the new law affect our income taxes?
    D. The plants were not affected by the long, cold winter, but they succumbed to the drought of summer.

2. A. He is one of the most able men who have been in the Senate.
    B. It is he who is to blame for the lamentable mistake.
    C. Haven't you a helpful suggestion to make at this time?
    D. The money was robbed from the blind man's cup.

3. A. The amount of children in this school is steadily increasing.
    B. After taking an apple from the table, she went out to play.
    C. He borrowed a dollar from me.
    D. I had hoped my brother would arrive before me.

4. A. Whom do you think I hear from every week?
    B. Who do you think is the right man for the job?
    C. Who do you think I found in the room?
    D. He is the man whom we considered a good candidate for the presidency.

5. A. Quietly the puppy laid down before the fireplace.
    B. You have made your bed; now lie in it.
    C. I was badly sunburned because I had lain too long in the sun.
    D. I laid the doll on the bed and left the room.

KEY (CORRECT ANSWERS)

1. A
2. D
3. A
4. C
5. A

PREPARING WRITTEN MATERIAL

PARAGRAPH REARRANGEMENT
COMMENTARY

The sentences that follow are in scrambled order. You are to rearrange them in proper order and indicate the letter choice containing the correct answer at the space at the right.

Each group of sentences in this section is actually a paragraph presented in scrambled order. Each sentence in the group has a place in that paragraph; no sentence is to be left out. You are to read each group of sentences and decide upon the best order in which to put the sentences so as to form a well-organized paragraph.

The questions in this section measure the ability to solve a problem when all the facts relevant to its solution are not given.

More specifically, certain positions of responsibility and authority require the employee to discover connection between events sometimes, apparently, unrelated. In order to do this, the employee will find it necessary to correctly infer that unspecified events have probably occurred or are likely to occur. This ability becomes especially important when action must be taken on incomplete information.

Accordingly, these questions require competitors to choose among several suggested alternatives, each of which presents a different sequential arrangement of the events. Competitors must choose the MOST logical of the suggested sequences.

In order to do so, they may be required to draw on general knowledge to infer missing concepts or events that are essential to sequencing the given events. Competitors should be careful to infer only what is essential to the sequence. The plausibility of the wrong alternatives will always require the inclusion of unlikely events or of additional chains of events which are NOT essential to sequencing the given events.

It's very important to remember that you are looking for the best of the four possible choices, and that the best choice of all may not even be one of the answers you're given to choose from.

There is no one right way to solve these problems. Many people have found it helpful to first write out the order of the sentences, as they would have arranged them, on their scrap paper before looking at the possible answers. If their optimum answer is there, this can save them some time. If it isn't, this method can still give insight into solving the problem. Others find it most helpful to just go through each of the possible choices, contrasting each as they go along. You should use whatever method feels comfortable and works for you.

While most of these types of questions are not that difficult, we've added a higher percentage of the difficult type, just to give you more practice. Usually there are only one or two questions on this section that contain such subtle distinctions that you're unable to answer confidently. And you then may find yourself stuck deciding between two possible choices, neither of which you're sure about.

EXAMINATION SECTION
TEST 1

DIRECTIONS: The following groups of sentences need to be arranged in an order that makes sense. Select the letter preceding the sequence that represents the BEST sentence order. *PRINT THE LETTER OF THE CORRECT ANSWER IN THE SPACE AT THE RIGHT.*

1. I. The keyboard was purposely designed to be a little awkward to slow typists down.
    II. The arrangement of letters on the keyboard of a typewriter was not designed for the convenience of the typist.
    III. Fortunately, no one is suggesting that a new keyboard be designed right away.
    IV. If one were, we would have to learn to type all over again.
    V. The reason was that the early machines were slower than the typists and would jam easily.
    The CORRECT answer is:
    A. I, III, IV, II, V
    B. II, V, I, IV, III
    C. V, I, II, III, IV
    D. II, I, V, III, IV

2. I. The majority of the new service jobs are part-time or low-paying.
    II. According to the U.S. Bureau of Labor Statistics, jobs in the service sector constitute 72% of all jobs in this country.
    III. If more and more workers receive less and less money, who will buy the goods and services needed to keep the economy going?
    IV. The service sector is by far the fastest growing part of the United States economy.
    V. Some economists look upon this trend with great concern.
    The CORRECT answer is:
    A. II, IV, I, V, III
    B. II, III, IV, I, V
    C. V, IV, II, III, I
    D. III, I, II, IV, V

3. I. They can also affect one's endurance.
    II. This can stabilize blood sugar levels, and ensure that the brain is receiving a steady, constant, supply of glucose, so that one is *hitting on all cylinders* while taking the test.
    III. By food, we mean real food, not junk food or unhealthy snacks.
    IV. For this reason, it is important not to skip a meal, and to bring food with you to the exam.
    V. One's blood sugar levels can affect how clearly one is able to think and concentrate during an exam.
    The CORRECT answer is:
    A. V, IV, II, III, I
    B. V, II, I, IV, III
    C. V, I, IV, III, II
    D. V, IV, I, III, II

4.
   I. Those who are the embodiment of desire are absorbed in material quests, and those who are the embodiment of feeling are warriors who value power more than possession.
   II. These qualities are in everyone, but in different degrees.
   III. But those who value understanding yearn not for goods or victory, but for knowledge.
   IV. According to Plato, human behavior flows from three main sources: desire, emotion, and knowledge.
   V. In the perfect state, the industrial forces would produce but not rule, the military would protect but not rule, and the forces of knowledge, the philosopher kings, would reign.
   The CORRECT answer is:
   A. IV, V, I, II, III
   B. V, I, II, III, IV
   C. IV, III, II, I, V
   D. IV, II, I, III, V

5.
   I. Of the more than 26,000 tons of garbage produced daily in New York City, 12,000 tons arrive daily at Fresh Kills.
   II. In a month, enough garbage accumulates there to fill the Empire State Building.
   III. In 1937, the Supreme Court halted the practice of dumping the trash of New York City into the sea.
   IV. Although the garbage is compacted, in a few years the mounds of garbage at Fresh Kills will be the highest points south of Maine's Mount Desert Island on the Eastern Seaboard.
   V. Instead, tugboats now pull barges of much of the trash to Staten Island and the largest landfill in the world, Fresh Kills.
   The CORRECT answer is:
   A. III, V, IV, I, II
   B. III, V, II, IV, I
   C. III, V, I, II, IV
   D. III, II, V, IV, I

6.
   I. Communists rank equality very high, but freedom very low.
   II. Unlike communists, conservatives place a high value on freedom and a very low value on equality.
   III. A recent study demonstrated that one way to classify people's political beliefs is to look at the importance placed on two words: freedom and equality.
   IV. Thus, by demonstrating how members of these groups feel about the two words, the study has proved to be useful for political analysts in several European countries.
   V. According to the study, socialists and liberals rank both freedom and equality very high, while fascists rate both very low.
   The CORRECT answer is:
   A. III, V, I, II, IV
   B. V, IV, III, I, II
   C. III, V, IV, II, I
   D. III, I, II, IV, V

7. I. "Can there be anything more amazing than this?"
    II. If the riddle is successfully answered, his dead brothers will be brought back to life.
    III. "Even though man sees those around him dying every day," says Dharmaraj, "he still believes and acts as if he were immortal."
    IV. "What is the cause of ceaseless wonder?" asks the Lord of the Lake.
    V. In the ancient epic, The Mahabharata, a riddle is asked of one of the Pandava brothers.
    The CORRECT answer is:
    A. V, II, I, IV, III
    B. V, IV, III, I, II
    C. V, II, IV, III, I
    D. V, II, IV, I, III

8. I. On the contrary, the two main theories—the cooperative (neoclassical) theory and the radical (labor theory)—clearly rest on very different assumptions, which have very different ethical overtones.
    II. The distribution of income is the primary factor in determining the relative levels of material well-being that different groups or individuals attain.
    III. Of all issues in economics, the distribution of income is one of the most controversial.
    IV. The neoclassical theory tends to support the existing income distribution (or minor changes), while the labor theory ends to support substantial changes in the way income is distributed.
    V. The intensity of the controversy reflects the fact that different economic theories are not purely neutral, *detached* theories with no ethical or moral implications.
    The CORRECT answer is:
    A. II, I, V, IV, III
    B. III, II, V, I, IV
    C. III, V, II, I, IV
    D. III, V, IV, I, II

9. I. The pool acts as a broker and ensures that the cheapest power gets used first.
    II. Every six seconds, the pool's computer monitors all of the generating stations in the state and decides which to ask for more power and which to cut back.
    III. The buying and selling of electrical power is handled by the New York Power Pool in Guilderland, New York.
    IV. This is to the advantage of both the buying and selling utilities.
    V. The pool began operation in 1970, and consists of the state's eight electric utilities.
    The CORRECT answer is:
    A. V, I, II, III, IV
    B. IV, II, I, III, V
    C. III, V, I, IV, II
    D. V, III, IV, II, I

10.
   I. Modern English is much simpler grammatically than Old English.
   II. Finnish grammar is very complicated; there are some fifteen cases, for example.
   III. Chinese, a very old language, may seem to be the exception, but it is the great number of characters/words that must be mastered that makes it so difficult to learn, not its grammar.
   IV. The newest literary language—that is, written as well as spoken—is Finish, whose literary roots go back only to about the middle of the nineteenth century.
   V. Contrary to popular belief, the longer a language is been in use the simpler its grammar—not the reverse.

   The CORRECT answer is:
   A. IV, I, II, III, V
   B. V, I, IV, II, III
   C. I, II, IV, III, V
   D. IV, II, III, I, V

KEY (CORRECT ANSWERS)

1.	D	6.	A
2.	A	7.	C
3.	C	8.	B
4.	D	9.	C
5.	C	10.	B

TEST 2

DIRECTIONS: This type of question tests your ability to recognize accurate paraphrasing, well-constructed paragraphs, and appropriate style and tone. It is important that the answer you select contains only the facts or concepts given in the original sentences. It is also important that you be aware of incomplete sentences, inappropriate transitions, unsupported opinions, incorrect usage, and illogical sentence order. Paragraphs that do not include all the necessary facts and concepts, that distort them, or that add new ones are not considered correct.

The format for this section may vary. Sometimes, long paragraphs are given, and emphasis is placed on style and organization. Our first five questions are of this type. Other times, the paragraphs are shorter, and there is less emphasis on style and more emphasis on accurate representation of information. Our second group of five questions are of this nature.

For each of Questions 1 through 10, select the paragraph that BEST expresses the ideas contained in the sentences above it. *PRINT THE LETTER OF THE CORRECT ANSWER IN THE SPACE AT THE RIGHT.*

1.   I. Listening skills are very important for managers.
   II. Listening skills are not usually emphasized.
   III. Whenever managers are depicted in books, manuals or the media, they are always talking, never listening.
   IV. We'd like you to read the enclosed handout on listening skills and to try to consciously apply them this week.
   V. We guarantee they will improve the quality of your interactions.

   A. Unfortunately, listening skills are not usually emphasized for managers. Managers are always depicted as talking, never listening. We'd like you to read the enclosed handout on listening skills. Please try to apply these principles this week. If you do, we guarantee they will improve the quality of your interactions.
   B. The enclosed handout on listening skills will be important improving the quality of your interactions. We guarantee it. All you have to do is take sometime this week to read and to consciously try to apply the principles. Listening skills are very important for manages, but they are not usually emphasized. Whenever managers are depicted in books, manuals or the media, they are always talking, never listening.
   C. Listening well is one of the most important skills a manager can have, yet it's not usually given much attention. Think about any representation of managers in books, manuals, or in the media that you may have seen. They're always talking, never listening. We'd like you to read the enclosed handout on listening skills and consciously try to apply them the rest of the week. We guarantee you will see a difference in the quality of your interactions.

1.____

D. Effective listening, one very important tool in the effective manager's arsenal, is usually not emphasized enough. The usual depiction of managers in books, manuals or the media is one in which they are always talking, never listening. We'd like you to read the enclosed handout and consciously try to apply the information contained therein throughout the rest of the week. We feel sure that you will see a marked difference in the quality of your interactions.

2.
I. Chekhov wrote three dramatic masterpieces which share certain themes and formats: Uncle Vanya, The Cherry Orchard, and The Three Sisters.
II. They are primarily concerned with the passage of time and how this erodes human aspirations.
III. The plays are haunted by the ghosts of the wasted life.
IV. The characters are concerned with life's lesser problems; however, such as the inability to make decisions, loyalty to the wrong cause, and the inability to be clear.
V. This results in sweet, almost aching, type of a sadness referred to as Chekhovian.

2.____

A. Chekhov wrote three dramatic masterpieces: Uncle Vanya, The Cherry Orchard, and The Three Sisters. These masterpieces share certain themes and formats: the passage of time, how time erodes human aspirations, and the ghosts of wasted life. Each masterpiece is characterized by a sweet, almost aching, type of sadness that has become known as Chekhovian. The sweetness of this sadness hinges on the fact that it is not the great tragedies of life which are destroying these characters, but their minor flaws: indecisiveness, misplaced loyalty, unclarity.
B. The Cherry Orchard, Uncle Vanya, and The Three Sisters are three dramatic masterpieces written by Chekhov that use similar formats to explore a common theme. Each is primarily concerned with the way that passing time wears down human aspirations, and each is haunted by the ghosts of the wasted life. The characters are shown struggling futilely with the lesser problems of life: indecisiveness, loyalty to the wrong cause, and the inability to be clear. These struggles create a mood of sweet, almost aching, sadness that has become known as Chekhovian.
C. Chekhov's dramatic masterpieces are, along with The Cherry Orchard, Uncle Vanya, and The Three Sisters. These plays share certain thematic and formal similarities. They are concerned most of all with the passage of time and the way in which time erodes human aspirations. Each play is haunted by the specter of the wasted life. Chekhov's characters are caught, however, by life's lesser snares: indecisiveness, loyalty to the wrong cause, and unclarity. The characteristic mood is a sweet, almost aching type of sadness that has come to be known as Chekhovian.
D. A Chekhovian mood is characterized by sweet, almost aching, sadness. The term comes from three dramatic tragedies by Chekhov which revolve around the sadness of a wasted life. The three masterpieces (Uncle Vanya, The Three Sisters, and The Cherry Orchard) share the same

theme and format. The plays are concerned with how the passage of time erodes human aspirations. They are peopled with characters who are struggling with life's lesser problems. These are people who are indecisive, loyal to the wrong causes, or are unable to make themselves clear.

3.
- I. Movie previews have often helped producers decide which parts of movies they should take out or leave in.
- II. The first 1933 preview of King Kong was very helpful to the producers because many people ran screaming from the theater and would not return when four men first attacked by Kong were eaten by giant spiders.
- III. The 1950 premiere of Sunset Boulevard resulted in the filming of an entirely new beginning, and a delay of six months in the film's release.
- IV. In the original opening scene, William Holden was in a morgue talking with thirty-six other "corpses" about the ways some of them had died.
- V. When he began to tell them of his life with Gloria Swanson, the audience found this hilarious, instead of taking the scene seriously.

3.____

   A. Movie previews have often helped producers decide what parts of movies they should leave in or take out. For example, the first preview of King Kong in 1933 was very helpful. In one scene, four men were first attacked by Kong and then eaten by giant spiders. Many members of the audience ran screaming from the theater and would not return. The premiere of the 1950 film Sunset Boulevard was also very helpful. In the original opening scene, William Holden was in a morgue with thirty-six other "corpses," discussing the ways some of them had died. When he began to tell them of his life with Gloria Swanson, the audience found this hilarious. They were supposed to take the scene seriously. The result was a delay of six months in the release of the film while a new beginning was added.
   B. Movie previews have often helped producers decide whether they should change various parts of a movie. After the 1933 preview of King Kong, a scene in which four men who had been attacked by Kong were eaten by giant spiders was taken out as many people ran screaming from the theater and would not return. The 1950 premiere of Sunset Boulevard also led to some changes. In the original opening scene, William Holden was in a morgue talking with thirty-six other "corpses" about the ways some of them had died. When he began to tell them of his life with Gloria Swanson, the audience found this hilarious, instead of taking the scene seriously.
   C. What do Sunset Boulevard and King Kong have in common? Both show the value of using movie previews to test audience reaction. The first 1933 preview of King Kong showed that a scene showing four men being eaten by giant spiders after having been attacked by Kong was too frightening for many people. They ran screaming from the theater and couldn't be coaxed back. The 1950 premiere of Sunset Boulevard was also a scream, but not the kind the producers intended. The movie opens

with William Holden lying in a morgue discussing the ways they had died with thirty-six other "corpses." When he began to tell them of his life with Gloria Swanson, the audience couldn't take him seriously. Their laughter caused a six-month delay while the beginning was rewritten.

D. Producers very often use movie previews to decide if changes are needed. The premiere of Sunset Boulevard in 1950 led to a new beginning and a six-month delay in film release. At the beginning, William Holden and thirty-six other "corpses" discuss the ways some of them died. Rather than taking this seriously, the audience thought it was hilarious when he began to tell them of his life with Gloria Swanson. The first 1933 preview of King Kong was very helpful for its producers because one scene so terrified the audience that many of them ran screaming from the theater and would not return. In this particular scene, four men who had first been attacked by Kong were eaten by giant spiders.

4.
I. It is common for supervisors to view employees as "things" to be manipulated.   4.____
II. This approach does not motivate employees, nor does the carrot-and-stick approach because employees often recognize these behaviors and resent them.
III. Supervisors can change these behaviors by using self-inquiry and persistence.
IV. The best managers genuinely respect those they work with, are supportive and helpful, and are interested in working as a team with those they supervise.
V. They disagree with the Golden Rule that says "he or she who has the gold makes the rules."

  A. Some managers act as if they think the Golden Rule means "he or she who has the gold makes the rules." They show disrespect to employees by seeing them as "things" to be manipulated. Obviously, this approach does not motivate employees any more than the carrot-and-stick approach motivates them. The employees are smart enough to spot these behaviors and resent them. On the other hand, the managers genuinely respect those they work with, are supportive and helpful, and are interested in working as a team. Self-inquiry and persistence can change even the former type of supervisor into the latter.
  B. Many supervisors all into the trap of viewing employees as "things" to be manipulated, or try to motivate them by using a carrot-and-stick approach. These methods do not motivate employees, who often recognize the behaviors and resent them. Supervisors can change these behaviors, however, by using self-inquiry and persistence. The best managers are supportive and helpful, and have genuine respect for those with whom they work. They are interested in working as a team with those they supervise. To them, the Golden Rule is not "he or she who has the gold makes the rules."
  C. Some supervisors see employees as "things" to be used or manipulated using a carrot-and-stick technique. These methods don't work. Employees often see through them and resent them. A supervisor who

wants to change may do so. The techniques of self-inquiry and persistence can be used to turn him or her into the type of supervisor who doesn't think the Golden Rule is "he or she who has the gold makes the rules." They may become like the best managers who treat those with whom they work with respect and give them help and support. These are the manager who know how to build a team.

D. Unfortunately, many supervisors act as if their employees are objects whose movements they can position at will. This mistaken belief has the same result as another popular motivational technique—the carrot-and-stick approach. Both attitudes can lead to the same result—resentment from those employees who recognize the behaviors for what they are. Supervisors who recognize these behaviors can change through the use of persistence and the use of self-inquiry. It's important to remember that the best managers respect their employees. They readily give necessary help and support and are interested in working as a team with those they supervise. To these managers, the Golden Rule is not "he or she who has the gold makes the rules."

5.
I. The first half of the nineteenth century produced a group of pessimistic poets—Byron, De Musset, Heine, Pushkin, and Leopardi.
II. It also produced a group of pessimistic composers—Schubert, Chopin, Schumann, and even the later Beethoven.
III. Above all, in philosophy, there was the profoundly pessimistic philosopher, Schopenhauer.
IV. The Revolution was dead, the Bourbons were restored, the feudal barons were reclaiming their land, and progress everywhere was being suppressed, as the great age was over.
V. "I thank God," said Goethe, "that I am not young in so thoroughly finished a world."

5.____

A. "I thank God," said Goethe, "that I am not young in so thoroughly finished a world." The Revolution was dead, the Bourbons were restored, the feudal barons were reclaiming their land, and progress everywhere was being suppressed. The first half of the nineteenth century produced a group of pessimistic poets: Byron, De Musset, Heine, Pushkin, and Leopardi. It also produced pessimistic composers: Schubert, Chopin, Schumann. Although Beethoven came later, he fits into this group, too. Finally and above all, it also produced a profoundly pessimistic philosopher, Schopenhauer. The great age was over.

B. The first half of the nineteenth century produced a group of pessimistic poets: Byron, De Musset, Heine, Pushkin, and Leopardi. It produced a group of pessimistic composers: Schubert, Chopin, Schumann, and even the later Beethoven. Above all, it produced a profoundly pessimistic philosopher, Schopenhauer. For each of these men, the great age was over. The Revolution was dead, and the Bourbons were restored. The feudal barons were reclaiming their land, and progress everywhere was being suppressed.

C. The great age was over. The Revolution was dead—the Bourbons were restored, and the feudal barons were reclaiming their land. Progress everywhere was being suppressed. Out of this climate came a profound pessimism. Poets, like Byron, De Musset, Heine, Pushkin, and Leopardi; composers, like Schubert, Chopin, Schumann, and even the later Beethoven; and above all, a profoundly pessimistic philosopher, Schopenauer. This pessimism which arose in the first half of the nineteenth century is illustrated by these words of Goethe, "I thank God that I am not young in so thoroughly finished a world."

D. The first half of the nineteenth century produced a group of pessimistic poets, Byron, De Musset, Heine, Pushkin, and Leopardi—and a group of pessimistic composers, Schubert, Chopin, Schumann, and the later Beethoven. Above it all, it produced a profoundly pessimistic philosopher, Schopenhauer. The great age was over. The Revolution was dead, the Bourbons were restored, the feudal barons were reclaiming their land, and progress everywhere was being suppressed. "I thank God," said Goethe, "that I am not young in so thoroughly finished a world."

6.
    I. A new manager sometimes may feel insecure about his or her competence in the new position.
    II. The new manager may then exhibit defensive or arrogant behavior towards those one supervises, or the new manager may direct overly flattering behavior toward one's new supervisor.

    A. Sometimes, a new manager may feel insecure about his or her ability to perform well in this new position. The insecurity may lead him or her to treat others differently. He or she may display arrogant or defensive behavior towards those he or she supervises, or be overly flattering to his or her new supervisor.
    B. A new manager may sometimes feel insecure about his or her ability to perform well in the new position. He or she may then become arrogant, defensive, or overly flattering towards those he or she works with.
    C. There are times when a new manager may be insecure about how well he or she can perform in the new job. The new manager may also behave defensive or act in an arrogant way towards those he or she supervises, or overly flatter his or her boss.
    D. Sometimes a new manager may feel insecure about his or her ability to perform well in the new position. He or she may then display arrogant or defensive behavior towards those they supervise, or become overly flattering towards their supervisors.

6.____

7.
    I. It is possible to eliminate unwanted behavior by bringing it under stimulus control—tying the behavior to a cue, and then never, or rarely, giving the cue.
    II. One trainer successfully used this method to keep an energetic young porpoise from coming out of her tank whenever she felt like it, which was potentially dangerous.
    III. Her trainer taught her to do it for a reward, in response to a hand signal, and then rarely gave the signal.

7.____

A. Unwanted behavior can be eliminated by tying the behavior to a cue, and then never, or rarely, giving the cue. This is called stimulus control. One trainer was able to use this method to keep an energetic young porpoise from coming out of her tank by teaching her to come out for a reward in response to a hand signal, and then rarely giving the signal.
B. Stimulus control can be used to eliminate unwanted behavior. In this method, behavior is tied to a cue, and then the cue is rarely, if ever, given. One trainer was able to successfully use stimulus control to keep an energetic young porpoise from coming out of her tank whenever she felt like it—a potentially dangerous practice. She taught the porpoise to come out for a reward when she gave a hand signal, and then rarely gave the signal.
C. It is possible to eliminate behavior that is undesirable by bringing it under stimulus control by tying behavior to a signal, and then rarely giving the signal. One trainer successfully used this method to keep an energetic porpoise from coming out of her tank, a potentially dangerous situation. Her trainer taught the porpoise to do it for a reward, in response to a hand signal, and then would rarely give the signal.
D. By using stimulus control, it is possible to eliminate unwanted behavior by tying the behavior to a cue, and then rarely or never give the cue. One trainer was able to use this method to successfully stop a young porpoise from coming out of her tank whenever she felt like it. To curb this potentially dangerous practice, the porpoise was taught by the trainer to come out of the tank for a reward, in response to a hand signal, and then rarely given the signal.

8. I. There is a great deal of concern over the safety of commercial trucks, caused by their greatly increased role in serious accidents since federal deregulation in 1981.
    II. Recently, 60 percent of trucks in New York and Connecticut and 70 percent of trucks in Maryland randomly stopped by state troopers failed safety inspections.
    III. Sixteen states in the United States require no training at all for truck drivers.

8._____

   A. Since federal deregulation in 1981, there has been a great deal of concern over the safety of commercial trucks, and their greatly increased role in serious accidents. Recently, 60 percent of trucks in New York and Connecticut, and 70 percent of trucks in Maryland failed safety inspections. Sixteen states in the United States require no training at all for truck drivers.
   B. There is a great deal of concern over the safety of commercial trucks since federal deregulation in 1981. Their role in serious accidents has greatly increased. Recently, 60 percent of trucks randomly stopped in Connecticut and New York and 70 percent in Maryland failed safety inspections conducted by state troopers. Sixteen states in the United States provide no training at all for truck drivers.
   C. Commercial trucks have a greatly increased role in serious accidents since federal deregulation in 1981. This has led to a great deal of concern.

8 (#2)

Recently, 70 percent of trucks in Maryland and 60 percent of trucks in New York and Connecticut failed inspection of those that were randomly stopped by state troopers. Sixteen states in the United States require no training for all truck drivers.

D. Since federal deregulation in 1981, the role that commercial trucks have played in serious accidents has greatly increased, and this has led to a great deal of concern. Recently, 60 percent of trucks in New York and Connecticut, and 70 percent of trucks in Maryland randomly stopped by state troopers failed safety inspections. Sixteen states in the U.S. don't require any training for truck drivers.

9. I. No matter how much some people have, they still feel unsatisfied and want more, or want to keep what they have forever.
    II. One recent television documentary showed several people flying from New York to Paris for a one-day shopping spree to buy platinum earrings, because they were bored.
    III. In Brazil, some people were ordering coffins that cost a minimum of $45,000 and are equipping them with deluxe stereos, televisions, and other graveyard necessities.

    A. Some people, despite having a great deal, still feel unsatisfied and want more, or think they can keep what they have forever. One recent documentary on television showed several people enroute from Paris to New York for a one day shopping spree to buy platinum earrings, because they were bored. Some people in Brazil are even ordering coffins equipped with such graveyard necessities as deluxe stereos and televisions. The price of the coffins start at $45,000.
    B. No matter how much some people have, they may feel unsatisfied. This leads them to want more, or to want to keep what they have forever. Recently, a television documentary depicting several people flying from New York to Paris for a one day shopping spree to buy platinum earrings. They were bored. Some people in Brazil are ordering coffins that cost at least $45,000 and come equipped with deluxe televisions, stereos and other necessary graveyard items.
    C. Some people will be dissatisfied no matter how much they have. They may want more, or they may want to keep what they have forever. One recent television documentary showed several people, motivated by boredom, jetting from New York to Paris for a one-day shopping spree to buy platinum earrings. In Brazil, some people are ordering coffins equipped with deluxe stereos, televisions and other graveyard necessities. The minimum price for these coffins—$45,000.
    D. Some people are never satisfied. No matter how much they have they still want more, or think they can keep what they have forever. One television documentary recently showed several people flying from New York to Paris for the day to buy platinum earrings because they were bored. In Brazil, some people are ordering coffins that cost $45,000 and are equipped with deluxe stereos, televisions and other graveyard necessities.

9.____

9 (#2)

10.
I. A television signal or video signal has three parts.
II. Its parts are the black-and-white portion, the color portion, and the synchronizing (sync) pulses, which keep the picture stable.
III. Each video source, whether it's a camera or a video-cassette recorder contains its own generator of these synchronizing pulses to accompany the picture that it's sending in order to keep it steady and straight.
IV. In order to produce a clean recording, a video-cassette recorder must "lock-up" to the sync pulses that are part of the video it is trying to record, and this effort may be very noticeable if the device does not have gunlock.

10.____

A. There are three parts to a television or video signal: the black-and-white part, the color part, and the synchronizing (sync) pulses, which keep the picture stable. Whether it's a video-cassette recorder or a camera, each video source contains its own pulse that synchronizes and generates the picture it's sending in order to keep it straight and steady. A video-cassette recorder must "lock up" to the sync pulses that are part of the video it's trying to record. If the device doesn't have gunlock, this effort must be very noticeable.
B. A video signal or television is comprised of three parts: the black-and-white portion, the color portion, and the sync (synchronizing) pulses, which keep the picture stable. Whether it's a camera or a video-cassette recorder, each video source contains its own generator of these synchronizing pulses. These accompany the picture that it's sending in order to keep it straight and steady. A video-cassette recorder must "lock up" to the sync pulses that are part of the video it is trying to record in order to produce a clean recording. This effort may be very noticeable if the device does not have gunlock.
C. There are three parts to a television or video signal: the color portion, the black-and-white portion, and the sync (synchronizing pulses). These keep the picture stable. Each video source, whether it's a video-cassette recorder or a camera, generates these synchronizing pulses accompanying the picture it's sending in order to keep it straight and steady. If a clean recording is to be produced, a video-cassette recorder must store the sync pulses that are part of the video it is trying to record. This effort may not be noticeable if the device does not have gunlock.
D. A television signal or video signal has three parts: the black-and-white portion, the color portion, and the synchronizing (sync) pulses. It's the sync pulses which keep the picture stable, which accompany it and keep it steady and straight. Whether it's a camera or a video-cassette recorder, each video source contains its own generator of these synchronizing pulses. To produce a clean recording, a video-cassette recorder must "lock up" to the sync pulses that are part of the video it is trying to record. If the device does not have gunlock, this effort may be very noticeable.

KEY (CORRECT ANSWERS)

1. C
2. B
3. A
4. B
5. D
6. A
7. B
8. D
9. C
10. D

FLOWCHARTING

When you program a computer, you must first think through what you want to get done. It is necessary to take small organized steps. The ordering of your thoughts is called an *algorithm*. It is a step-by-step process to complete a certain task.

For instance, imagine that you are looking for a new job. You need a plan of action. Your algorithm:

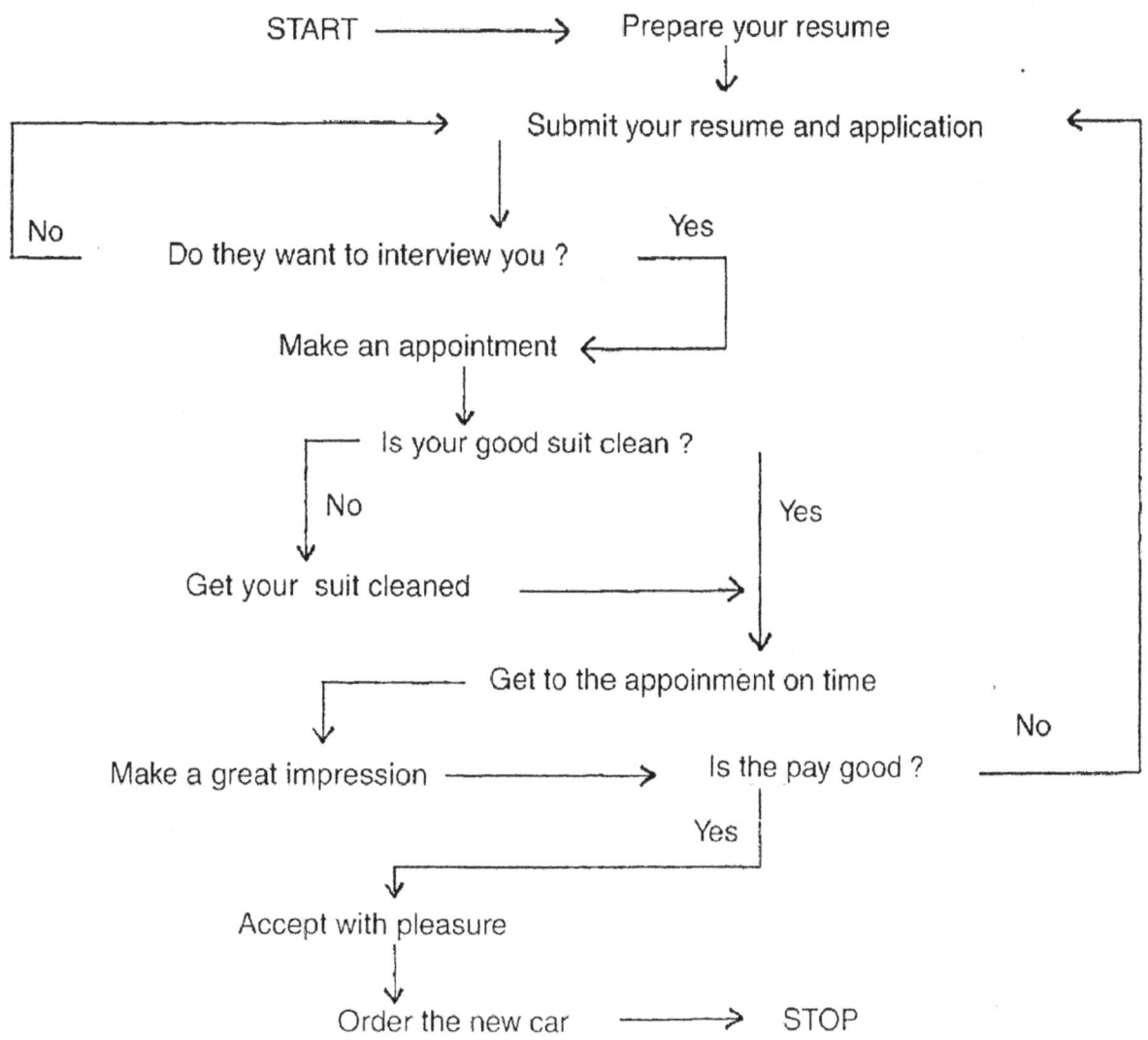

This is the flowchart that goes with your algorithm. Compare them. Note the use of shapes for each step. These are symbols.

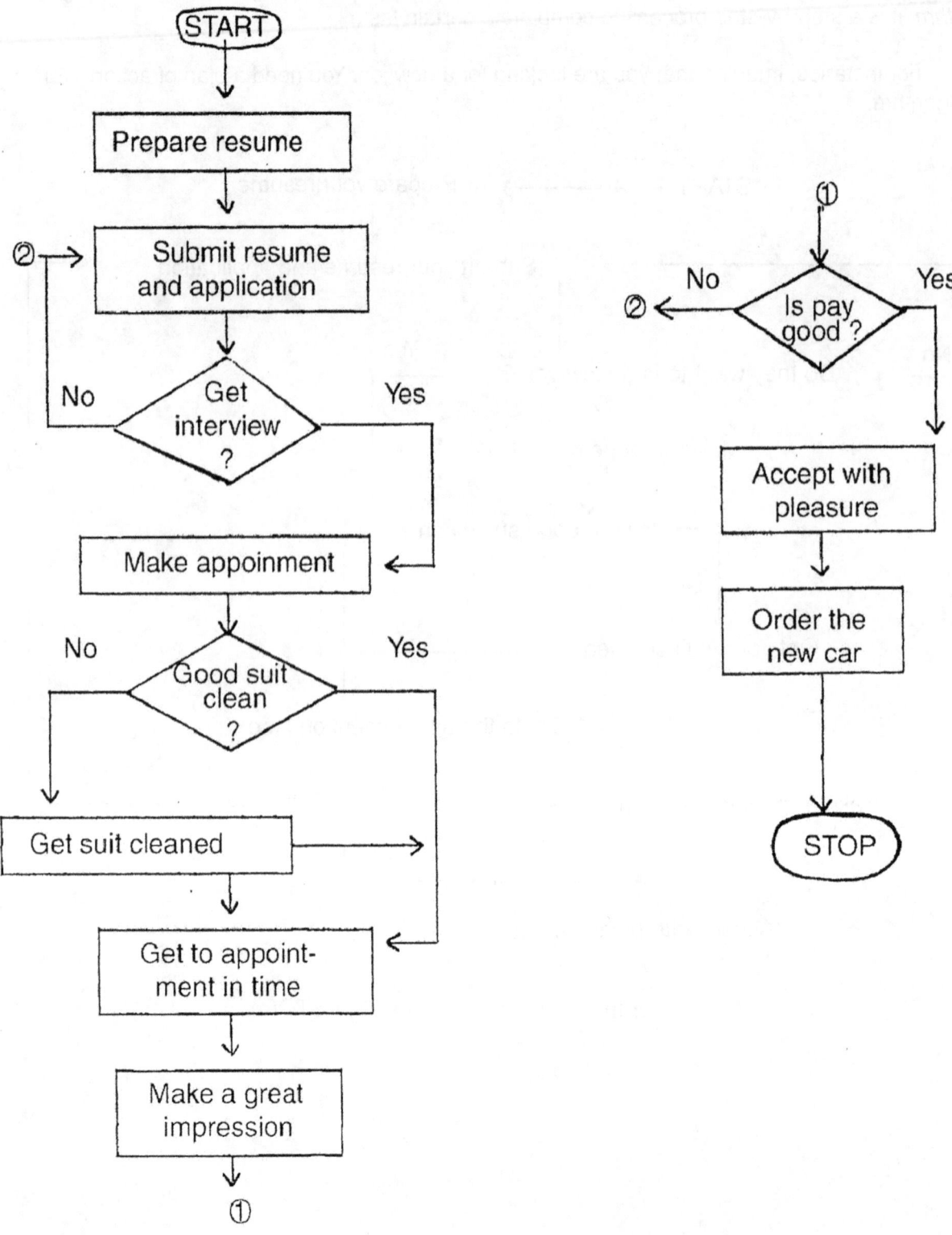

182

FLOWCHART SYMBOLS make flowcharts uniform and easier to read:

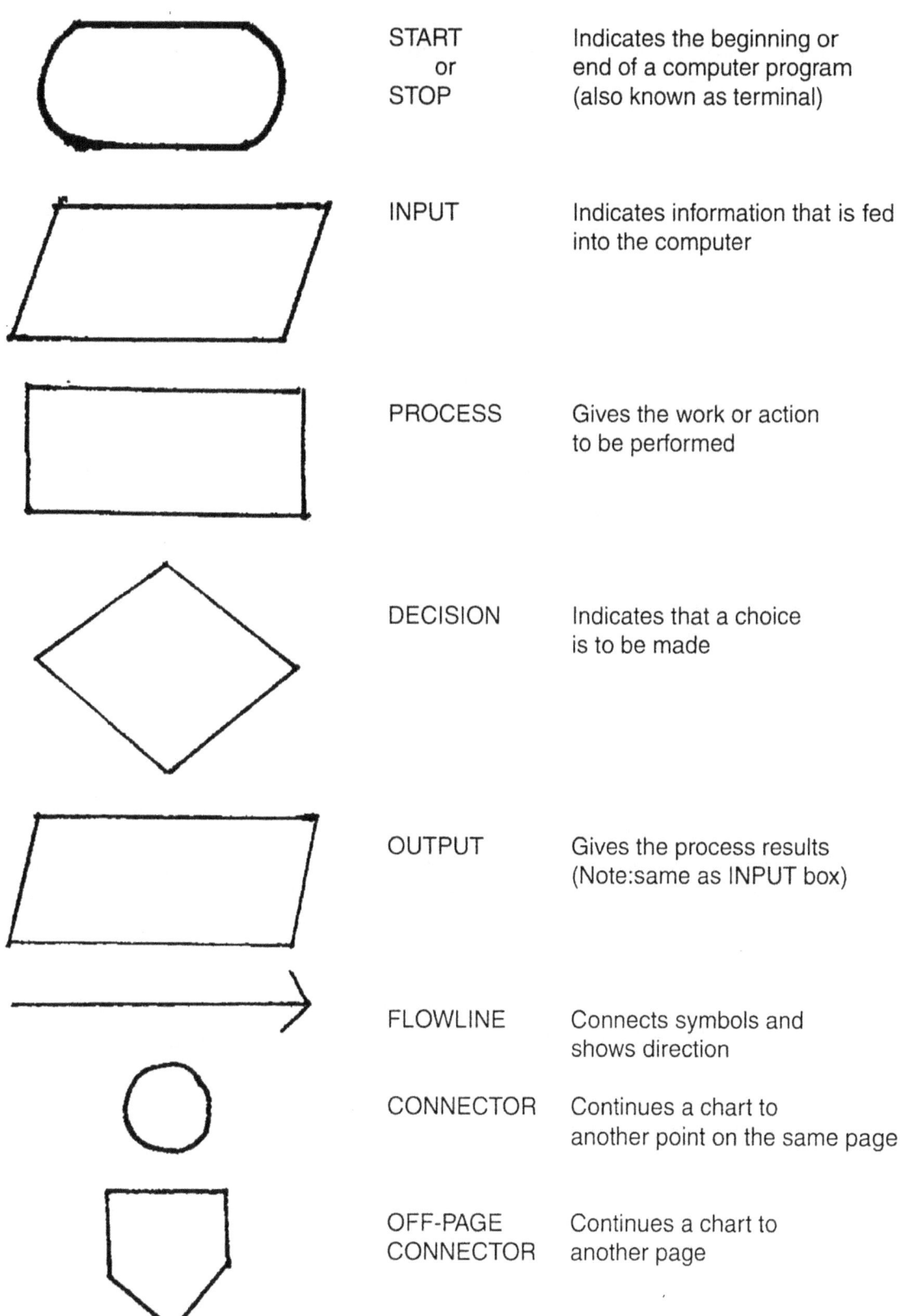

POINTS TO REMEMBER:

An <u>OVAL</u> means the beginning and end of a flowchart; it indicates the terminal points. If you trace it, you will see that one "flowline leads out from START and into STOP.

A <u>PARALLELOGRAM</u> has two purposes, to show input and to show output. Input is information given to the computer. Information gotten from the computer is called output and is also put into a parallelogram. A parallelogram should have one line leading in and one line leading out.

A <u>RECTANGLE</u> represents work done. One task is presented in each box. It will always have one flowline leading in and one leading out.

A <u>DIAMOND</u> represents a decision.It is always phrased as a question which can be answered yes or no. A diamond will have one flowline leading in and two leading out, one marked YES and one marked NO.

A <u>LINE</u> with arrows indicates the direction of the flowchart. These <u>FLOWLINES</u> are always vertical or horizontal and meet each other at right angles. They must <u>never</u> cross each other.

A <u>CIRCLE</u> is used when the flowchart does not fit in the space. One circle has a number which corresponds to another circle on the sane page.

A <u>PENTAGON</u> means that a flowchart will be continued on the next page. The number put in the first pentagon matches the number in a second pentagon found on the following page.

NOTE: Flowcharts should follow a top-to-bottom and left-to-right progression a's much as possible.

Once the job is yours, a flowchart such as the one below may be used to determine what your weekly paycheck is.

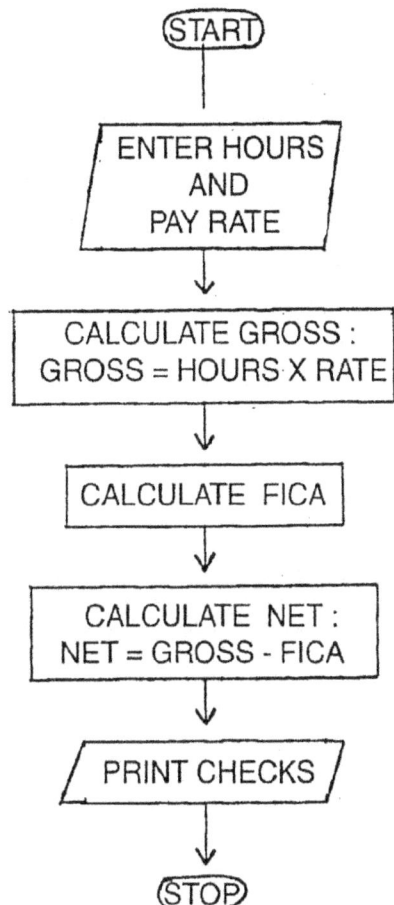

This is a very simple program flowchart, but may be all that is necessary to show the basic procedure. Note the two parallelograms and how their messages differ from those of the rectangles. A programmer might then take this and expand it to show other things — how FICA is determined, for example. You might want to try this if you know the formula for calculating FICA.

Below you will see three flowcharts which are used to solve math problems. The first is an incomplete chart for finding the average of five numbers. The second computes the batting average (B) of a baseball player, given his at-bats (A) and his hits (H). The third determines whether a given number is positive or negative. Complete each by enclosing the steps with the correct symbols and connecting with arrows. Since page 7 gives you the answers, you might want to fold the booklet over or cover the page as you are working to keep from looking at it.

6

#1	#2	#3
START	START	START
ENTER 29,467, 53,902,84	ENTER H, A	AENTER X=50, Y=30
8=29+467+53+902+84	B=H/A	D=X-Y
A=S/5	PRINT B	D>0? (YES / NO)
PRINT A	STOP	PRINT NEGATIVE NUMBER
STOP		PRINT POSITIVE NUMBER
		STOP

Did your charts look like this? If so, great! If not, review pages 3-4. You may be wondering why there is an option to print negative number when the answer is obviously positive. Both options are needed in order to cover all variations of a problem. What if this were a *real* program and it had to handle a problem in which D = Y - X? Then the answer would have been 30-50, or -20.

7

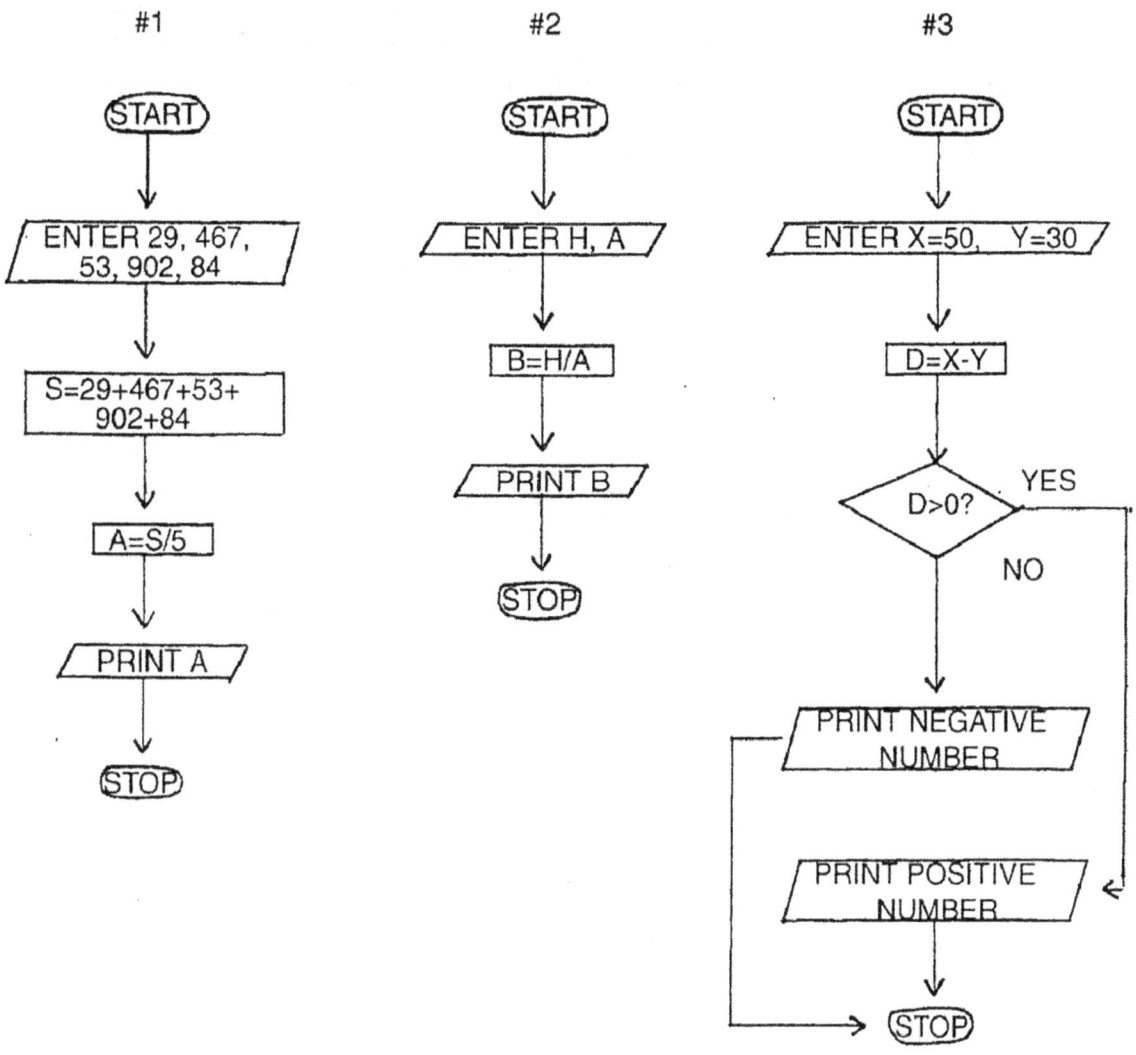

LOOPS:

A loop in a flowchart comes out of a decision box and enables you to return to an earlier point in the chart. To understand the use of the loop, let's look back at the flowchart for job-hunting which was on page 2. There are two loops represented by this flowchart.

The first came out of the diamond-shaped decision box reading *Get interview?* If the answer was *Yes,* you proceeded to make an appointment. If *No,* you *looped* back up to an earlier point and continued the job-hunt by submitting resume and application to another possible employer.

The second loop came from a *No* response to the decision box, *Is pay good?* When you decided *Yes,* the pay was good, you proceeded to accept the job. If you decided *No,* the pay was not good, you returned to an earlier point, submitting your resume and application elsewhere. The flowchart then guided you to repeat the same steps you had taken before. (NOTE:, Loops always flow from, decisions, symbolized in this guide by diamond-shaped boxes, and always return you to an earlier point. Understanding this simple process will help you trace through and understand the most complex flowchart.)

The flowchart that follows shows how to divide a number between 10 and 100 by a number that is less than 10. Study it and then answer the following:

1. This flowchart shows how many loops?

2. What decision is made first?

3. What should you do if the answer is *Yes*?

4. What should you do if the answer is *No*?

5. What is the second decision?

6. What should you do if the answer is *No*?

9

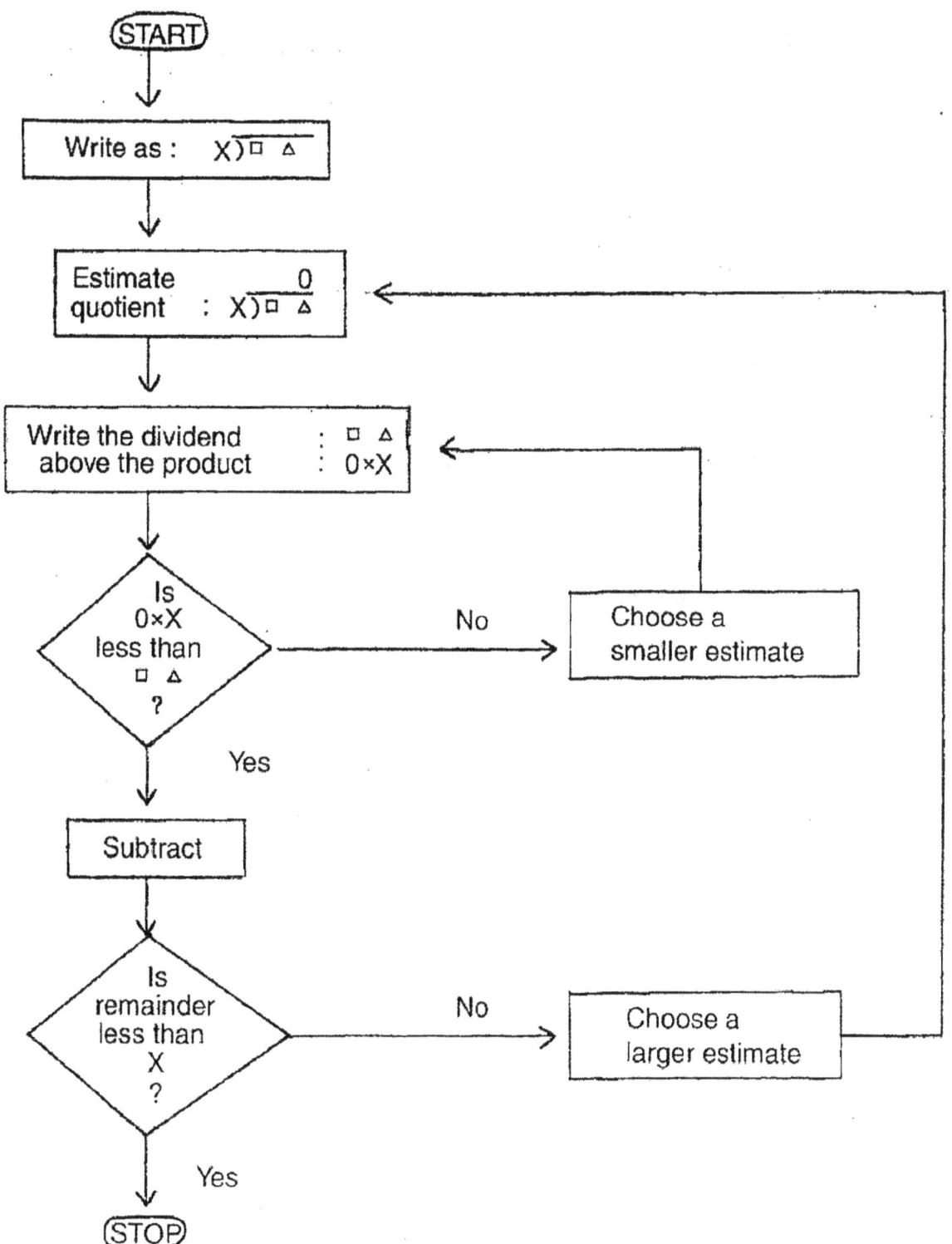

On the following page is an old, almost classic example of flowcharting, which has been titled *How to Get to Work in the Morning*. Use it to answer the questions that follow below. Answers to these questions can be found on the last page of this section.

7. Look at point ⓐ Does this represent a loop? Why or why not?

8. Bow many loops do you find in the chart? Do all the decision boxes in the chart produce loops? How can you tell?

9. What is the first decision? 10. If *Yes*, what do you do?

11. Look at the box that contains ⓑ. Could that box read *How cold?* Why or why not?

12. Which step comes next if the answer at point ⓒ is *No?*

13. If the answer to the step at point ⓓ is *Yes*, what happens?

14. How many times does someone who is married more than 5 years get kissed?

15. How many times does a newlywed get kissed?

16. If point ⓓ had to be located on another page because of space limitations, what should Ⓐ be changed to?

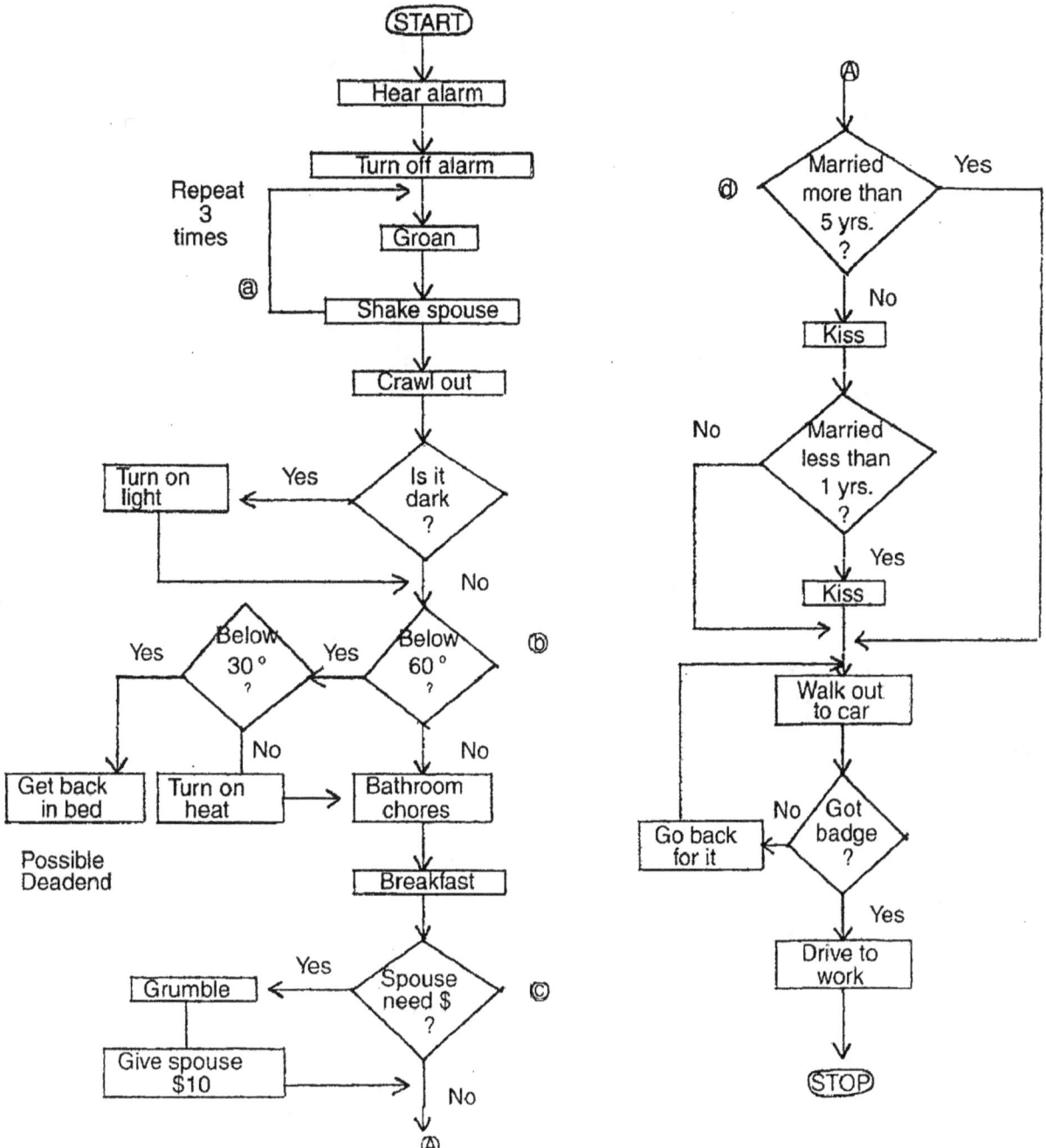

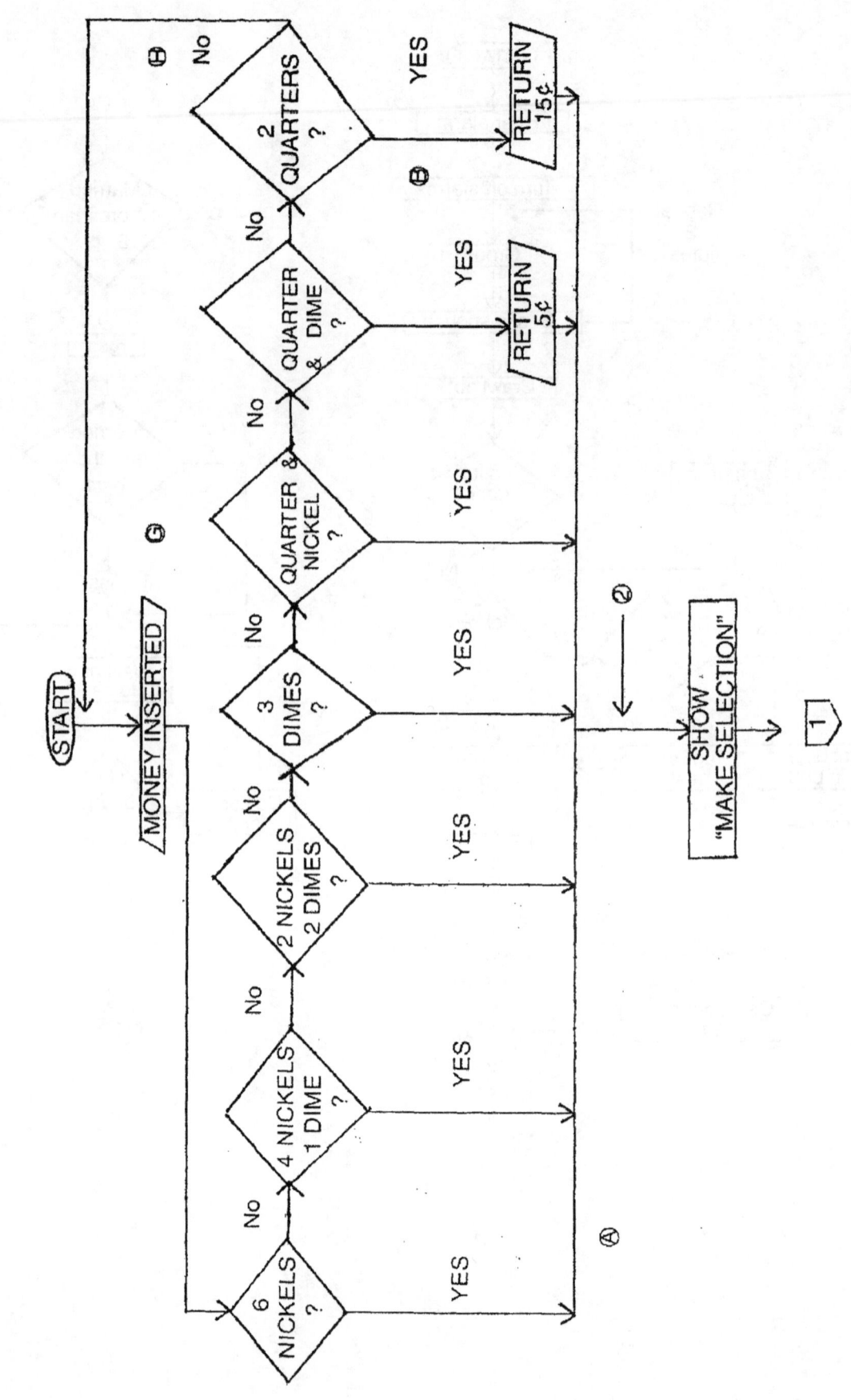

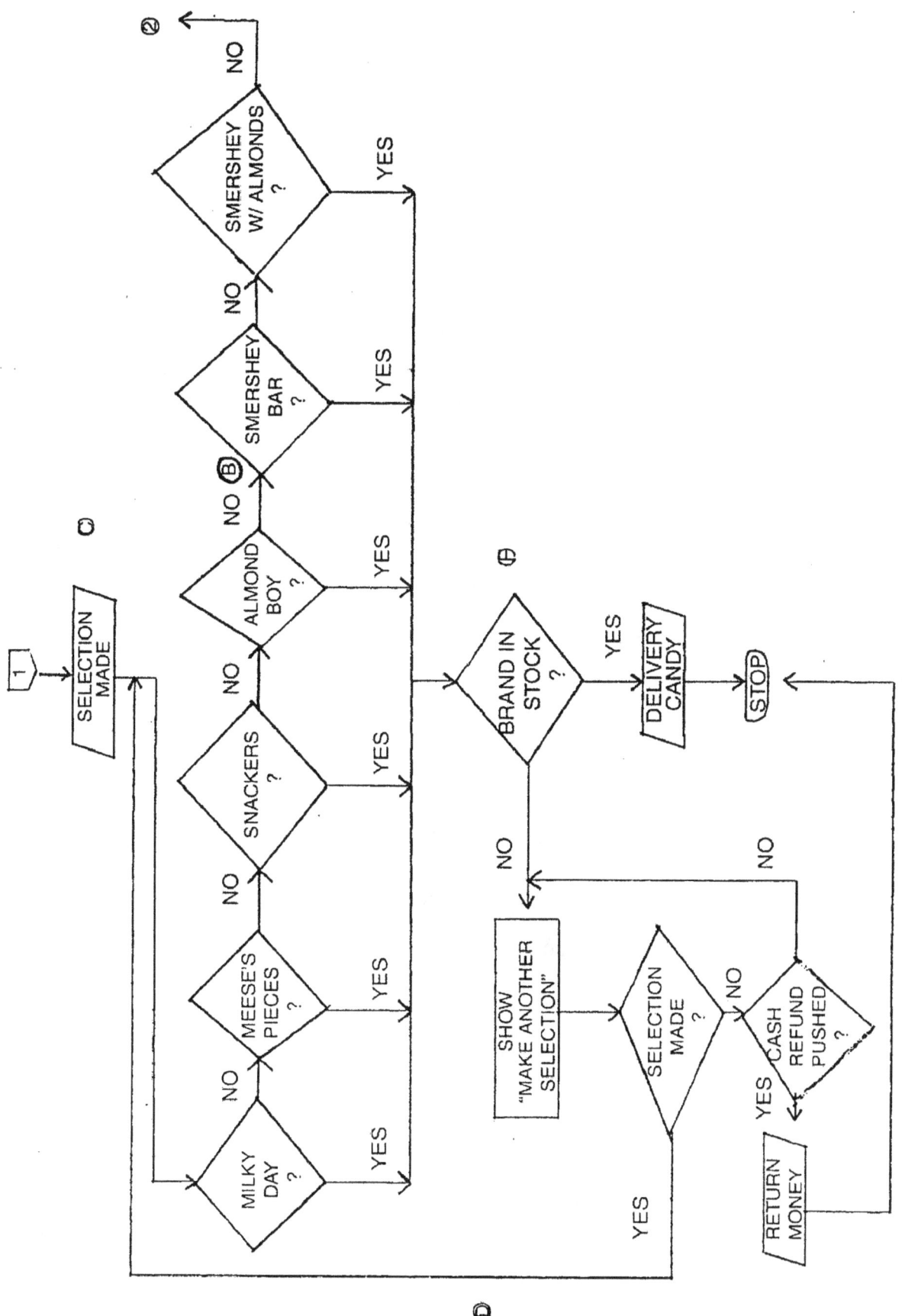

Please study the flowchart for a candy vending machine, then answer the following questions. The answers are at the end of the section.

17. How many brands of candy are available?

18. What is the price of each?

19. What coins may be used?

20. At point Ⓐ, what is the next function?

21. At point Ⓑ what is the next function?

22. Why is point Ⓒ a parallelogram?

23. What three steps immediately preceded point Ⓓ ?

24. If one were to reach point Ⓗ what would that MOST likely mean?

25. What might we call point Ⓓ?

26. At point Ⓔ what brands have been eliminated as selection options?

27. At point Ⓔ, what brands are still selection options?

28. Why is the box at Ⓕ a diamond shape?

29. What does a *Yes* decision at Ⓕ lead to?

30. Name two indicated input points.

31. Name two output boxes.

15
KEY (CORRECT ANSWERS)

ANSWERS TO QUESTIONS 1-6.

1. Two.

2. Is OxX (the product) less than ?? (the dividend)?

3. Subtract the product from the dividend.

4. *Choose a smaller estimate* and go back to *Write the dividend* ?? *above the product* OxK to then see if the product is less than the dividend. In other words, you repeat the steps as the loop indicates.

5. *Is the remainder less than X (the divisor)?*

6. *Choose a larger estimate* and loop back to repeat the steps as the arrows indicate. You go all the way back to the rectangle immediately preceding the first decision box.

NOTE: Now look back at the flowchart again. See that the lines forming the loops never intersect (cross) each other.

ANSWERS TO *HOW TO GET TO WORK IN THE MORNING*

7. No, point ⓐ doesn't represent a loop. You know this because it doesn't flow from a decision box, a diamond-shaped box that requires a *Yes* or *No* answer.

8. There is only one loop in the chart. No, all the decision boxes in the chart don't produce loops. Only once does it come from a decision box <u>and</u> direct you <u>back</u> to repeat steps. This is at *Got badge?* Remember, loops refer you back to an earlier part in the chart. The only other item that looks like a loop is from *Shake spouse.* It's not a loop, however, it's a way of telling you to repeat an action without taking up space.

9. *Is it dark?* is the first decision.

10. If the answer is *Yes,* then you should *Turn on light.*

11. No, because decision boxes must be able to be answered *Yes* or *No* <u>only</u>.

12. The next step is point ⓓ, *Married more than 5 years?*

13. If the answer to the step at point ⓓ your car. is *Yes,* you walk out to

14. Someone who is married more than 5 years doesn't get kissed at all.

195

15. A newlywed gets kissed twice.

16. Under these circumstances, Ⓐ should be changed to ⌂A⌂; it would become an *off-page connector*.

ANSWERS TO THE *CANDY MACHINE FLOWCHART*

17. 6

18. 30 cents

19. Quarters, nickels and dimes

20. Show *make selection*

21. *Return 15¢*

22. It's a parallelogram because that shape signals input. We are assuming that a candy machine is a computer. In that case, the *keyboard* is the knobs or buttons that are pushed to make a selection or to get a refund. The *keyboard operator* is any person who comes to buy candy. He/she *enters* the data (the selection or the money), and so this is considered input.

23. (1) The selection made was not in stock.
    (2) The consumer was signaled to make another selection.
    (3) Another selection was made.

24. The *operator* did not put in enough money, he or she put in the wrong coins or wrong combination of coins, or the machine is out of order. By the time we get to point Ⓗ, all likely, possible combinations of the coins that will be taken have been exhausted. The flaw here is that there is no detailed provisio for occurrences like: putting in pennies, or putting in too much money. If the person were to put in three quarters, how would he or she get one back? This flowchart doesn't tell us, and this is a flaw in the algorithm.

25. A loop.

26. Milky Day, Meese's Pieces, Snackers, and Almond Boy.

27. Smershey Bar and Smershey with Almonds.

28. It is a decision box. It asks whether or not the brand is in stock.

29. *Deliver sandy*

30. Ⓖ and Ⓒ

31. *Deliver candy, Return 5¢, Return 15¢,* and/or *Return money*

TABLE OF CONTENTS
LOGICAL DATABASE DESIGN

Page

1. INTRODUCTION 2

    1.1 What Is Logical Database Design? 2

        1.1.1 LDD's Relation to Other Life Cycle Phases . 2
        1.1.2 Characteristics of LDD 6

    1.2 An Ideal Logical Database Design Methodology . 8

        1.2.1 LDD Practices 8
        1.2.2 Data Dictionary System 9

    1.3 Intended Audience for this Guide 10

    1.4 Purpose of this Guide 10

    1.5 Assumptions 11

    1.6 Scope of this Guide 11

    1.7 Structure of this Guide 12

2. THE FRAMEWORK THAT SUPPORTS LDD 14

    2.1 The Role of LDD in the Life Cycle 14

        2.1.1 Needs Analysis 15
        2.1.2 Requirements Analysis 16
        2.1.3 Logical Database Design 17
        2.1.4 Physical Database Design 18

    2.2 Detailed Framework for LDD 19

        2.2.1 LDD Information Requirements 19
        2.2.2 LDD Phases 20
        2.2.3 Strategies for LDD Development 23
        2.2.4 Summary of LDD Features 25

3. PROJECT ORGANIZATION 26

    3.1 Functional Roles Needed for LDD 26

    3.2 Training Required for LDD 28

    3.3 Project Planning and Management Requirements . 29

4. LOCAL INFORMATION-FLOW MODELING 30

    4.1 Information Used to Develop the LIM 31

    4.2 Functions of the LIM 34

    4.3 Procedure for Developing the LIM 34

         4.3.1 Review Need for Analysis 36
         4.3.2 Determine Subsystems 37
         4.3.3 Plan Development of the LIM 39
         4.3.4 Develop LIM 40
         4.3.5 Develop Workload With Respect to LIMs 44

5. GLOBAL INFORMATION-FLOW MODELING 47

    5.1 Information Used to Develop the GIM 48

    5.2 Functions of the GIM 49

    5.3 Procedure for Developing the GIM 49

         5.3.1 Verify the LIMs 51
         5.3.2 Consolidate LIMs 52
         5.3.3 Refine Boundary of Automated Information
               System (AIS) 54
         5.3.4 Produce GIM 57

6. CONCEPTUAL SCHEMA DESIGN 58

    6.1 Information Used to Develop the CS 59

    6.2 Functions of the CS 59

    6.3 Procedure for Developing the CS 60

         6.3.1 List Entities and Identifiers 62
         6.3.2 Generate Relationships among Entities 64
         6.3.3 Add Connectivity to Relationships 69
         6.3.4 Add Attributes to Entities 72
         6.3.5 Develop Additional Data Characteristics .. 74
         6.3.6 Normalize the Collection 75

7. EXTERNAL SCHEMA MODELING 77

    7.1 Information Used to Develop the ES 77

    7.2 Functions of the ES 77

    7.3 Procedure for Developing the ES 78

	7.3.1 Extract an ES from the CS 80
	7.3.2 Develop Workload With Respect to ESs 82
	7.3.3 Add Local Constraints to the ES 84

8. CONCLUSIONS 85

9. ACKNOWLEDGMENTS 86

10. REFERENCES AND SELECTED READINGS 87

LIST OF FIGURES

FIGURES	DESCRIPTION	PAGE
1	Information Systems Life Cycle	5
2	Diagram of the Four LDD Phases	22
3	Local Information-Flow Modeling (LIM) Procedure	35
4	Example of a LIM	41
5	Global Information-Flow Modeling (GIM) Procedure	50
6	Example of a GIM	56
7	Conceptual Schema (CS) Design Procedure	61
8	Example of an E-R Diagram	66
9	Alternate Notation for an E-R Diagram	67
10	Replacing a Relationship with an Entity	68
11	Example of an E-R Diagram with Connectivity	71
12	Example of an E-R-A Diagram	73
13	External Schema (ES) Modeling Procedure	79

LIST OF ABBREVIATIONS

AA	Application Administrator
AIS	Automated Information System
BSP	Business Systems Planning
CS	Conceptual Schema
DA	Data Administrator
DBA	Database Administrator
DBMS	Database Management System
DD	Data Dictionary
DDA	Data Dictionary Administrator
DDS	Data Dictionary System
EKNF	Elementary Key Normal Form
E-R	Entity-Relationship
E-R-A	Entity-Relationship-Attribute
ES	External Schema
GIM	Global Information-flow Model
IRDS	Information Resource Dictionary System
LDD	Logical Database Design
LIM	Local Information-flow Model
PERT	Program Evaluation and Review Technique
QA	Quality Assurance

LOGICAL DATABASE DESIGN

Logical Database Design. The methodology includes four phases: Local Information-flow Modeling, Global Information-flow Modeling, Conceptual Schema Design, and External Schema Modeling. These phases are intended to make maximum use of available information and user expertise, including the use of a previous Needs Analysis, and to prepare a firm foundation for physical database design and system implementation. The methodology recommends analysis from different points of view--organization, function, and event-- in order to ensure that the logical database design accurately reflects the requirements of the entire population of future users. The methodology also recommends computer support from a data dictionary system, in order to conveniently and accurately handle the volume and complexity of design documentation and analysis. The report places the methodology in the context of the complete system life cycle. An appendix of illustrations shows examples of how the four phases of the methodology can be implemented.

Key words: data dictionary system; data dictionary system standard; data management; data model; database design; database management system, DBMS; Entity-Relationship-Attribute Model; Information Resource Dictionary System, IRDS; logical database design.

1. INTRODUCTION

1.1 What Is Logical Database Design?

Logical Database Design (LDD) is the process of determining the fundamental data structure needed to support an organization's information resource. LDD provides a structure that determines the way that data is collected, stored, and protected from undesired access. Since data collection, storage, and protection are costly, and since restructuring data generally requires expensive revisions to programs, it is important that the LDD be of high quality. This guide describes procedures that lead to the development of a high quality LDD.

A high quality LDD will be: (1) internally consistent, to reduce the chances of contradictory results from the information system; (2) complete, to ensure that known information requirements can be satisfied and known constraints can be enforced; and (3) robust, to allow adaptation of the data structure in response to foreseeable changes in the information requirements. To fulfill these considerations, a good LDD should be independent of any particular application, so that all applications can be satisfied, and independent of any particular hardware or software environment, so that the data structure can be supported in any environment. A good LDD will ensure that modularity, efficiency, consistency, and integrity are supported in the data structure underlying the databases of the information system.

1.1.1 LDD's Relation to Other Life Cycle Phases.

LDD is closely related to the life cycle phases of Needs Analysis, Requirements Analysis, and Physical Database Design. Needs analysis and requirements analysis provide the information requirements needed to perform LDD. LDD produces data models and schemas for use in physical database design. The Physical Database Design phase receives the data structures prepared during LDD and adapts them to the specific hardware and software environment to form the internal schema of each database.

Figure 1 shows LDD's place in the life cycle and depicts the functional and data activities that can be performed in parallel. LDD can be performed in parallel to the phases of Requirements Analysis, Systems Specification, and Systems Design. The synchronized performance of these phases will assist in providing the information needed for a good LDD and will result in speeding the systems development process.

By taking a brief overview of the development of an information system, we can see how LDD is used. The life cycle of an information system should consist of the following phases:

1. Needs Analysis

    Also known as Enterprise Analysis, this phase is conducted before other work on the systems development project begins. Its purpose is to establish the context and boundaries of the systems development effort, and provide the focus, scope, priorities, and initial requirements for the target system.

2. Requirements Analysis

    The results of the Needs Analysis are carried further in this phase, which provides both the functional and the data requirements for the system under development. Requirements analysis is performed in parallel to the LDD and Systems Specification phases. Prototyping may be performed during this phase to refine requirements.

3. Systems Specification

    During this phase, the functional information provided by requirements analysis is used to produce specifications for: input and output reports that are both external and internal to the system; the functions, processes, and procedures of operational subsystems; and decision support capabilities.

4. Logical Database Design

    This phase is performed concurrently with the phases of Requirements Analysis, Systems Specification, and Systems Design. During this phase, the data requirements provided by the Needs Analysis and Requirements Analysis phases are used to perform the following iterative data modeling and design activities:

A. Local and Global Information-flow Modeling

The following are defined: data flows throughout the system; information models for each application (i.e., local) and for the entire system (i.e., global); and, data classifications, requirements, and sources for the subsystems including those for decision support. The LDD data modeling activities correspond to the functional specification activities of to the Systems Specification phase.

B. Conceptual and External Schemas

The following are defined: data structures for system-wide (i.e., conceptual) and application-oriented (i.e., external) views of the system; user views of the databases including those providing decision support capabilities; and logical database schema designs and constraints. LDD schema design activities correspond to the functional design activities of the Systems Design phase.

5. Systems Design

This phase delineates: the functional control flows using the data flows from LDD; high level and detailed system architectures; the software structure design; and the module external design (i.e., the design for interfaces among modules of code).

6. Physical Database Design

This phase produces physical data flows and the detailed internal schema for the specific hardware, software, and database implementations to be used, in order to balance maximum data storage efficiency, data retrieval performance, and data update performance. Physical database design is performed in parallel to the Implementation phase.

7. Implementation

This phase produces: logic definition for programs; module design; internal data definitions; coding; testing and debugging; acceptance testing; and conversion from the old system to the new one.

INFORMATION SYSTEMS LIFE CYCLE

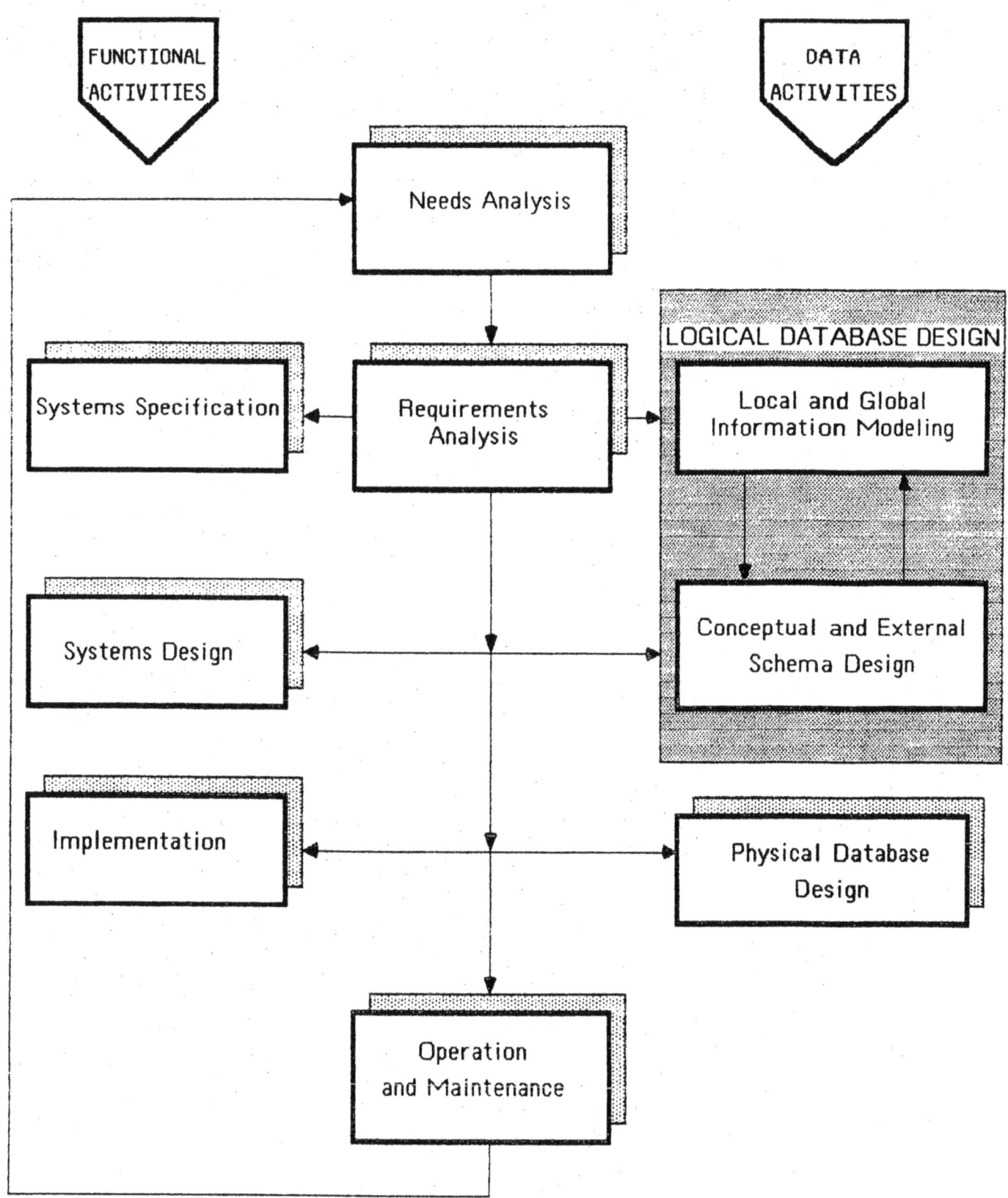

FIGURE 1

8. Operation and Maintenance

   During this phase the information system performs to serve the users' information needs and to collect data about the system's ongoing operation. Programmers and analysts continue to debug the system and modify it to support changing users' needs. Database designers continue to maintain database effectiveness and efficiency during system modifications and data changes. When modifications to the system are no longer adequate to support user needs, the current system should evolve to a new target system and the cycle will begin again.

As this description of the information system's life cycle shows, LDD plays a major role in development. LDD greatly enhances the performance of the Quality Assurance (QA) process, which would be ongoing from the Systems Specification and LDD phases through the Operation and Maintenance phase. Because LDD emphasizes the iterative approach, QA will have many opportunities to check the results of one iteration against the results of other iterations. Since LDD is performed in parallel to the Requirements Analysis, Systems Specification, and Systems Design phases, QA will be able to compare both the interim and final results of concurrent phases to resolve any difficulties sooner than through the traditional approach. The automated Data Dictionary System (DDS), described in Section 1.2.2, should be used during Requirements Analysis and LDD to provide immediate, shared access to data requirements and database designs, and to support the QA process.

1.1.2 Characteristics of LDD.

The potential benefits of LDD to the development life cycle can only be gained, however, through a good quality LDD. For LDD to perform its role well, the results of the logical design process must have certain characteristics. A LDD should be:

- o Independent of the hardware and software environment, so that the design can be implemented in a variety of environments and so the design will remain relevant even if the hardware and software selected to support the information system eventually change.

- o Independent of the implementation data model or the Database Management System (DBMS) in use, so that the design will apply to any present or future data model or data management system, which would not necessarily be a DBMS.

o Comprehensive in representing present and future applications so that all known, anticipated, and probable needs can be included or considered in the design, to avoid costly system alterations in the future.

o Able to satisfy the information requirements of the entire organization, encompassing all possible applications rather than being limited to one or two; this way the information system will have the capacity to be an organizational resource, not just the resource of one department or application area.

A good LDD should also fulfill a set of precise technical goals to provide a firm foundation for:

o Maintainability and reusability, achieved through the use of modularity in the database design.

o Robustness, allowing both the design and the system to be adaptable to hardware and software changes.

o Security, controlled through compartmentalization in the database design which will limit specified types of data access to designated personnel or organizational units.

o Update and storage efficiency, achieved through controlled redundancy that limits the number of places where the same data will be stored.

o Retrieval efficiency, so that data can be organized to be readily accessible by system users.

o Consistency and integrity, achieved through several measures including data integrity constraints and controlled redundancy.

If done correctly, logical database design for a complex information system is a massive undertaking. The short-term cost of LDD is great, but the long-term benefits of better information and greater flexibility provide substantial savings over the system's life cycle.

1.2 An Ideal Logical Database Design Methodology

A methodology is an organized system of practices and procedures applied to a branch of knowledge to assist in the pursuit of that knowledge, which in this case is database design. In other words, a LDD methodology is a planned approach to database design that assists in database development in support of an information system.

1.2.1 LDD Practices.

This guide describes a methodology that includes the preferred practices and procedures characterizing the development of a good quality LDD and a successful information system. Although normalization is often considered the primary activity of LDD, normalization is only one of many procedures performed in LDD. Normalization is a valuable but limited tool in that it only considers functional data dependencies. Other procedures should be used in conjunction with normalization for a coherent database design. An ideal LDD methodology should be supported by:

1. A LDD guide, such as the one provided in this document, that describes clearly defined steps for analysts and designers to follow in order to produce a good LDD.

2. Analytical methods, such as the ones described in this guide, to assist in the detection of redundancies, incompleteness, and possible errors in the conceptual and functional data modeling. Some of these methods include: (a) a hierarchical, iterative approach to organizational or functional concept development; (b) differentiation of various points of view in information development, such as organizational components, higher and lower level functions, and event, control, and decision structures; and (c) normalization procedures.

3. A series of specified checkpoints for progress reviews by designers and management, and for information exchange meetings with the personnel of LDD's parallel phases, Requirements Analysis, Systems Specification, and Systems Design.

4. A mode of notation (i.e., graphic or symbolic) to describe and build a detailed conceptual model of the data and functions under study.

5. A specification language (e.g., the language used by a Data Dictionary System) to specify information requirements and the LDD design in a consistent, unambiguous manner.

6. An automated tool such as a Data Dictionary System, capable of supporting the documentation and analysis of LDD complexity, especially for large systems development projects. This tool should be used to assist in: (a) describing the conceptual model; (b) describing the data needed to support the functions of the conceptual model; (c) performing completeness and consistency checking of the conceptual model and the data needed to support the functions of the conceptual model [AFIF84].

1.2.2 Data Dictionary System.

A Data Dictionary System (DDS) is a computer software system used to record, store, protect, and analyze descriptions of an organization's information resources, including data and programs. It provides analysts, designers, and managers with convenient, controlled access to the summary and detailed descriptions needed to plan, design, implement, operate, and modify their information systems. The DDS also provides end-users with the data descriptions that they need to formulate ad hoc queries. Equally important, it provides a common language, or framework, for establishing and enforcing standards and controls throughout an organization.

The data dictionary (DD) is the data that is organized and managed by the Data Dictionary System. The DD is a resource that will be of great value long after a logical database design is completed. The data dictionary can provide support for information about all aspects of system development to be stored, updated, and accessed throughout the system's life cycle.

The term Information Resource Dictionary System (IRDS) is beginning to replace the term Data Dictionary System due to recognition of the flexibility and power of the software [ANSI84, FIPS80, KONI84]. This paper uses the terms Data Dictionary System (DDS) and data dictionary (DD) to conform to the current practice of software vendors.

1.3 Intended Audience for this Guide

This guide is intended primarily to provide information and guidance to: Data Administrators (DAs) and Database Administrators (DBAs) in leading their LDD projects; Applications Administrators (AAs) and application specialists in the types of data and data validation that LDD will require; and, end-users and systems analysts in how they can best contribute to the LDD project to maximize its benefits.

1.4 Purpose of this Guide

This guide provides a coherent plan of action that will allow management and database designers to direct and perform the database design successfully. The LDD plan offered here is sufficiently general to be compatible with existing tools and techniques in use for database design. By defining a methodology that provides a more stable view of the relationships among data items, this guide can be used to increase the effectiveness of an information system over its life cycle.

When the LDD approach described here is used, particularly if used with the assistance of a Data Dictionary System, an increase in clear communication can result among the end-users, systems analysts, designers, and the applications programmers who will actually code and implement the system. By providing a detailed and unambiguous description of the system's information requirements in relation to the users' perspectives, LDD offers a bridge between the end-users and the physical database designers and applications programmers.

This guide describes a methodology to be used in optimizing the flexibility and integrity of an information system. Flexibility will be ensured through the identification of the least changing characteristics of the system, which give a stable foundation upon which to build the information system. Data integrity will be optimized through the centralized control, completeness, and consistency that a quality LDD will provide. The information system that results from these LDD procedures will perform better over the system's life cycle because it will address current and probable future needs more completely and will allow requirements changes to be incorporated more effectively.

1.5 Assumptions

Several assumptions have been made in the preparation of this guide about the types of information systems in which LDD will be used. Because LDD is a non-trivial process to be undertaken when a need for it exists, it is assumed that:

- The information system's databases will be sizable and complex to support multiple applications, may have no single dominant application, and will probably contain tens or hundreds of data collections and relationships, and thousands of data elements. DBMS support is not assumed, although it is usually desirable.

- The information system and its databases are intended for use over a long period of time so that the benefits to the life cycle costs will justify the investment of time, money, and effort in LDD.

- The data requirements of the information system will be significant and include the use of ad hoc queries where the precision of the database structure will prove important.

1.6 Scope of this Guide

This guide is limited in scope to the LDD phase. The interaction of LDD with the immediately preceding and subsequent life cycle phases is mentioned, since these determine LDD's information resources and products. Because LDD works from the results of the preceding Needs Analysis and concurrent Requirements Analysis phases, and prepares a foundation for the subsequent Physical Database Design phase, these phases will be described briefly.

1.7 Structure of this Guide

Chapter 2 addresses the relationship between LDD and the phases of Needs Analysis, Requirements Analysis, and Physical Database Design. The major phases of the LDD approach are further discussed along with the types of analysis strategies that will be needed to accompany LDD. Figure 2, in Section 2.2.2, illustrates the interaction of the four phases of the LDD methodology to assist the reader in visualizing the LDD process.

In Chapter 3, the organizational aspects of the LDD project are described, including the key roles in LDD development, the training required for the personnel in these roles, and the part played by management in planning for and monitoring the LDD process.

The following chapters, 4 through 7, define the four phases of the LDD approach in detail. Chapters 4 through 7 are identically structured so that each chapter has three sections: (1) the first section of each phase discusses the information used by that phase, (2) the second section discusses the general functions of that phase, and (3) the third section discusses the procedure for accomplishing that phase. The third section of each phase includes a diagram of the steps within that phase, followed by a subsection on each step. Each step is followed by a summary chart.

Chapter 4 discusses Local Information-flow Modeling and describes three modes of analysis corresponding to the target system's (1) organizational components, (2) functions, and (3) the events to which the target information system will respond. These three analysis modes are examined in relation to data flow and data structure design techniques.

Chapter 5 addresses Global Information-flow Modeling and emphasizes the need to balance the perspectives of data flow and data structure in the development of a design that will favor both equally. The Conceptual Schema Design is described in Chapter 6 in relation to the use of Entity-Relationship-Attribute (E-R-A) data modeling diagrams and normalization techniques. Chapter 7 defines External Schema Modeling (i.e., subschema modeling) as it reflects the data structure and data flow from the end-user's perspective in the development of workload specifications for physical database design.

A glossary of acronyms used in this guide is included at the beginning of the document for reference. An appendix of examples has been included at the end of the document to illustrate the types of graphics that will be used and analysis that will occur during the four phases of LDD.

2. THE FRAMEWORK THAT SUPPORTS LDD

LDD plays an important part in the life cycle of the information system. This chapter describes: (1) the relationship between the database design and the functioning of the information system; (2) the interactions between LDD and the Needs Analysis, Requirements Analysis, and Physical Database Design phases; (3) the information requirements needed to perform LDD; (4) the phases within LDD; and (5) strategies for LDD development and their impact.

2.1 The Role of LDD in the Life Cycle

LDD defines the data structure that supports the databases of an information system. The database system and the information system are inextricably linked, but they are different.

An information system is one or more multi-purpose computer systems that may be supported by a network through which many types of users, perhaps in different locations, update, query, and provide data to the system in order to have current information available on a variety of topics. Decision support capabilities may be incorporated in the information system's structure to assist end-users in the decision-making process.

A database is a component of an information system and may contain a variety of general and detailed information that is made available to the information system's end-users through queries. The information system's ability to respond to user's queries is directly related to logical database design.

The design of the information system's databases will determine the ways in which the information system will function. If the information system will be required to answer ad hoc queries, the data structures within the databases should be modeled to provide maximum flexibility in data accessibility and retrieval. If the system will be required to respond quickly to certain predefined queries, then the structural modeling should be constructed to support rapid retrieval performance, which will generally require indexes or redundant data. If the time and expense needed to update the data in the system are of paramount importance, then ease in locating and changing data values should be stressed in the database design. If the storage cost of large databases is a primary consideration, then the minimization of physical redundancy should be emphasized in the database design.

Usually a combination of such requirements exist for an information system, with conflicting implications for the design of the underlying databases. These requirements and their implications for the databases that support the information system are defined during the LDD phase, and their conflicts are resolved during the Physical Database Design phase.

The structure of the logical design of the database plays a crucial role in determining the capabilities and performance of an information system. A good physical database design cannot be developed without adequate preparation. A good logical database design prepares the groundwork for a quality physical database design and a successful system implementation.

The phases of Needs Analysis, Requirements Analysis, Logical Database Design, and Physical Database Design are closely linked. The ability to perform the subsequent phases is determined by the performance of the previous and parallel phases. Each of these phases must be performed well for the resulting database to represent the desired system accurately. These phases are described below.

2.1.1 Needs Analysis.

As we have seen in Chapter 1, a Needs Analysis describes the primary needs a new information system should fulfill. Without this formal expression of the organization's perception of its needs, the analysts and designers will have to work from their own assumptions of the information system's purposes. Their assumptions could unknowingly conflict with the organization's vaguely described or unstated purposes. The resulting lack of clarity in direction would be costly.

A specific Needs Analysis methodology should be adopted and used by an organization previous to undertaking any extensive systems development project. The use of a well-defined methodology assures that most, if not all, of the important questions about the purpose of the proposed system will have been asked and answered at the end of the Needs Analysis phase. One of the most familiar and extensively used Needs Analysis methodologies available at this time is IBM's Business Systems Planning (BSP) approach [MART82].

In the Needs Analysis methodology adopted, the following minimum set of questions should be posed:

1. What organizational problems require a solution that the target information system could effect?

2. What new or improved information is needed to perform what types of functions?

3. What are the boundaries and interfaces of the target system?

4. What possible improvements in information availability could be expected from the target information system? The following are goals of many system development projects:

    o Greater accuracy of information.
    o Improved timeliness.
    o Better end-user interfaces.
    o Improved privacy and security.
    o Rapid access to distant information centers by information sources and end-users.

Once a Needs Analysis methodology has been adopted and these types of questions have been answered in detail, the purposes and plans for the systems development project can be made available to the systems development personnel. If the Needs Analysis has been performed well and a comprehensive methodology has been used, sufficient information has probably been collected for LDD to begin. Close coordination with the Requirements Analysis phase is needed for LDD to continue.

2.1.2 Requirements Analysis.

The requirements analysis effort will verify and supplement the results of the Needs Analysis phase. Since LDD and Systems Specification are directly supported by the concurrent Requirements Analysis phase, it is critical that the procedures and performance of requirements analysis be planned carefully to coordinate with these other phases.

The Requirements Analysis phase will involve two types of analysis: (1) analysis of the types of data and data flows needed within the organization; and (2) analysis of the functions performed within the organization which will require the use of this data. The purpose of requirements analysis is to provide data requirements to support the LDD phase, and functional requirements to support the Systems Specification phase.

Requirements analysts verify which functions and subsystems will remain external to the system and require interfaces. By defining the information products of external subsystems or systems that are inputs to the target system, and by defining the information products of the target system that are used by external subsystems or systems, the analysts can designate the high level input/output transformations of information that must take place within the target system. The specific functions and subfunctions performed within the target system are logically organized and described. Further, the analysts define the known constraints on accuracy, timeliness, and other performance requirements, which will be further defined in LDD. Once general requirements have been described, further refinements of the requirements are developed. Prototyping may be used in conjunction with the LDD and Systems Specification phases to refine and model requirements.

As requirements are defined, the information may be stored in the form of a data dictionary to be manipulated by a Data Dictionary System. The use of a DDS will provide automated support for the storage, analysis and querying of data, for the definition and presentation of technical and management reports, and for the simultaneous access of requirements information for use in concurrent phases. Requirements information stored in a data dictionary can be supplemented with information from LDD and other phases, and can be maintained for on-line use throughout the system's life cycle.

2.1.3 Logical Database Design.

The LDD designers decide which data must be stored and maintained to support the functions and subfunctions of the target system. By abstracting from the functions to the data structures, the designer defines the data objects to be modeled and decides which properties and constraints are relevant in modeling these objects. The Conceptual Schema is the primary product of LDD.

The Entity-Relationship-Attribute modeling technique has been chosen to define the LDD data structure (see Chapter 6). Organizations that prefer other equivalent data modeling techniques may easily adapt this LDD methodology to those techniques.

An important consideration for LDD is to ensure that all information required from the LDD phase is developed and provided to the Physical Database Design phase at the appropriate time. This information required from LDD includes the volume of data, the priority and frequency of the logical access paths to be implemented in the physical database, and constraints on performance, integrity, security, and privacy.

2.1.4 Physical Database Design.

The first step of the Physical Database Design phase is to select the appropriate data model (e.g., relational, network, or hierarchical) and the data management system to support it. This selection may, unfortunately, be dictated by the software that the organization is currently using, or by the availability of software for hardware that has already been procured. Preferably, the data model and the data management system will be selected to match the requirements defined by the LDD Conceptual Schema and the workload. A useful reference in the selection process is [GALL84].

The second step, once the selection has been made, is to translate the Entity-Relationship-Attribute model from the Conceptual Schema into the selected data model. This translation is a rather simple matter for the relational model: entities become tables, relationships are implemented by means of foreign keys, and attributes become columns. The network model translation is not much more difficult: entities become records, relationships become sets or repeating groups, attributes become data items, and attributes are omitted from a member record if they are in the owner. The hierarchical model is difficult: entities become records, attributes become data items, but relationships may become either true hierarchical relationships or logical children. These translations are discussed in detail in [CHEN82] and papers referenced therein.

The next step is to develop a detailed physical data structure, including the development of indexes and other access paths, detailed record structures (perhaps combining the logical records to reduce physical accesses), loading factors, and so on. Detailed methodologies are discussed in [CARL80, CARL81, MARC78].

2.2 Detailed Framework for LDD

The information requirements needed for the performance of LDD are described in Section 2.2.1. Although LDD has previously been presented as a single phase within the information system life cycle, in Section 2.2.2 LDD will now be subdivided into four simpler phases to be performed iteratively. Strategies for analysis and the information requirements of these phases will be described in detail in Section 2.2.3.

2.2.1 LDD Information Requirements.

In addition to information obtained from Needs Analysis, LDD designers will need other information to be collected and analyzed during the Requirements Analysis phase, conducted in parallel to LDD and Systems Specification. The following information must be available to LDD designers:

- Predefined constraints on the system, such as the use of existing hardware or software, the need to convert an existing system, and the scope of the projected information system.

- Project constraints, such as the amount of time, money and personnel allocated by the organization for the development project.

- Processing requirements, such as the type of functions that the information system will be expected to perform, and the general application areas that it will be expected to support.

- Organizational, functional and data subsets, such as departments, types of actions, and types of information that the target system will be expected to supply or support.

- Performance requirements, such as maximum retrieval and update times.

- Capacity requirements, such as the number of data objects within the target system, and storage restrictions if the limitations of existing hardware are applicable.

o Data integrity requirements, such as the control needed over redundant data, and the need for automated integrity checks during data input and update, including edit and validation rules.

o Security and privacy requirements, such as the need for encryption for some types of data, or the limitation of access for certain types of data to specific personnel.

o Reliability and maintainability requirements that define the need for the continuous functioning of the system.

o Distributed processing and data requirements, such as the need for network connections among databases in multiple locations, or the need for shared or replicated data in multiple locations.

2.2.2 LDD Phases.

As we have seen from Chapter 1, LDD generally involves information modeling and database design that are largely hardware and software independent. LDD focuses attention on the subsystems that generate the information comprising the target system. Throughout the phases of LDD, each subsystem is examined and described in terms of: (1) the organizational components, (2) the application areas or functions, and (3) the events, which occur within or affect that subsystem. The number and type of these subsystems to be analyzed during each phase of LDD will depend on the type of analysis strategy selected, as described in Section 2.2.3.

LDD consists of four distinct phases during which all the subsystems within the system, the data flows, data structures, and user views of the databases are described. These phases are performed iteratively and in sequence until the LDD is completed. The phases of LDD are the subject of this paper and are described more fully beginning at Chapter 4. In brief, the four phases of LDD are:

1. Local Information-flow Modeling

   During this phase, data flows are modeled for individual subsystems within the target system, including each organizational component, function, and event. Subsystems are modeled one at a time. A data flow is the information that is exchanged, or "flows," within and between subsystems. Data is defined at a general rather than specific level, in terms of general formats or packages (e.g., all the data contained within a particular type of report). The products of this phase are Local Information-flow Models (LIMs).

2. Global Information-flow Modeling

During this phase, individual data flows are combined and global data flows are modeled for collections of individual subsystems (i.e., organizational components, applications, or events) viewed as a whole. Data will continue to be viewed at the format or package level. The products of this phase are Global Information-flow Models (GIMs).

3. Conceptual Schema Design

During this phase, the data within the data flows, defined in the previous phases, is abstracted from the packages in which it resides, and defined in terms of its functional use. The data is described in terms of: (a) entities, the basic data components; (b) relationships, the ways in which entities are associated with each other or share characteristics; and (c) attributes, the data that describes the data entities. Entity-Relationship-Attribute (E-R-A) diagrams may be used as an analysis method. The E-R-A abstraction provides the basis for a conceptual data structure. The products of this phase are Conceptual Schemas (CSs).

4. External Schema Modeling

During this phase, the conceptual schema is adapted to conform to the needs of the application areas within the information system. By modeling the data from the user's perspective, the designer is able to verify the Conceptual Schema and derive a structured user's view of the data. The products of this phase are External Schemas (ESs) and are also known as subschemas.

Figure 2 depicts the iterative relationship of the four LDD phases. The vertical line through the center indicates a division between the phases on the left that are oriented

DIAGRAM OF THE FOUR LDD PHASES

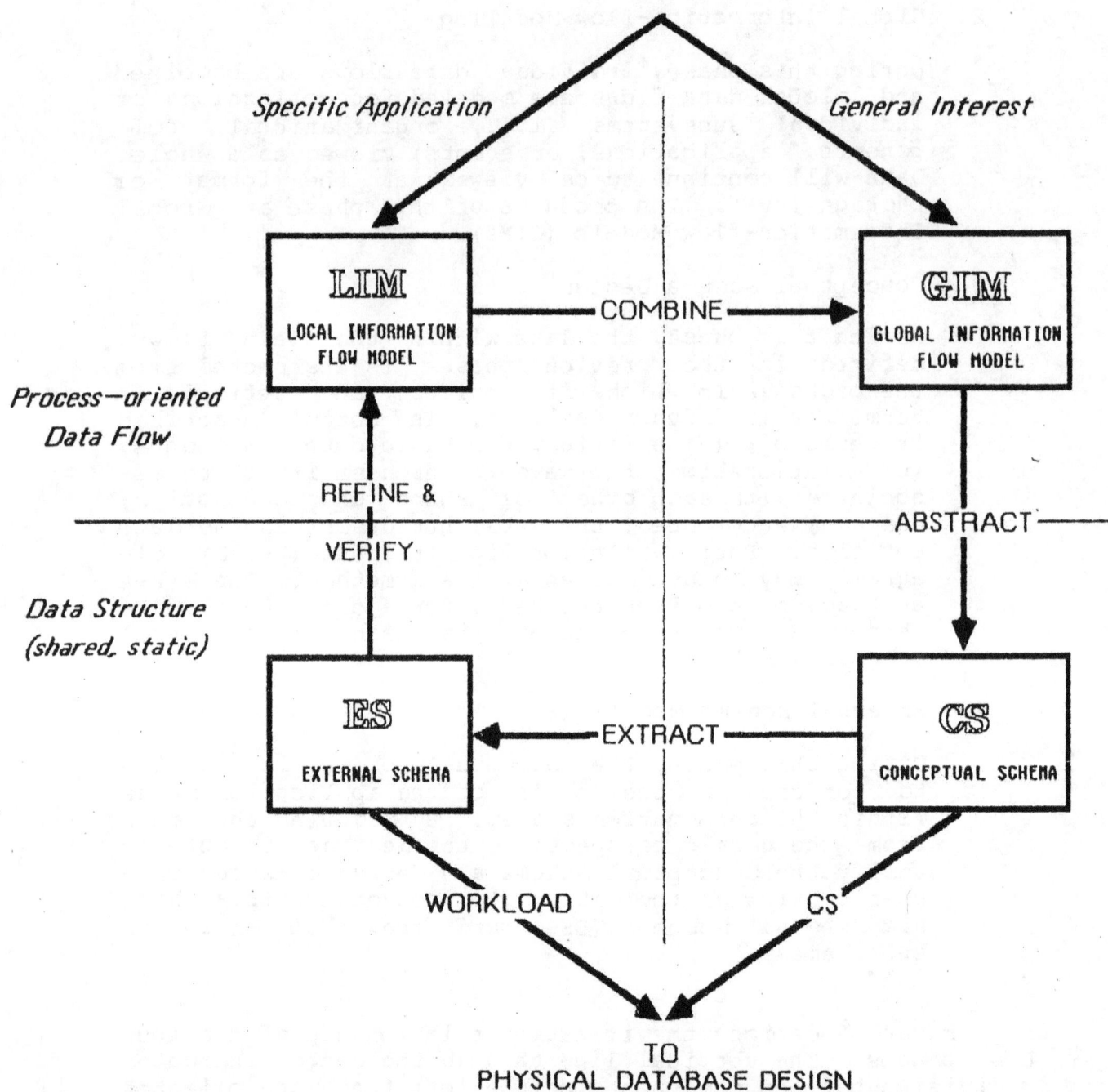

FIGURE 2

toward a specific application (e.g., toward one organizational component, function, or event), and those phases on the right that are oriented toward organizing these specific applications into areas of general interest.

The horizontal line across the diagram indicates a division between the upper phases that are oriented toward the performance of functions and the dynamic data flow among these functions, and the lower phases that are oriented toward relatively static, shared data structures.

At the top of the diagram, Needs Analysis and Requirements Analysis indicates that these phases provide information to LDD. The results of Needs Analysis may be sufficient to begin the initial iterations of the LIM and GIM phases, particularly if the Business Systems Planning (BSP) methodology has been used. Subsequent iterations will require further information from the Requirements Analysis phase.

The diagram in Figure 2 should be read clockwise, beginning at Local Information-flow Modeling (LIM), where data flows are modeled. In Global Information-flow Modeling (GIM), the individual data flows from LIM are combined into global data flows. These are abstracted to the underlying shared entities, relationships and attributes in the Conceptual Schema (CS). Parts of the CS are then extracted to form each External Schema (ES), which is a particular user's view of the shared data. At this point, each ES is then compared with the appropriate, previously developed LIM, to ensure that the data required by the LIM has been included in the ES view. When errors are detected in this comparison, the ES, and possibly the CS, will require modification. The workload data that was originally developed for the LIM is translated into operations on data in the ES. Finally, the workload data and the CS are passed on to the next life cycle phase, Physical Database Design, for the development of the internal schema.

2.2.3 Strategies for LDD Development.

Several analysis strategies are possible in approaching LDD. The choice of the strategy will depend on the type of system to be developed and the definition of the data that will need to be integrated in its design. The scope of the data can be described as horizontal and the level of detail as vertical. The system can be viewed horizontally in the breadth of functions that the information system will support. If the system will provide many functions to many departments or locations, then the system and its data will have a broad, horizontal scope. If the system performs few functions but performs them in great detail, then the system and its data will have a depth of detail. A large system will generally include both a breadth of scope and a depth of detail. Three possible strategies for approaching the logical design phases are described, with their ramifications for system development success. Refer to Figure 2 in following the sequence of LDD procedures for the following strategies. The three strategies for approaching LDD are:

1. Breadth First.

    In this strategy, a large number of Local Information-flow Models (LIMs) will be developed at first, but in limited detail. The LIMs will then be consolidated into one Global Information-flow Model (GIM) with a broad scope but limited detail. One or more Conceptual Schemas (CSs) will be developed with broad scope but limited detail. The External Schemas (ESs) extracted from the CS will provide quality control and structure for the next iteration of LIM. The LDD phases will be repeated for the various subsystems, adding greater detail for each LIM, until the data element level is reached. This strategy is analogous to top-down system design.

    Impact: This strategy is appropriate for the development of very large, very complex information systems, where a great depth and breadth of data must be integrated through the development process.

2. Depth First.

    In this strategy, a small number of LIMs will be developed through iterations of the LDD phases to the data element level. The LIMs will be consolidated into a GIM having depth of detail but a limited horizontal scope. A small number of ESs will be developed, again with depth of detail but limited scope. Further iterations of the entire process are developed until the desired horizontal scope is attained.

    Impact: This strategy is inappropriate for the development of an information system that requires the integration of design components of considerable scope and many levels of detail. The use of this strategy may result in the need to redesign the system to effect integration. This strategy is appropriate only for the development of throw-away or expendable training or prototype projects, such as a prototype system used to verify a development concept, or an experimental system used to train personnel in other systems development concepts or in Data Dictionary System use.

3. Critical Factors First.

In this strategy, a large number of LIMs are developed, including details for the critical aspects of the target system (e.g., critical functional requirements, critical performance characteristics, proof of concept, etc.). The LIMs will be consolidated into a GIM with broad scope but uneven detail. One or more CSs will be developed with the same broad scope but uneven levels of detail. The process will be repeated with increasing levels of detail for each LIM, with subsystems analyzed in order of priority, until the data element level is reached. The critical subsystems will be processed through the LDD cycle first, and the non-critical subsystems will follow later.

Impact: This strategy is appropriate for the development of a very large system if the critical factors of the target system can be identified and accepted. It is also appropriate for prototype development and for evolutionary development, where some functions will be implemented first and other functions will follow.

2.2.4 Summary of LDD Features.

The four phases of LDD use a variety of symbologies to assist in analysis. These include the use of bubble diagrams in the analysis of data flows, Entity-Relationship-Attribute (E-R-A) diagrams in CS development, normalization analyses where applicable, and Data Dictionary System (DDS) contents and automated analysis reports throughout LDD.

The outputs of LDD's phases are: Local Information-flow Models (LIMs) and Global Information-flow Models (GIMs) that model data flows for the organizational components, functions, and events; Conceptual Schemas (CSs) that provide an E-R-A model, or another type of data model, for use by programmers and designers; and External Schemas (ESs) that present an application-oriented user view for use within the organization as a representation of the data to be included in the target system.

3. PROJECT ORGANIZATION

For LDD to be performed successfully, plans should be made to support the information requirements of LDD and to incorporate LDD roles into the organization. In this chapter, LDD functional roles, training, and project planning needs are described.

3.1 Functional Roles Needed for LDD

The following functional roles are described in terms of the development of LDD. A role may be performed by many people, or one person may perform several roles, depending on the complexity of the database. Some LDD roles may overlap with roles to be performed in Requirements Analysis and other phases. The roles required for LDD are the following:

- Application Administrators (AAs) who will work with designers and analysts to define and validate the data and functions. One or more AAs may be needed according to the size of the system and the complexity of the application areas. AAs will work with a number of application specialists.

- Application Specialists who are knowledgeable about the application data being modeled, or about the application functions that use the data, or about both. The application specialists will assist the designers and analysts in preparing an accurate LDD.

- Data Administrator (DA) who will facilitate the LDD and systems development process by ensuring consistency in data definition, and overseeing the data management, data integrity, and data security functions performed in LDD development. The DA will continue to perform this role in regulating these facets of the information system once it is completed, and so will also use the LDD once it is developed. The DA may have a sizable staff, depending on the complexity of the data resource and the time available to perform LDD and other tasks. The DA staff may include the Database Administrator and the Data Dictionary Administrator. The DA staff will work closely with the AAs.

- Database Administrator (DBA) who will control the database and the DBMS, facilitate the LDD and systems development process, assist in data maintenance, and use the LDD as it is developed. The DBA is concerned primarily with technical aspects of the database, in contrast to the DA, who is more concerned with information policy and interacts with management and users. The DBA will continue in this role once the information system is operational. The DBA may have a small staff to support this function. This function will continue throughout the life cycle of the target system.

- Data Dictionary Administrator (DDA) who will oversee the operation of the Data Dictionary System (DDS), and assist in the data maintenance process for LDD. The DDA may be supported by a staff, including a Librarian and possibly data entry personnel. Data entry may also be performed directly by designers and analysts in the course of their work. The DDA function should continue throughout the life cycle of the target system, to continue to maintain documentation about the system.

- Data Dictionary Librarian who will maintain the data in the data dictionary (DD), and support the LDD and systems development effort.

- Database Designers/Analysts who will develop the information requirements, logical database diagrams, models and schemas. They will be expert in database design, familiar with the DDS, and become familiar with the application areas. They will perform the functions that are the focus of this report. Database designers will be needed throughout the life cycle of the information system, to maintain high performance and efficiency as the database changes through time.

- Project Managers who will direct the LDD and systems development projects. They will be familiar with the application areas, computer systems, systems development practices, and become familiar with LDD procedures.

- End-users of the DDS and the information system under development who will access and update information in the databases, and who will generate reports and decisions from this information. End-users will include personnel from all organizational levels and will perform the following roles:

- Data Entry and Update
- Data Retrieval
- Data Analysis
- Data Management and Control
- Project Management
- Upper Management

3.2 Training Required for LDD

The personnel involved in the LDD phase of development, particularly AAs and Application Specialists, will require training so that they will be able to work with database designers as a team. Some personnel will already be knowledgeable in these areas, but many will need to be trained. Project management should arrange to have LDD personnel trained in:

o The purpose and general procedures of LDD.

o The points of view to be represented within the system (i.e., organizational components, functions, and events).

o Use of the symbology, such as how to construct and interpret E-R-A and bubble diagrams.

o Use of the Data Dictionary System or other automated tool.

End-users who review the LDD may require any of three levels of training in the use of the Data Dictionary System, depending on the extent of each end-user's responsibility:

o Reading knowledge of LDD reports that are generated via the DDS, to be able to recognize when the report indicates a modeling error.

o Interpretive capability to understand LDD reports generated via the DDS, to be able to recognize what is wrong in a report that indicates a modeling error.

o Expert knowledge of the DDS procedures and an understanding of the products of LDD, to be able to correct errors in modeling detected in DDS reports.

3.3 Project Planning and Management Requirements

The systems development Project Manager and the LDD Manager should plan for and control the systems development project so that a high quality LDD results. In addition to the activities of traditional management roles, managers in these positions must determine that several procedures have been adopted before the project begins.

The Project Manager must be sure that good methodologies have been selected or developed for the Needs Analysis, Requirements Analysis, LDD, and other phases. In addition, it is necessary to determine that these methodologies are coordinated according to a schedule so that the results of previous and parallel phases are available for use by other phases. The schedule should also include various types of training for personnel working on parallel phases. Further, the Project Manager must decide on a strategy for LDD development that will support the breadth of scope and depth of detail to be encountered in analyzing the target system.

The Logical Database Design Manager will fill a similar role for the LDD phase. The LDD Manager will: (1) select a good LDD methodology and analysis strategy suitable to the type of system under development; (2) coordinate LDD training with the managers for parallel phases; (3) coordinate LDD activities with the Requirements Analysis Manager, so that information will be available for LDD to conform to appropriate schedules; (4) define checkpoints to review the progress of the LDD work; (5) determine the types and characteristics of the DDS documentation and analysis reports to be generated to support the LDD phases; and (6) manage the synthesis and integration of information from many sources within the organization to support LDD.

4. LOCAL INFORMATION-FLOW MODELING

A Local Information-flow Model (LIM) is a description of the movement of data collections such as reports, forms, memos, messages, transactions, and files to, from, and within a particular focal point. The focal point may be an organizational component (e.g., the personnel department), a function or application (e.g., payroll processing), or an event (e.g., a milestone in the budget cycle). The first iteration of this phase will produce a single LIM summarizing the inputs and outputs of the entire organization served by the database being designed. During subsequent iterations multiple LIMs will be produced, each describing a part of the next higher-level LIM. The level of detail may be very high (e.g., very general types of data going into or out of an entire organization), intermediate (e.g., reports and other data going into, out of, or processed within an office), or very low (e.g., transformation of an employee number into an employee name), depending on the number of iterations through the four phases of logical database design.

There are two reasons for choosing this approach:

1. Complexity is controlled at every stage of the iteration by restricting the scope of each LIM. Interviews with users can concentrate on the most critical aspects of the user's organization, function, or event, with the assurance that a higher-level context has already been developed and that details can be filled in later. The interviewer need not be overwhelmed with trying to understand everything all at once. Note that a top-down approach is advisable--starting from data elements and working up is more likely to end in a disastrous lack of direction and an abundance of confusion.

2. The different aspects--organization, function, and event--represent the fact that organizational structures are important, but they do not give a complete model of information processing. Functions and responsibilities are shared by sequential or simultaneous access to and transformation of data. All aspects may be required to give a true picture of database requirements. Note that manual functions should be analyzed if there is a significant chance that they will be automated during the life of the database.

The general objective is for a LIM to represent whatever an application specialist knows about his or her job and organization. The LIM does not represent details about how information is captured or derived before it reaches the application specialist or how it is used or processed after it leaves her or him.

The emphasis of the LIM should be on business functions and events--that is, data, operations, and products that are basic to achieving organizational objectives--rather than on any particular technology for implementing those functions. One reason for this particular emphasis is the fact that technology changes much more rapidly than the business functions (the need for payroll is constant, but the policies and technologies implementing it are changeable). A database should be relatively stable and retain its value over a long period of time--the time and cost of data collection and organization are too great to permit the database to be considered anything less than a major capital investment. Another reason for the emphasis on business functions is that these are familiar and well-understood by the data users, who are the people responsible for achieving organizational objectives. The abstract concepts of data modeling, introduced in the phase concerned with the development of the Conceptual Schema, are generally not meaningful to the user unless there is some familiar context of business functions. One way of viewing the LIM is that it is a means for relating the abstract External Schema (a part of the Conceptual Schema) to a concrete business context.

4.1 Information Used to Develop the LIM

Information that is relevant to the development of the LIM may be obtained through examination of documents or through interviews, or, preferably, through interviews based on thorough preparation via documents. The following information is generally needed:

1. The nature, objectives, structure, and scope of the subsystem must all be analyzed to ensure compatible LIMs. Both the present and the future should be considered. Non-routine operations, or operations that are performed infrequently, may be particularly important--for example, end-of-year accounting operations may have unique but critical requirements. Interactions with customers, vendors, and other parts

of the external environment may be very important.

2. Existing automated systems and other available hardware, software, and data resources should be studied to determine how they interact with the subsystem being studied; the emphasis should be on the queries, reports, and transactions that are actually relevant rather than on what is currently produced. It is important to maintain continuity with the present while still ensuring sufficient flexibility for long term growth of the information resource. Existing systems may already have replaced certain functions and as such should themselves be "interviewed." This can be difficult since existing systems may be poorly structured and documented. However, existing systems have already solved problems -- what are those problems? Existing systems may be enforcing policies that the people are no longer aware of -- what are those policies? Existing systems may also be creating data that everyone takes for granted -- how are existing systems combining files, applying algorithms, etc.?

3. The subsystem's perspective on decisions must be analyzed. The position titles and descriptions held by decision-makers, the business models that they use, the information that they require, and the relationships that they have with other decision-makers must all be analyzed. Senior management views (strategic planning), middle management views (control and tactical policy), and applications views (operations) are all required to give balance to the total collection of LIMs. Historical and "what if" data are particularly important in analyzing the data flow of higher-level decision makers.

4. Real-world rules and policies should be studied. Geographic location requirements are particularly important (e.g., there is little point in designing a highly integrated central database if the policy is to maintain local control of data). Policies on data retention and archiving may also be important (e.g., archiving may constitute a major information subsystem). Security, privacy, integrity, and error handling policies (including policies and procedures for recovery from both data processing and organizational mistakes) may have major effects on the data structures (for example, classified and unclassified data may have to be stored separately).

5. A catalog of reports and forms needed for routine tasks is clearly relevant to the LIM. Collections of reports and forms are relevant to high-level LIMs, individual reports and forms are relevant to intermediate-level LIMs, and parts of reports and forms are relevant to low-level LIMs. The timeliness and quality of the reports and forms should be recorded. Reports that have outlived their usefulness are irrelevant to LDD.

6. Collections of informal data are also very important. This data can include files or folders of memos and letters (e.g., Freedom of Information Act requests, and customer complaints in writing), notes on telephone conversations (e.g., payroll inquiries), and databases on personal computers.

7. Formal reference data collections such as FIPS codes, ZIP codes, pay scale tables, and address or telephone directories are relevant.

8. "Log" books or lists may be used to assign unique numbers, organize office functions, record significant events, or otherwise coordinate activities.

9. Other regular sources of information, such as telephone contacts, should be carefully studied, since these may be very relevant to getting the job done.

10. Information from the higher-level GIM and the higher-level LIM which is being subdivided provide context for developing more detailed LIMs in successive iterations of the LDD cycle. Once LDD has begun, the examination of this information will be the first step in providing a LIM.

11. Quantitative information on volume of data and frequency of processing for all of the above. This information will be used to help develop an estimate of the database workload.

Since each LIM is a refinement of the previous iteration of the design cycle, the LIM is constrained by the previous higher-level LIM and External Schema. If deeper analysis uncovers an error at the higher level, then that higher-level should be corrected before proceeding further. Otherwise, other lower-level LIMs, based on the erroneous LIM and External Schema, may contain errors or be inconsistent with each other.

4.2 Functions of the LIM

The primary function of the LIM is to serve as part of the Global Information-flow Model (GIM). Other functions of the LIM are:

1. The LIM provides a guide for the development of further details. Each iteration is based on a decomposition of a previously developed LIM, unless the focus is switched from an organizational component to a function or event, in which case the new LIMs are based on combinations of previously developed LIMs.

2. The LIM may be used as a guide to planning the development of a new application program or system, modifying an old application program or system, or modifying the organizational structure. In each case, the LIM is analyzed to see whether the flow of data is efficient and effective; changes are suggested if unused reports are being produced, if similar functions are being performed unnecessarily, if functions that should be performed by a computer system are being performed manually, or if the data flow can be reduced by combining organizational components that sequentially process the same data.

3. The LIM is also used to collect information concerning the database workload. This information is eventually used to optimize and evaluate the physical database design.

4.3 Procedure for Developing the LIM

Figure 3 shows the five sequential steps in the development of the LIM. The steps are described in the following paragraphs.

LOCAL INFORMATION-FLOW MODELING (LIM) PROCEDURE

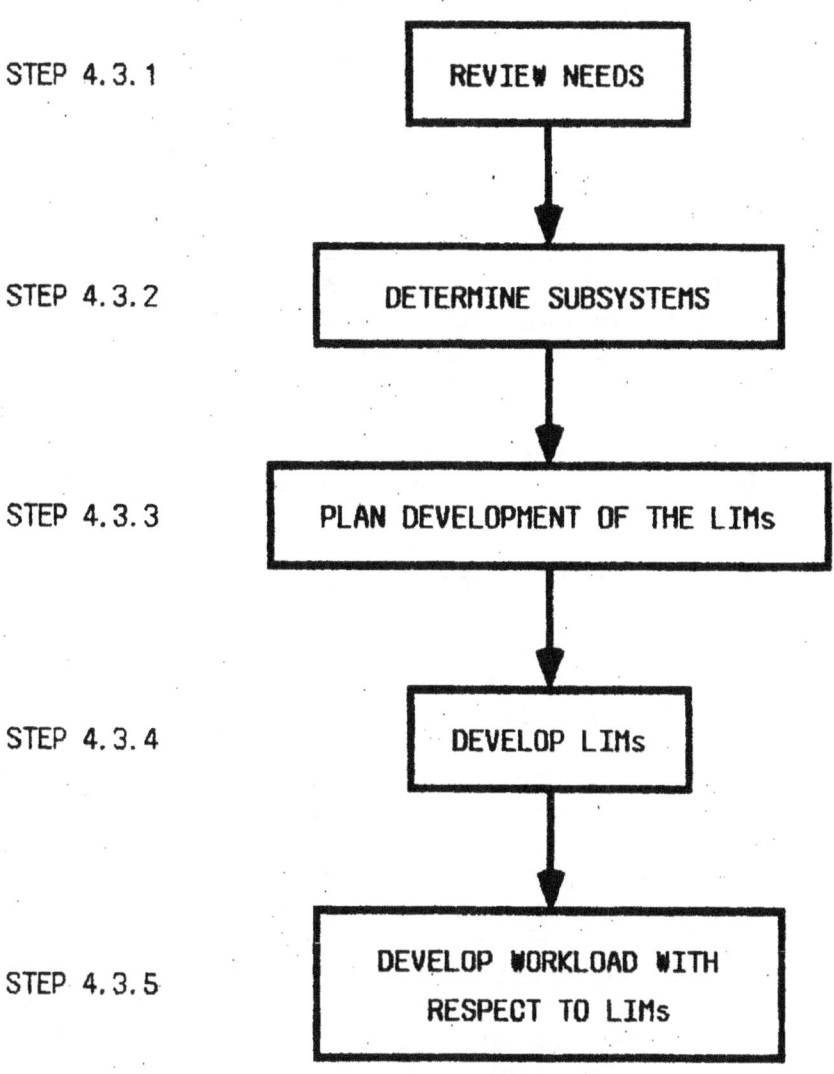

FIGURE 3

4.3.1 Review Need for Analysis.

The primary function of this step is to determine whether the organizational component, function, or event under consideration should be subdivided for further analysis, or whether it has already been analyzed sufficiently.

The first iteration of the logical database design methodology will begin with a preliminary determination of boundaries--that is, which organizational components, functions, and events require interaction with the proposed database. Next, it is necessary to determine the best method for subdividing the design problem--by organizational components, by functions, or by events. Generally, the first few subdivisions will be along organizational boundaries. These boundaries are usually well-defined, familiar, and non-threatening to the application specialists. They serve very well in identifying broad classes of data, major functions and events, and data flows.

Organizational decomposition may be insufficient, however, for the detailed development of data structures which are shared among different organizational components. Later iterations should concentrate on subdividing the functions and events that have been identified during the study of organizational subdivisions; such functions and events must provide data to the database and use data from it, so are directly relevant to the structure of the database.

Since functions and events frequently cross organizational boundaries, their analysis may suggest the need for reorganization to eliminate duplicate or unnecessary jobs, and will almost certainly require cooperation among application specialists from different organizational components. Consequently, such analysis is very delicate and should not be attempted too early in the LDD process.

Eventually it will be determined that there is no need to subdivide any more functions or events; the logical database design process is then "complete," although maintenance of the LIMs and other products must continue indefinitely.

```
-----------------------------------------------------------------
|  Step 4.3.1    Review Need for Analysis                        |
|                                                                |
|  Function:     To determine whether more detail is             |
|                required                                        |
|                                                                |
|  Output:       Determination of whether to subdivide a         |
|                subsystem                                       |
|                                                                |
|  Team Members: User - AA, DA                                   |
|                Developer - AA, DA                              |
|                                                                |
|  Tools:        Use DD to report on previous work               |
|                                                                |
|  Guidelines:   Decision involves both technical and            |
|                management issues                               |
-----------------------------------------------------------------
```

4.3.2 Determine Subsystems.

Once a decision has been made to subdivide an organizational component, function, or event, the next step is to determine the appropriate subdivisions. Two situations may be distinguished:

1. The subdivision involves a further refinement of an organizational component, function, or event. This is the normal case in business systems analysis, so various methodologies from business systems planning, organizational analysis, and software engineering may be applied. Either function-oriented methodologies [DEMA78, GANE79, MYER78, ROSS77] or data-oriented methodologies [JACK83, ORRK82] may be used as measures of the relative merit of different decompositions.

2. The subdivision involves a switch from one type of analysis to another. For example, the previous iteration of subdivision was based on organizational components, but this iteration is to be based on functions. In this case, the primary activity is composition, rather than decomposition--the various aspects of a function that appear in different organizational components must first be joined together to form a coherent statement of the whole function, and

then functional decomposition can proceed at later iterations. Clearly, it is extremely important that data flow has been carefully documented during previous iterations; data flow is the primary clue to the common basis for different organizational perspectives on a single function. The effect of a Data Dictionary System is to allow the DA to combine an organizational hierarchy, a functional hierarchy, and an event hierarchy into a consistent network which can be supported by the database structure.

In either case, the result will be a list of well-defined subsystems--organizational components, functions, or events-- of the LIM being analyzed. The subsequent steps will determine how each subsystem interacts with the data flowing into or out of that LIM, and the data flowing from or to the other subsystems.

Step 4.3.2   Determine Subsystems

Function: Determination of how to subdivide a
                subsystem

Output: List of lower-level subsystems

Team Members: User - AA, DA
                Developer - AA, DA

Symbology: Organization charts, data-flow or
                event diagrams

Tools: Use DD to represent organizational
                components, functions, or events

Guidelines: Care is required -- poorly chosen
                subsystems will have overly complex
                interfaces

4.3.3 Plan Development of the LIM.

This step involves the development of a detailed plan for this iteration of the analysis. The plan may include priorities, so that decomposition will consider critical factors first. Two strategies are possible:

1. Each step in the subdivision spawns a set of independent plans. Detailed work may proceed in parallel, given a sufficiently large staff, with the results coordinated primarily through the data dictionary. The advantage of this approach is that planning is minimized. The disadvantage is that quality control of the data dictionary becomes extremely critical during and after execution of the plan. Synonyms and homonyms for functions and data must be detected and resolved quickly or different analysis paths will unknowingly overlap, resulting in confusion and duplication of effort. The philosophy of this strategy is to move quickly and solve problems later (possibly during the development of the GIM).

2. Each step in the subdivision involves the development of a single, coordinated plan. Detailed work is coordinated in advance, so that problems of synonyms, homonyms, and duplicated effort are minimized. The advantage of this approach is that overall control of the effort is maintained. The obvious disadvantage is that this approach requires extremely knowledgeable DA and AA staff to formulate, monitor, and control the execution of the plan. Also, more work must be done serially rather than in parallel.

In either case, it is necessary to develop a detailed project management plan, with milestones, time and cost estimates, and assignments for application specialists as well as for AA and DA personnel.

```
-------------------------------------------------------------
Step 4.3.3   Plan Development of the LIM

Function:       Develop project management plan for
                this subsystem

Output:         Milestones, time and cost estimates

Team Members:   User - AA, DA
                Developer - AA, DA, Managers

Symbology:      Project management charts

Tools:          Use DD to represent project management
                data and boundaries

Guidelines:     Assignments must be very specific
-------------------------------------------------------------
```

4.3.4 Develop LIM.

Various system analysis and design methodologies may be used in conjunction with a data dictionary to document the data flows that are developed. Either function-oriented methodologies [DEMA78, GANE79, MYER78, ROSS77] or data-oriented methodologies [JACK83, ORRK82] are suitable. Whereas previous steps have involved consultation with management, this step and the following are best accomplished by short interviews (no more than two hours per iteration) with application specialists. Reference material and the LIM developed during the previous iteration are used to prepare for the interview and to verify the analyst's interpretation of the application specialist's statements. All materials may be made available to the application specialists in advance of the interview. (Note that discrepancies revealed during an interview should prompt further questions rather than challenges--the interview should not be threatening.) Graphical simplicity is very desirable, so that untrained users can judge the correctness of the LIMs that are relevant to them.

Useful types of diagrams include the following:

1. An organization chart can be used to show the hierarchical relationships among organizational LIMs.

2. A "bubble" diagram with an organizational focal point connected to other organizations by data flows can be used to represent an organizational LIM, as in the following:

EXAMPLE OF A LOCAL INFORMATION-FLOW MODEL

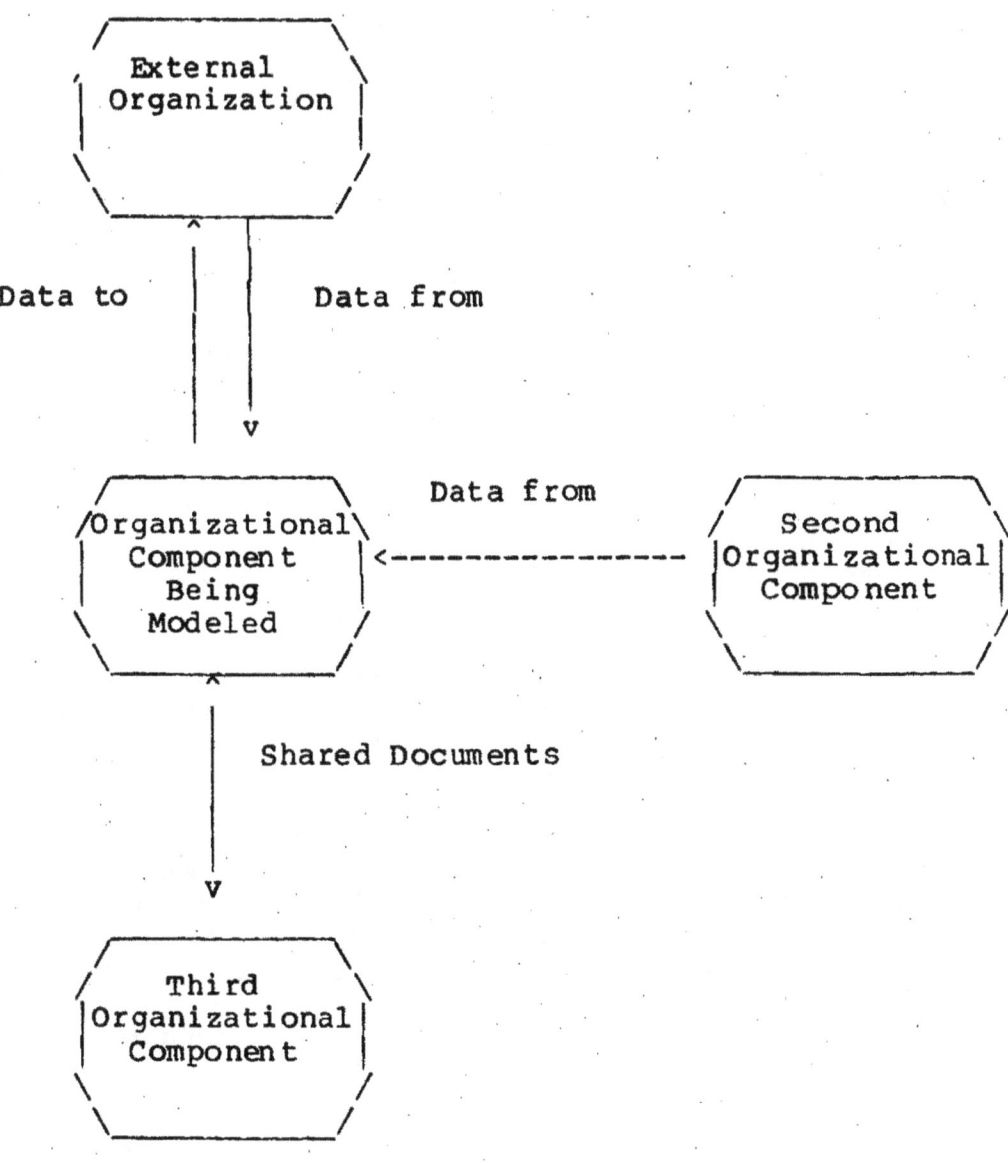

Figure 4

3. A functional hierarchy can be used to show the hierarchical relationships among the functional LIMs.

4. A data-flow diagram [DEMA78, GANE79, MYER78] or action diagram [ROSS77] can be used to show inputs, outputs, subfunctions, and data flows among the subfunctions of a functional LIM. (Note that this type of diagram shows two levels of the LIM hierarchy.)

5. A Gantt chart can be used to show the temporal relationships among events.

6. A PERT chart can be used to show the relationships, especially time dependencies, among functions and events.

7. A state-vector diagram [JACK83] or a decision table can be used to show additional details of functions and events.

The data dictionary is used to record detailed information that would only confuse a diagram; automated analysis of program code, job control language, and audit trails may provide much of the detail. The selectivity of data dictionary queries and reports helps to make the details comprehensible. Diagrams should be produced automatically from the data dictionary. Also, graphic input could be a means of populating the data dictionary when this capability becomes automated in the future.

A special but important example of data flow is storage and retrieval of information by an organizational component, function, or event; the storage medium is treated like another organizational component, function, or event.

Data flow is used to determine the formal consistency and completeness of the analysis--for example, whether each data flow has a source and a sink (either may be some internal storage medium). The use of a data dictionary is extremely important in this situation to ensure that all of the various aspects of the function are considered. The views of all users who interact with a function must be reflected in that function.

The description of data flows should generally include one level of decomposition. For example, if the data flows in a top-level functional analysis are collections of reports, then each data description in the data dictionary should include a list of the component reports. At a lower level, if the data flows are reports, then their descriptions should include subdivisions of the reports--selected columns, or rows between subtotals, or the subtotals themselves, for example. At a very detailed level, the data descriptions would be data elements.

Information which is useful in understanding the relative importance of the functions and in planning the next iteration of this phase includes the following:

1. Staff time, in work-years or other convenient unit, expended on performing the function.

2. The number of staff personnel performing the function.

3. The number of locations where the function is performed.

4. Whether there is a single step that consumes 80% or more of the time spent on the function.

Step 4.3.4 Develop LIMs

Function: Provide guidance to the development
                of the GIM and CS

Output: LIMs

Team Members: User - AA, DA
                Developer - AA, DBA

Symbology: Use bubbles to represent organizational
                components, events, functions, or
                external interfaces. Use lines to
                represent data flows.

Tools: Use DD to represent subsystems
                and interfaces

Guidelines: Graphical simplicity is desirable
                Use selectivity of DD reports
                Should be easy for users to understand
                and critique

4.3.5 Develop Workload With Respect to LIMs.

The primary function of this step is to develop a preliminary description of the workload: the frequency, sequence, and selectivity with which functions use or produce data, and the volume of stored data [JEFF82, SUST84]. The workload will be used during the development of the External Schemas to determine whether the Conceptual Schema can support the LIM, and what paths must be taken through the Conceptual Schema to obtain the data required by the LIM. It will also be used to determine whether certain functions should be automated. The workload must be used during the development of the Internal Schema (physical database design) to determine appropriate physical record structures, record placement in areas, access methods, loading factors, indexes, and other parameters. Accordingly, this step must be performed during the most detailed iteration of functional analysis; it may be performed at earlier steps to provide additional quality control for the LIMs and Conceptual Schema.

At this phase, the workload is described in terms of data collections that may be very different from the logical records that will eventually constitute the final Conceptual Schema. In particular, the level at this phase may be very high (e.g., data objects like "employee," "project," and "part" rather than data elements like "employee-first-name," "estimated-project-cost," and "part-quantity-in-warehouse") and the grouping of data may be quite arbitrary (e.g., "employee" may include data about skills, projects, and organizations associated with the employee). Eventually these data objects will be restructured to form a database, so it is important to be able to map this preliminary workload into appropriate paths through that database.

The information to be collected and stored in the data dictionary should include the following:

1. The volume (number of instances) of each data collection (e.g., the number of employees, projects, and parts).

2. The priority of the function (e.g., "an airline reservation must be confirmed within 20 seconds" and "a marketing analysis on advance reservations must be available within 2 hours of a request").

3. The frequency of execution of the function.

4. The sequence with which data collections are accessed by the function, and the source of the data from input or database (e.g., start with "employee," then access "project," then access "project-manager" to determine who "manages" a given employee).

5. The parts of each data collection that are used to decide whether a given instance of that data collection is relevant (e.g., "employee-name" identifies the required "employee" data).

6. For each of the parts of data collection, the number of relevant instances (e.g., "1").

7. For each relevant data collection accessed by the function, the parts that are needed for retrieval by the function (e.g., "employee-project" is the only retrieved part of the "employee" data). If applicable, the preferred order is desirable (e.g., the "employee-project" data is to be sorted by "project-number").

8. The parts of each relevant data collection that are needed for update by the function (e.g., "employee-hours" is the only updated part of the "employee" data).

9. At each point where the function branches, the fraction of the time each branch is taken (e.g., 90% of the time "employee-project" will be non-null, so "project" will be accessed, and 10% of the time it will be null so the path will terminate).

Step 4.5.3 Develop Workload with Respect to LIMs

Function: Develop preliminary specifications for physical design

Output: LIMs with volume, frequency, sequence, and selectivity

Team Members: User - AA, DBA
                Developer - AA, DBA and Analysts

Symbology: LIM diagrams

Tools: Use DD to store workload information to be used for physical design

Guidelines: Keep the scope limited to a single application

5. GLOBAL INFORMATION-FLOW MODELING

A Global Information-flow Model (GIM) is basically an interconnected collection of all of the Local Information-flow Models (LIMs). Its structure is quite complex: it combines up to three hierarchies of LIMs (a hierarchy based on organizational components, another based on functions, and possibly another based on events); these must be interconnected in terms of data flow, which itself may be a complex network of data objects, as well as other interrelationships such as organizational authority and responsibility. A Data Dictionary System (DDS) is strongly recommended to manage the GIM. In an extremely complex situation, where even a DDS is unable to present the mass of information in a meaningful way, multiple GIMs may be developed, each representing a major subsystem loosely connected to the other GIMs. Note, in particular, that the GIM, like the LIM, must generally represent both automated and manual data, and both current and planned functions.

The major task involved in developing the GIM is simply adding the new details represented by each new LIM. The new LIMs must be verified for consistency with higher-level LIMs, names must be reconciled with existing names, and the different perspectives (organization, function, and event) must be interrelated. These are basically responsibilities of the DA with assistance from the AAs in detecting and resolving potential problems in performance, cost, reliability, security, and the like. The DA should not require direct access to the users.

The GIM may be represented in various forms according to the methodology chosen. A diagram may consist of ovals or rectangles representing the subsystems, and labelled lines representing the data flows. This is a simple source-sink model which is very useful for communicating with users. Other representations of the GIM include many different types of matrices showing the interactions of organizational components, functions, events, and data objects with each other [MART82]. A data dictionary is recommended for the primary means of representation, from which diagrams and matrices can be produced selectively and automatically. Also, the data dictionary is quite suitable for representing details that would be very confusing in a diagram or matrix, such as the Local Information-flow Models (LIMs) and their relationships with the GIM, the relationships between names in the GIM and in the LIMs, and details of database workload.

Some methodologies dispense with the GIM [NAVA82] and begin the design of the Conceptual Schema with a small number of applications, then add more applications, continually integrating the new applications with the old Conceptual Schema. This has the advantage of facilitating quick development of a prototype, but has the disadvantage of possible major revisions of the Conceptual Schema [JEFF82]. The safer procedure is to develop a GIM with careful control of detail, so that the level of effort is reasonable yet the GIM provides sufficient detail to guide the development of a relatively stable Conceptual Schema. This procedure is also likely to uncover important new interrelationships among LIMs, such as unexpected interrelationships among organizational components, and dependencies within them.

Note the similarity of the Local Information-flow Model and Global Information-flow Model development to Business Systems Planning (BSP) [MART82], which is also based on data flow. The primary difference, which is extremely important, is that each iteration of the Local Information-flow Model and Global Information-flow Model is followed by the development of the Conceptual Schema and External Schemas in the procedures described in this paper. This cyclical and iterative approach balances the data flow perspective with the data structure perspective, so that neither will be emphasized at the expense of the other. BSP, however, emphasizes the data flow perspective almost to the exclusion of the data structure perspective; high level data objects are identified, but their relationships and detailed structures must be developed by another methodology.

5.1 Information Used to Develop the GIM

Information that is relevant to the development of the GIM is obtained primarily from the previous iteration of the GIM and the newly developed LIMs. Other types of information are similar to those used to develop the LIM, except that they are at a higher organizational level.

1. The nature, objectives, and scope of the organization must be analyzed to ensure a compatible GIM.

2. The organizational perspective on decisions must be determined.

3. Organizational rules and policies must be analyzed.

4. Reports and forms must be examined.

5. Available resources must be determined.

5.2 Functions of the GIM

The primary function of the GIM is to guide the development of the Conceptual Schema. Other functions of the GIM are:

1. The GIM provides context for the development of the next iteration of the LIMs.

2. The GIM, like the LIMs, may assist in management planning to increase efficiency; the GIM provides a wider perspective on reducing data flow through changes in functions and organizational structures.

3. The GIM may also be used to design the interfaces among separate, loosely connected Conceptual Schemas, as may be appropriate among several large systems or a distributed database system.

5.3 Procedure for Developing the GIM

Figure 5 shows the four sequential steps in the development of the GIM. The steps are described in the following paragraphs.

GLOBAL INFORMATION-FLOW MODELING (GIM) PROCEDURE

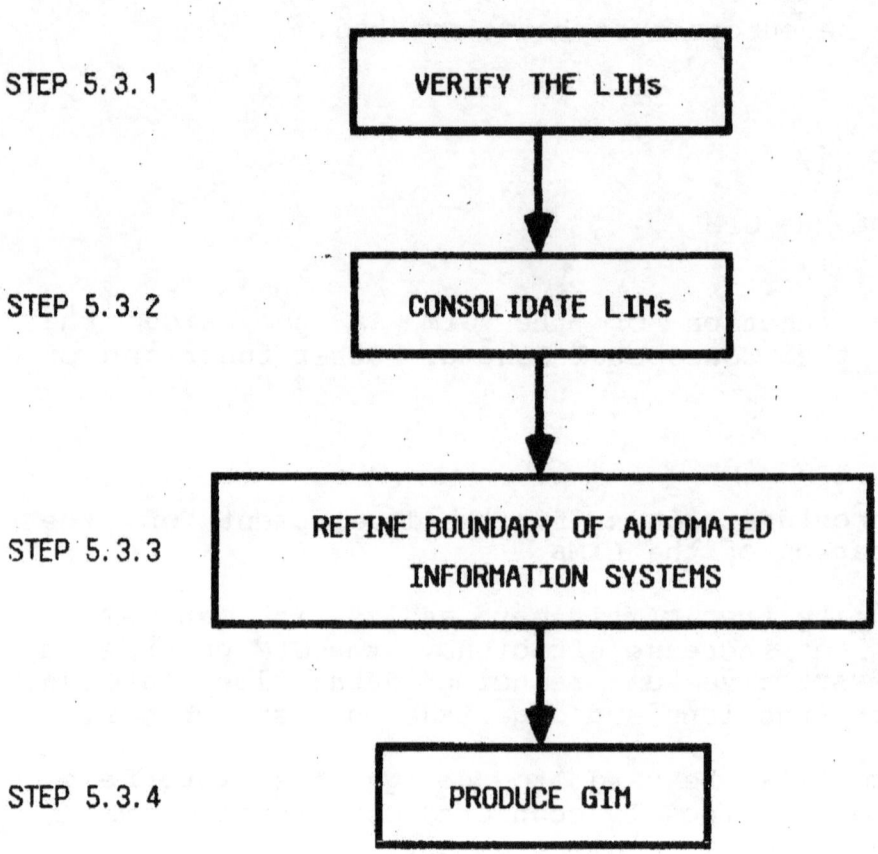

FIGURE 5

5.3.1 Verify the LIMs.

The LIMs are organized into a hierachy of organizational components, a separate but interrelated hierarchy of functions, and, possibly, a separate but interrelated hierachy of events. The function of this step is to verify that each new LIM is consistent with the objectives and constraints of the next higher level LIM in its hierarchy. Any inconsistencies require modification of either the lower-level LIM or the higher-level LIM. In the latter case, modifications may propagate all the way up the hierarchy and possibly affect the other hierarchies as well: such modifications may also propagate to the GIM, Conceptual Schema, and External Schemas. The following are the major considerations:

1. The data flow of a LIM must be consistent with that of its higher-level LIM. Each data object at the lower level should either appear at the higher level, or be a part of a higher-level data object, or have both source and sink within the lower-level LIMs. For example, assume that the higher level is a department, and the lower level consists of the branches within it. Data received by one branch from an outside source must be traceable to a departmental data source, but data sent to another branch might not appear at the departmental level.

2. Similarly, the data flow of the higher-level LIM must not be greater than the data flow of the LIMs that comprise it.

3. More generally, the scope of a lower-level LIM must be consistent with the scope of the higher-level LIM, where scope includes such non-data considerations as timing, resources, general objectives, and interrelationships with other hierarchies. For example, the branch should not have more time to perform a task than is available to the department, and should not perform functions that are not assigned to the department.

4. Similarly, the scope of the higher-level LIM must not be greater than the scope of the LIMs that comprise it.

5. If workloads have been developed, the workload of a LIM must be consistent with that of its higher-level LIM. Data volumes should be consistent. Each path through the lower-level data must either be entirely contained within the lower-level LIM or must be traceable to a path in the higher-level data. Priority, frequency, timing dependencies, and numbers of instances should be consistent.

6. Similarly, all of the paths in the higher-level LIM must appear in the lower-level LIM.

Step 5.3.1 Verify the LIMs

Function: To verify that each new LIM is consistent with the objectives and constraints of the next higher level

Output: LIMs organized in a hierarchy of organizational components, functions, or events

Team Members: User - AA, DA
Developer - AA, DA

Symbology: LIM diagram

Tools: Use DD to change entries and determine effects of change

Guidelines: Verify LIMs from top down

5.3.2 Consolidate LIMs.

The function of this step is to resolve synonyms that arise when different subsystems use different names for the same data flow and homonyms that arise when different subsystems use the same name for different data flows. Once detected, synonyms and homonyms are relatively easy to resolve. One of the synonyms is chosen for the GIM name, while the others are retained in the data dictionary as alternate names for the appropriate LIMs. For example, "part#" could be the preferred, global name, while "part-number" could be used within the context of a particular function, and be represented in the data dictionary as an alternate name. Only one object can be assigned the homonym for its GIM name; each of the other objects is assigned a new, unique name, and the homonym is assigned as an alternate name. For example, if "price" refers to both retail and wholesale price, then "price" could be used globally to refer to retail price, or locally within a particular function to refer to wholesale price; "wholesale-price" could be used to refer to wholesale price globally. Alternatively, "retail-price" and "wholesale-price" could be used globally, and "price" only locally.

Detection of synonyms is largely a manual process, but there are some clues that can be provided by the DDS or other computerized tool:

1. The primary means for detecting possible synonyms is data flow analysis, which can be performed by the DDS--for example, the DDS may be able to produce groups of data objects that have identical sources and sinks, which would indicate that the group members could be the same data object with different names in different subsystems.

2. Name analyses, such as keyword in context, are useful for suggesting possible synonyms.

3. Data element analysis may also help in suggesting possible synonyms by identifying data elements that have similar characteristics, such as their COBOL pictures or legal values.

Detection of homonyms should be primarily a process performed by the DDS--the DDS should reject any attempt to add conflicting characteristics to any data object. Situations in which two distinct objects have the same names and all other characteristics must be detected manually; however, if each object has a meaningful textual description, it is relatively simple to compare descriptions to determine whether they should be combined, or should be given separate names. Homonyms that are not resolved at this step may be resolved at a later step or later iteration of this step when more characteristics are known and therefore there is more likelihood of a conflict being detected by the DDS. Resolution at this step is a convenience but not a necessity.

```
-------------------------------------------------------
| Step 5.3.2    Consolidate LIMs                      |
|                                                      |
| Function:      Resolution of synonyms and honomyms  |
|                                                      |
| Output:        One uniform model                    |
|                                                      |
| Team Members:  User - DA                            |
|                Developer - DA                       |
|                                                      |
| Symbology:     Bubbles and lines                    |
|                                                      |
| Tools:         Use DD to store alternate names      |
|                Use name analyses such as keyword in |
|                context to detect synonyms           |
|                                                      |
| Guidelines:    Standardize names in GIM             |
|                Use local synonyms whenever appropriate |
|                in LIMs                              |
-------------------------------------------------------
```

5.3.3 Refine Boundary of Automated Information System (AIS).

The function of this step is to refine the boundary of the automated information system that is being designed. This may reduce the scope of the logical database design and therefore reduce the effort expended in subsequent phases. Note that the final boundary will generally be three dimensional: organizational components, functions, and events. They must all be included in or excluded from the logical database design.

The criteria for drawing the boundary are primarily based on upper management goals as applied by the DA with possible technical advice from the DBA.

The boundary may be represented on a data flow diagram by a line, in a subsystem/data matrix by highlighting subsystems within the boundary or omitting subsystems outside the boundary, and in the data dictionary by a keyword or by relationships between a specific system and the subsystems within the boundary.

```
-------------------------------------------------------------

Step 5.3.3    Refine Boundary of Automated Information
              System (AIS)

Function:      Reduce scope and refine the boundaries
               of the AIS

Output:        Models of the AIS

Team Members:  User - DA and upper level managers
               Developer - DA and DBA

Symbology:     Bubbles and lines

Tools:         Use DD to represent specific system and
               subsystems within the boundary

Guidelines:    Criteria for refining boundary are
               based on upper management goals

-------------------------------------------------------------
```

EXAMPLE OF A GLOBAL INFORMATION-FLOW MODEL

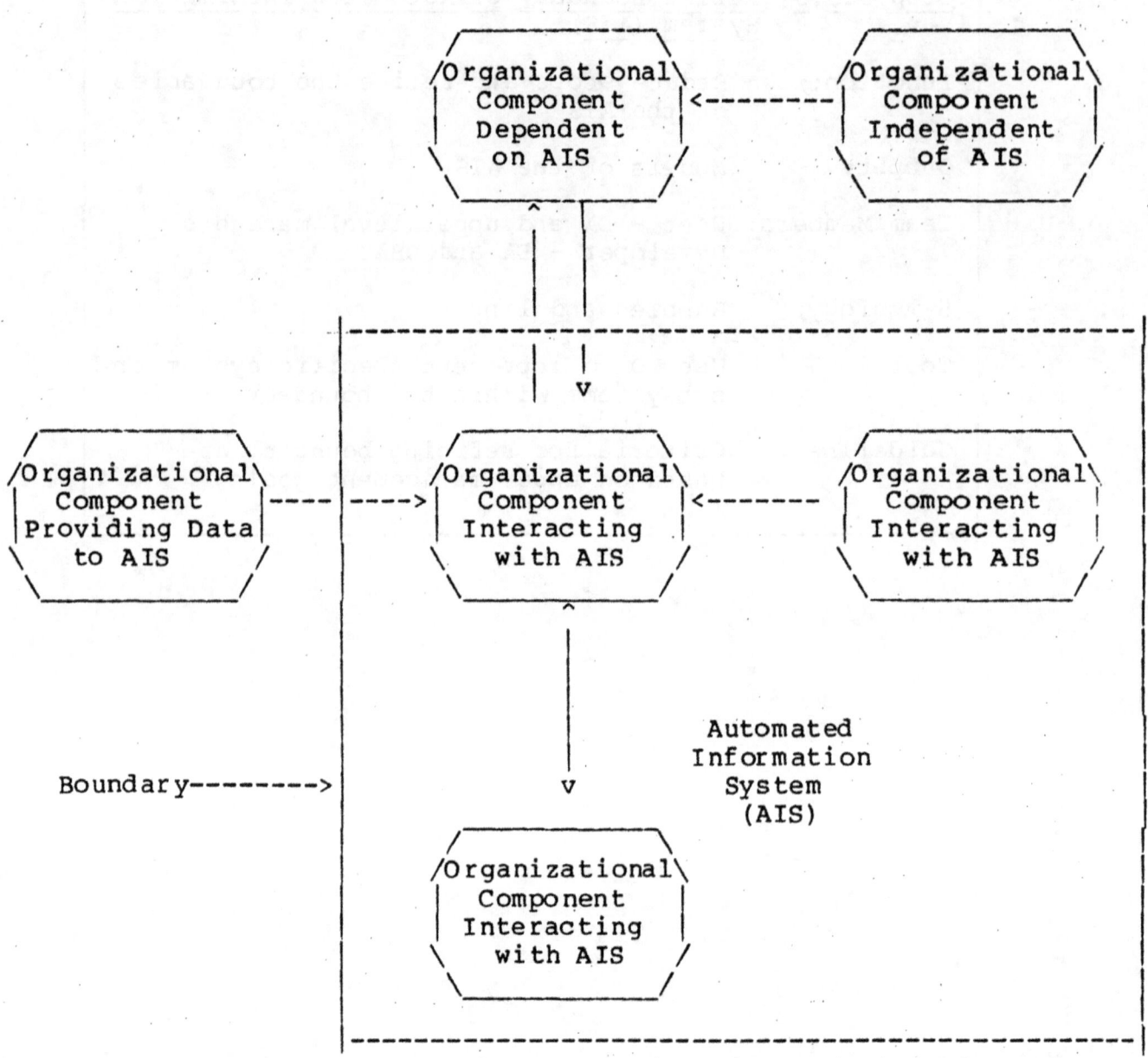

Figure 6

5.3.4 Produce GIM.

The function of this step is to provide additional quality assurance and documentation for the GIM. Use of a data dictionary is recommended. Details of how the data dictionary represents the GIM, what quality assurance reports are provided, and what documentation is to be produced must be determined by each organization to suit its own capabilities.

```
Step 5.3.4   Produce GIM

Function:      Provide final review and documentation
               for the GIM

Output:        Specification of components of GIM

Team Members:  User - DA and DBA
               Developer - DA and DBA

Symbology:     Bubbles and lines

Tools:         Use DD for corrections

Guidelines:    Quality assurance must be provided
               by application experts
```

6. CONCEPTUAL SCHEMA DESIGN

A Conceptual Schema (CS) is a description of the logical (hardware- and software-independent) structure of the data required by an organization. The phases concerned with development of the Local Information-flow Models (LIMs) and Global Information-flow Model (GIM) concentrated on the interactions between data and organizations, functions, or events; the structure and meaning of the data were not analyzed beyond the relatively simple resolution of synonyms and homonyms. This phase concentrates on the deep exploration of structure and meaning in terms of three important concepts: entity, relationship, and attribute. These concepts correspond very closely to the natural language constructs of noun, verb, and adjective. The following paragraphs, which define these concepts and provide brief examples, may be omitted by readers familiar with the Entity-Relationship-Attribute Model [CHEN80, CHEN81, CHEN82].

1. An entity is a type of real-world object or concept. For example, "employee," "project," and "position description" may be entities of interest to an organization. Note that only "employee" is a physical object--"project" and "position description" are both concepts. To appreciate the difference, consider that a "position description" may be recorded on a piece of paper. If the paper is copied or reproduced electronically in a database, the medium is changed, but the concept--the position description--is still the same. Therefore, the entity of interest is the message, not the medium.

2. A relationship is a type of association or correspondence among entities. For example, "works on" may be a relationship between "employee" and "project." An instance of a relationship is a fact or assertion--e.g., the phrase ´"12345" "works on" "design"´ could express the fact that the "employee" identified by the "employee number" "12345" is associated with the "project" entity identified by the "project-name" "design" through the relationship "works on." This example involves two entities and two instances of entities. A relationship may involve only one entity. For example, ´"design" "precedes" "implementation"´ is a relationship involving two instances of the entity "life-cycle phase." A relationship may also involve more than two entities-- e.g., ´"12345"

"works on" "design" "using" "Entity-Relationship-Attribute Approach"´ is an instance of a relationship ("works on" ... "using") among three entities ("employee," "project," and "technique").

3. An attribute is a property or characteristic which describes an entity or relationship. For example, the "employee" entity may have attributes such as "birth date," "marital status," and "annual salary," while the "works on" relationship may have attributes such as "hours per week," or "hours to date." Every entity must have an attribute or collection of attributes that distinguishes among entity instances (e.g., an "employee number" identifies a particular "employee"). A relationship may be without attributes, since each instance is identified by the entities that it associates (e.g., the relationship instance ´"design" "precedes" "implementation"´ is uniquely identified by "design" and "implementation," in that order).

6.1 Information Used to Develop the CS

Most of the information that is relevant to the development of the CS is provided indirectly by the GIM. Entities are the subjects of the data flows that were identified by the GIM, but they are generally not the data flows themselves. For example, a personnel report is not an entity unless there is system for tracking the production or distribution of the report, in which case each instance of the report might be identified by a control number. The subjects of the personnel report, e.g., "employee" and "project," would be entities.

6.2 Functions of the CS

The primary function of the CS is to provide a single logical structure for the database. Other functions include:

1. The CS provides input to the External Schema Design Phase.

2. The CS provides guidance in the choice of a data model (e.g., either a hierarchical, network, or relational data model may most easily represent the CS).

3. The CS provides guidance in the choice of a DBMS (e.g., a DBMS that easily represents the CS).

4. The CS provides guidance in the development and evaluation of the physical database design (the CS provides the definition of the logical data structure that the physical database must support).

The output of this phase may include the following:

1. For each entity of fundamental interest to the organization, its name, identifier (key), other attributes, synonyms, textual description, and relationships with other entities.

2. Entity-Relationship-Attribute diagrams [CHEN82].

3. Security, privacy, and integrity constraints.

4. Normalized relations [BEER79, BERN76, ZANI82].

6.3 Procedure for Developing the CS

Figure 7 shows the six steps in the development of the CS. The last step may reveal redundancies that will suggest repeating some or all of the preceding steps. The steps are described in the following paragraphs.

CONCEPTUAL SCHEMA (CS) DESIGN PROCEDURE

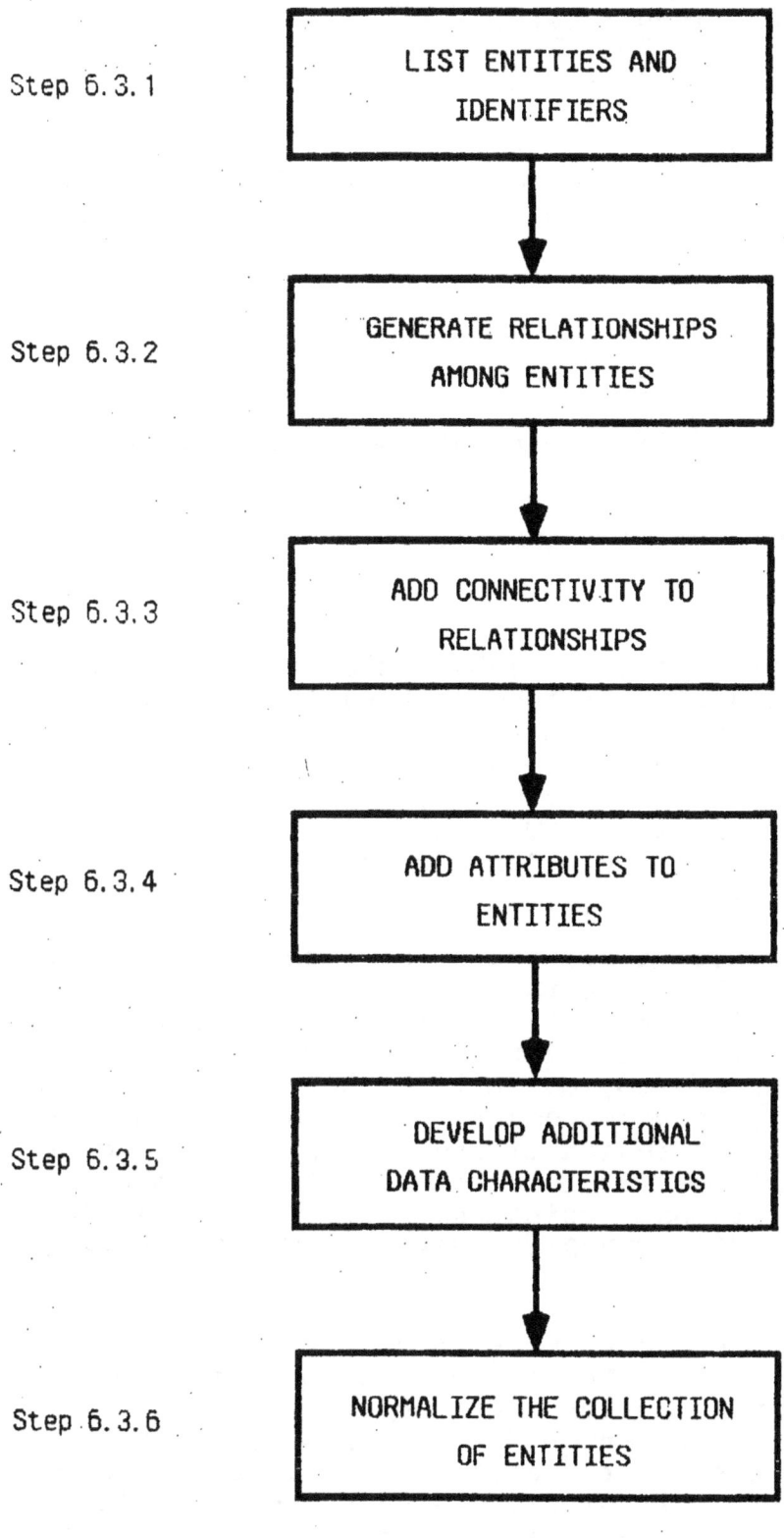

FIGURE 7

6.3.1 List Entities and Identifiers.

The primary function of this step is to develop a list of entities that must be represented in the CS. Because of the inherent complexity of the real world that the CS models, this is considerably more difficult than one might assume. Some reasonable guidelines are presented below and discussed in the following paragraphs.

1. A data flow may suggest one or more entities.

2. An entity must have a meaningful name and description.

3. An entity must have an identifier.

In general, entities are the subjects of the GIM data flows; an entry in a report or form is usually an attribute which can identify or describe an entity. For example, an assignment matrix could have "project#" as the column heading, "employee-number" as the row title, and an "X" or blank as an indicator of assignment. The matrix itself is not an entity in most cases, but the "project#" and "employee-number" identify entities.

An entity should have a meaningful name consisting of a noun or noun phrase. If there is no obvious choice for the name of a proposed entity, then it is likely that it is not an entity. In addition, the entity must have an extended description that addresses topics such as the lifetime of an entity instance (e.g., is a "dependent" removed from the database when an "employee" resigns?) and criteria for inclusion (e.g., does "employee" include both hourly and salaried personnel?). For additional guidance, refer to [ATRE80, CHEN82, CURT82, KAHN79, ROUS81, SHEP76, SMIT78, SUST83, TEOR82].

An entity must have one or more identifiers (or keys). Each identifier is an attribute or combination of attributes which distinguishes among entity instances. For example, "employee-number," "project-name," and "PD#" could be the identifiers of "employee," "project," and "position description." The identifier of an entity may be composed of identifiers of other entities. For example, the identifier of "assignment" could be composed of the combination of the attributes "employee-number" and "project-name." Note that neither single attribute would uniquely identify a particular "assignment." Note also that "assignment" could equally well be identified by "SS#" and "project#," or even by a unique "assignment-number"--the important fact at this point is that an identifier can be found, so that "assignment" is a legitimate entity.

Analysis of the preceding example demonstrates that care must be exercised in finding an identifier and defining an entity:

o If the "employee" is released from the "project," is a record of the "assignment" retained?

o If so, how can such an assignment be distinguished from a current assignment?

o If the "employee" is returned to the "project," is the "assignment" still the same?

This analysis may indicate that the "employee-number" and "project-name" cannot constitute the identifier. Another attribute, such as "assignment-starting-date-and-time," may be needed for uniqueness. Another possibility is the "assignment-number;" the rules for handling multiple assignments could then be represented by the algorithm for determining the "assignment-number." For example, if the first "assignment-number" is 1, and each succeeding "assignment-number" is increased by 1, then multiple assignments of a given "employee" to a given "assignment" can always be distinguished.

Entities may be determined "top-down" by abstracting from the data flows and the GIM, or "bottom-up" by synthesizing from identifiers and their attributes [SHEP76]. The latter approach is greatly simplified by the use of a computer-based normalization program, as described in step 6.3.6. However, "top-down" is recommended because it forces the developer to concentrate on the semantic characteristics of the data; normalization can then be used to confirm the design.

```
---------------------------------------------------------------
|                                                             |
| Step 6.3.1   List entities and identifiers                  |
|                                                             |
| Function:      Abstract data flows to determine             |
|                entities                                     |
|                                                             |
| Output:        List of entities with descriptions           |
|                and identifier                               |
|                                                             |
| Team Members:  User - DA and DBA                            |
|                Developer - DA and DBA                       |
|                                                             |
| Symbology:     Text                                         |
|                                                             |
| Tools:         Use DD to enter entities and identifier      |
|                                                             |
| Guidelines:    Be careful in defining an entity             |
|                and finding the identifier for it            |
|                Determine entities top-down                  |
|                                                             |
---------------------------------------------------------------
```

6.3.2 Generate Relationships among Entities.

The primary function of this step is to examine individual entities to see whether they can be subdivided into simpler, related entities, and to examine collections of entities to see whether they are related components of a more complex entity. A general guideline is to look at entities that share components. For example, "employee" and "assignment" share "employee-number;" obviously, there is a relationship between them. The data dictionary can be of great help in comparing entity structures.

The following are examples of common types of relationships [SUST83]:

1. Membership--a collection of similar secondary entities constitute another, primary, entity. The fiscal years in a five-year plan, the quarters in a fiscal year, or the cities in a state are examples of membership relationships. The relationship between the secondary and primary can be expressed by "in," "of," or "is a member of." The identifier of the primary may be required to identify each secondary; for example, a city name may be ambiguous unless the state is identified. The primary entity would

include properties common to all the secondary entities, while the secondary entities would have unique properties.

2. Aggregation--a collection of dissimilar secondary entities describes another, primary, entity. Generally all primary entities are related to similar collections of secondary entities. For example, each "employee" is described by the aggregation of "address," "salary-history," "education," etc., which are themselves entities. The relationship between the secondary and primary can be expressed by the phrase "is a property of" or "is a part of." The existence of a secondary entity is usually dependent on the existence of the primary entity.

3. Generalization--each of a collection of similar secondary entities can be considered to represent a special case of another, primary, entity. Different primary entities may be related to different types of secondary entities. For example, "salaried-employee" and "hourly-employee" are each roles of the primary entity "employee." The relationship between the secondary and primary can be expressed by the phrases "is a" or "is a type of." The existence of each secondary entity may be dependent on the existence of the primary entity; for example, every "salaried-employee" or "hourly-employee" must also be an "employee." The primary entity would include properties common to all the secondary entities, while the secondary entities would have unique properties.

These relationships correspond to the programming constructs of iteration (looping through the members of a collection), sequence (manipulating one after another of the aggregated properties), and selection (determining whether a particular role is played by the entity). All of these relationships can be developed bottom-up (from a given collection of secondary entities to the primary), to produce a simplified high-level structure, or top-down (from a primary to a collection of secondaries), to add more detail.

Another type of relationship which is occasionally useful is the following:

4. Precedence--the existence of one entity in the database must precede the existence of another entity in the database. For example, a "proposed-budget" must precede an "approved-budget;" once an "approved-budget" has been entered, however, its existence is independent of the "proposed-budget."

Other, more specialized relationships are discussed in [SUST83].

Diagrams are recommended as a convenient way of communicating with the application specialists. Examples are given below.

EXAMPLE OF AN ENTITY-RELATIONSHIP DIAGRAM

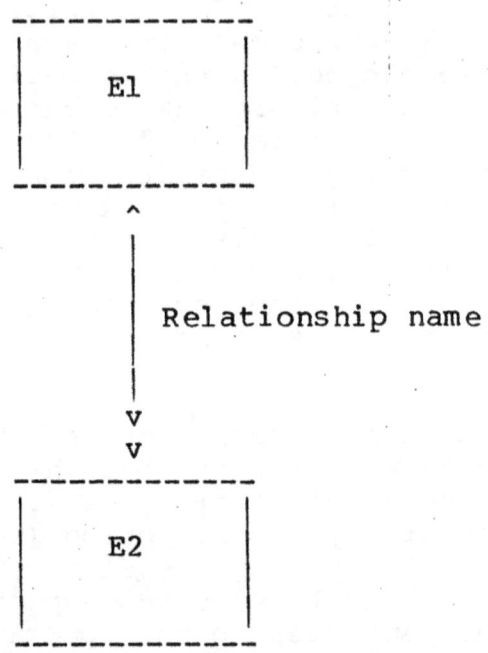

Figure 8

This example states that entity "E1" has a relationship with another entity "E2." The single and double arrows indicate that an instance of "E1" may be associated with many instances of "E2," while each instance of "E2" is associated with one instance of "E1."

ALTERNATE NOTATION FOR AN ENTITY-RELATIONSHIP DIAGRAM

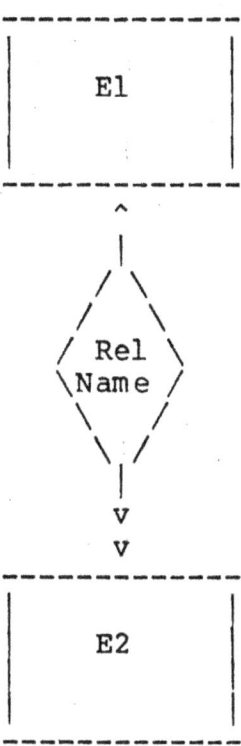

Figure 9

The alternate notation is somewhat more cumbersome but it does have the advantage of emphasizing the importance of relationships, and is readily extended to include relationships among more than two entities and relationships with attributes.

In general, the simplicity of labeled lines is preferred. A relationship among more than two entities should usually be transformed into an entity which has simple relationships with those entities. For example,

REPLACING A RELATIONSHIP WITH AN ENTITY

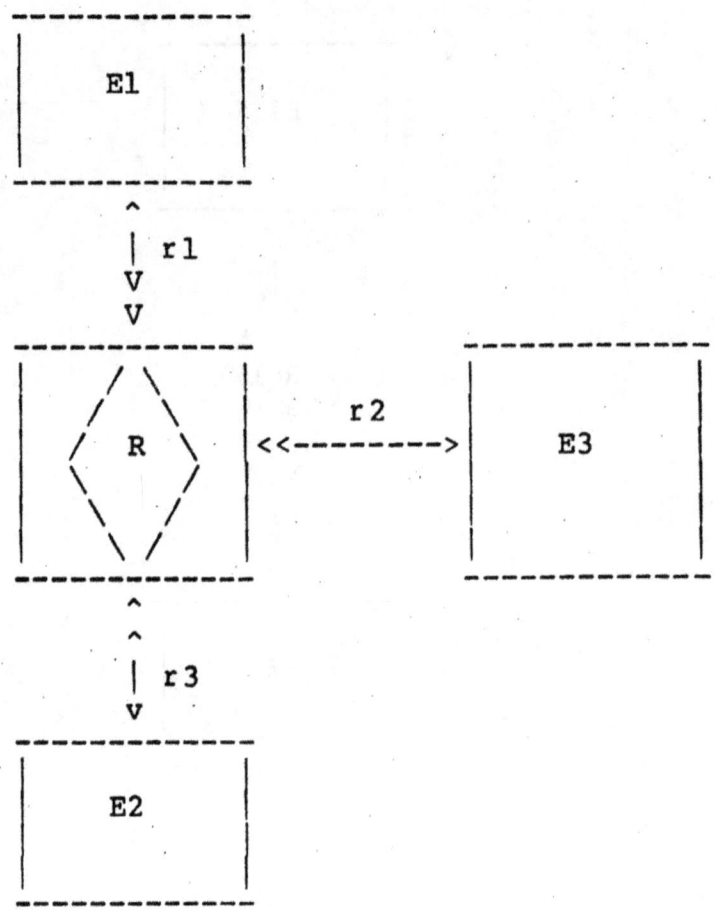

Figure 10

The complex relationship R has been replaced by an entity; the diamond within the rectangle indicates that R may be an entity on one diagram and a relationship on a less detailed diagram. New relationships, r1, r2, and r3 must be added unless they are obvious. The fact that an "employee" uses a particular "skill" on a particular "project" would be represented by such a diagram; E1, E2, and E3 would represent "employee," "skill," and "project," while R could be a relationship or an entity identified by the "employee," "skill," and "project" identifiers.

```
-------------------------------------------------------
| Step 6.3.2    Generate relationships among entities |
|                                                     |
| Function:      Revise entities                      |
|                                                     |
| Output:        Entities and relationships           |
|                                                     |
| Team Members:  User - DA and DBA                    |
|                Developer - DA and DBA               |
|                                                     |
| Symbology:     Entity-Relationship diagrams         |
|                                                     |
| Tools:         Add relationships to DD              |
|                                                     |
| Guidelines:    Look for common types of             |
|                relationships                        |
-------------------------------------------------------
```

6.3.3 Add Connectivity to Relationships.

The primary function of this step is to suggest new entities or ways in which entities can be combined. A secondary function is to provide quantitative data useful to physical database design.

Connectivity describes a relationship between two entities-- how many instances of one entity are associated with how many instances of the other entity. For example, if an "employee" can have only one "manager," but a "manager" can manage many employees, then the relationship "manages" is "1 to many." If a reasonably good number can be given for the "many," that may assist in physical database design. However, the most important situations for logical database design are the following:

o Most relationships will have connectivity "1 to many" or "many to 1."

o If the connectivity is "1 to 1," then the two entities should be combined, provided that the result can be given a meaningful name and description. For example, if a "project" always has exactly one "manager," and a "manager" always has exactly one "project," then the two entities can be combined.

(Note the use of the word "always." In the real world it is likely that there will be periods of transition when a "manager" has no "project," or more than one "project," or a "project" has no "manager." In reality, then, the connectivity might be "0,1 to 0,1,2," and the entities should not be combined.)

o If the connectivity is "1 to 0,1" then this often indicates generalization. For example, the relationship between "employee" and "salaried-employee" is "1 to 0,1," since the "employee" could be an "hourly-employee." The "salaried-employee" entity cannot exist unless the "employee" entity exists.

o If the connectivity is "many to many" (or numbers indicating a similar situation), then the relationship should be replaced by an entity. For example, if there is a "many to many" relationship between "employee" and "manager" (i.e., matrix management), then a new entity, such as "assignment of employee to manager" should be created, and the "many to many" relationship replaced by two "1 to many" relationships. This leads to more entities but simplifies relationships and also simplifies the mapping of the logical database design into a conventional data model.

An example of a diagram with connectivity is shown below.

EXAMPLE OF AN ENTITY-RELATIONSHIP DIAGRAM WITH CONNECTIVITY

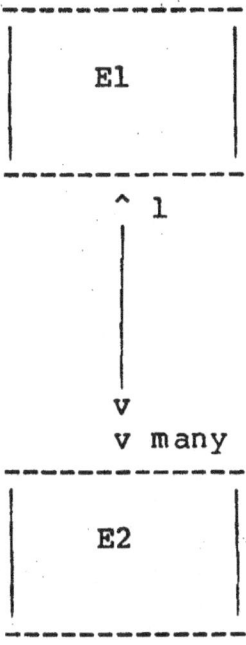

Figure 11

```
Step 6.3.3    Add connectivity to relationships

Function:      Determine connectivity and provide
               quantitative data to physical
               database design

Output:        Annotated relationships

Team Members:  User - DA and DBA
               Developer - DA and DBA

Symbology:     Extended E-R diagrams

Tools:         Add connectivity information to DD

Guidelines:    Eliminate 1 to 1 and many to many
               relationships
```

6.3.4 Add Attributes to Entities.

The primary function of this step is to add detail to the entity descriptions in the data dictionary and diagrams. Two strategies are possible:

1. If there is a collection of known attributes (e.g., data elements), then this step can be performed "bottom-up." Each attribute is assigned to an entity (or entities) which identifies a unique instance of that attribute. If no entity is appropriate, one is created, relationships are developed, and so on.

2. This step can be performed "top-down" by examining each entity to determine appropriate descriptors. This procedure is recommended during high-level iterations, when attributes are data collections rather than data elements.

The attributes are represented in the data dictionary by being "contained in" an entity [FIPS80], and in the diagrams by some notation such as that in the following example, where "A1" is the attribute:

EXAMPLE OF AN ENTITY-RELATIONSHIP-ATTRIBUTE DIAGRAM

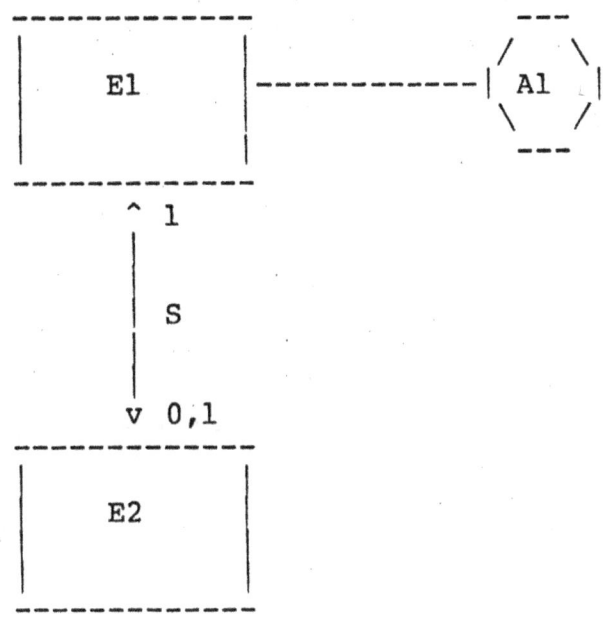

Figure 12

The relationship S could be an agreed-upon symbol to indicate that E2 is a subtype of the entity E1.

Another function of this step is to simplify the CS by eliminating unnecessary entities. The rule for doing this is very simple:

o If an entity is single-valued in every relationship with other entities, then it can be eliminated by moving its attributes (including the identifier) into those entities.

For example, suppose that "hourly-pay-scale" is an entity with the attribute and identifier "dollar-amount," and its only relationships are "many to 1" from "salaried-employee" and "hourly-employee" to "hourly-pay-scale." Then "dollar-amount" should be assigned to "salaried-employee" and "hourly-employee," and "hourly-pay-scale" should be eliminated. The justification is simple: "dollar-amount" is single-valued in every relationship, so it acts like a descriptor--i.e., an attribute.

```
------------------------------------------------------------
| Step 6.3.4    Add attributes to entities                 |
|                                                          |
| Function:      Add attributes to the entity              |
|                descriptions                              |
|                                                          |
| Output:        E-R-A diagrams                            |
|                                                          |
| Team Members:  User - DA and DBA                         |
|                Developer - DA and DBA                    |
|                                                          |
| Symbology:     E-R-A diagrams                            |
|                                                          |
| Tools:         Add attributes to DD                      |
|                                                          |
| Guidelines:    Simplify by eliminating unnecessary       |
|                entities                                  |
------------------------------------------------------------
```

6.3.5 Develop Additional Data Characteristics.

The function of this step is to add additional constraints, such as security and integrity, to the entity and relationship descriptions in the data dictionary. These constraints are important but are not easily represented on a diagram; the recommendation is to keep the diagrams simple by representing these constraints only in the data dictionary.

Step 6.3.5 Develop additional data characteristics

Function: Add security, integrity, and other
                constraints

Output: E-R-A diagrams and updated DD
                with detailed description of data

Team Members: User - DA and DBA
                Developer - DA and DBA

Symbology: E-R-A diagrams

Tools: Add constraints to DD

Guidelines: Keep the diagrams simple

6.3.6 Normalize the Collection.

The primary function of this step is to ensure that the collection of entities is optimal in the following sense:

1. Each non-key attribute is identified only by the simplest possible identifiers. For example, "supplier-address" should not be in a "supplier-part" entity (identified by the combination of "supplier-name" and "part-number") if "supplier-address" is uniquely identified by "supplier-name" alone.

2. Redundant non-key attributes are eliminated. For example, if the "branch" entity contains "division#" and "department#," and the "division" entity (identified by "division#") also contains "department#," then "department#" can be eliminated from "branch." The "department#" can be determined from the unique "division" entity identified in the "branch," so "department#" is redundant in "branch."

3. Entities with the same identifier are combined.

4. Entities with equivalent identifiers (identifiers that identify each other) are combined.

The first two conditions, plus the condition that attributes are single-valued (which was required in step 6.3.4), are sufficient to ensure that the entities are in Third Normal Form [BERN76]. The third and fourth conditions ensure that the entities are in the more rigorous Elementary Key Normal Form (EKNF) [ZANI82], which minimizes the total number of entities. A computer algorithm to obtain EKNF is described in [BEER79, BERN76]; the proofs of correctness and minimality are complex, but the algorithm itself is quite simple.

Commercially available programs perform various levels of normalization [MART77]. A good program should interface to a data dictionary to obtain identifiers and the attributes that they identify, and should provide EKNF as well as various reports, traces, and diagrams. The objective of the preceding steps of this phase is to do such a good job of identifier analysis that the normalization program will produce exactly the entities that are input to it. Experience indicates that discrepancies between the input and output entities are often caused by more serious and subtle errors than those found by the normalization program; the program exposes errors, but its "corrections" are sometimes difficult to understand, and should not be accepted without thorough analysis. A normalization program should definitely not be used as a substitute for careful thought.

Step 6.3.6 Normalize the collection of entities

Function: Remove redundancies and detect errors

Output: Normalized entities

Team Members: User - System analyst and DBA
                Developer - DA and DBA

Tools: Normalization program

Guidelines: Careful manual analysis as well as use of the automated tools

---

7. EXTERNAL SCHEMA MODELING

An External Schema (ES) is a subschema (part) of a Conceptual Schema (CS) that is relevant to a Local Information-flow Model (LIM). A LIM, in turn, represents the information requirements of a user, group of users, application program, or application system. An ES includes all entities, relationships, and attributes needed by the LIM. Local names are possible--for example, the Conceptual Schema may have an entity called "employee-number" which is "emp-no" in the personnel ES. An ES reflects the way information is used by an individual task or decision.

7.1 Information Used to Develop the ES

The primary sources of information needed to develop an ES are the CS and the relevant LIM as represented in the data dictionary. If the LIM is inadequate in scope or detail, then it should be expanded using additional information from the sources listed in section 4.1.

7.2 Functions of the ES

The primary function of an ES is to help users and programmers interact with the database by presenting a simplified view of the database in terms which are familiar to them. An ES has the following secondary functions:

1. Detailed iterations of the ES provide one of the inputs to physical database design--they describe the workload, originally developed in terms of LIMs, in terms of the CS.

2. An ES is a piece of the CS which can be assigned privacy and security locks during physical database design and implementation phases.

3. An ES provides quality control of the CS--if the ES cannot be constructed from the CS, then the CS is incomplete. Also, if there are portions of the CS which are not required by any ES, then those portions

are unnecessary or are information sources that are not being utilized by any LIMs. During the early iterations of the logical database design process the ESs will be useful only for comparing high-level descriptions of very general categories of data (e.g., data needed for the support of management decisions), since the relevant LIMs will be based on an organizational perspective and will not have much detail. In addition, the LIMs may not indicate what information is to be in the database and what is to be provided by some other source. During later iterations, the ESs will provide a much more accurate means for ensuring CS quality.

7.3 Procedure for Developing the ES

Figure 13 shows the three sequential steps in the development of the ES. The steps are described in the following paragraphs.

EXTERNAL SCHEMA (ES) MODELING PROCEDURE

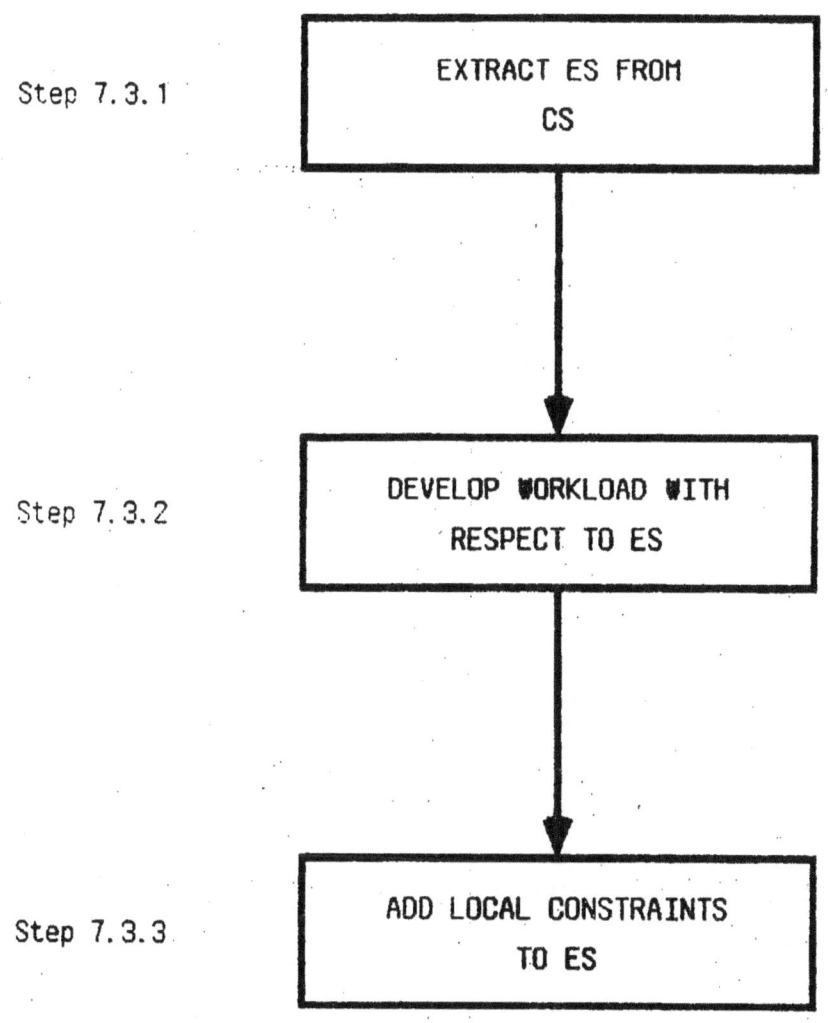

FIGURE 13

7.3.1 Extract an ES from the CS.

The primary function of this step is to decide what parts of the CS are required by a particular LIM. First, data flows must be classified into those requiring data from the database and those that are independent of the database [JEFF82]. The data collection may be obtained from or stored in a private file or other non-database location if any of the following are true:

1. The data collection is of interest to only a single user or application and therefore need not be shared.

2. The data collection is transitory, as in a temporary working file, and would not exist long enough to be relevant to other users or applications.

3. The data collection is incomplete or inconsistent, as in a partially completed update, or consists only of references or keys to other data, as in a file of references to data of particular interest to decision support.

In general, a data collection should be obtained from or stored into the database if all of the following are true:

1. The data collection is of interest to many users or applications and should therefore be shared.

2. The data collection is sufficiently long-lived to have many uses.

3. The data collection represents a consistent, complete view of the real world.

There are then two situations that can be distinguished:

o This LIM is not a part of any LIM for which an ES has already been constructed. For example, this LIM might be a top-level organization, function, or event. In this case, the ES will consist of high-level entities, relationships, and attributes from the CS. If a Data Dictionary System (DDS) is available, it should be employed to extract only high-level data objects. These objects will then be manually compared with the data flows of the LIM to determine what parts of the CS are needed by the LIM.

o Alternatively, this LIM is a part of a higher-level LIM for which an ES has already been constructed. For example, this LIM may be a part of a function for which there is an ES. In this case, the ES is based on the higher-level ES. The DDS should be used to extract the data objects relevant to the higher-level ES, and the lower-level data objects which are contained within them. The resulting collection of data objects must then be compared with the data flows of the LIM to verify that all data required by the LIM is in the higher-level ES, or is a part of some data object in the higher-level ES (the DDS can greatly reduce the effort involved in this comparison). If not, the higher-level ES must be extended to include the missing data. The lower-level ES will then consist of the relevant parts of the higher-level ES plus additional entities, relationships, and attributes required by the more detailed level of analysis.

The final result of this step is a diagram of selected parts of the CS plus additional entries in the data dictionary to relate the selected data to the LIM.

```
Step 7.3.1    Extract an ES from the CS

Function:      Decompose CS based upon the
               particular LIM

Output:        Decomposed E-R-A diagram

Team Members:  User - Programmers, analysts, and DBA
               Developer - DA and DBA

Symbology:     E-R-A diagrams

Tools:         Use DD to relate data to LIM

Guidelines:    Verify the extracted ES with LIM
```

7.3.2 Develop Workload With Respect to ESs.

The primary function of this step is to translate the workload, originally developed in terms of data flow in the LIM, into data access and update in the ES. The preceding step determined what parts of the database, if any, are required for each data flow, while step 4.3.5 determined the frequency, sequence, and selectivity with which each function uses and updates data. Therefore, this step involves two alternatives for each data collection in the LIM workload sequence:

- If the data collection is not database data, then nothing need be done.

- If the data collection is database data, then an appropriate access path must be determined. That is, given the data available at that point in the sequence, what entities and relationships must be accessed to arrive at the required entities? If a path cannot be found, there is an error, which must be corrected by modifying the LIM (e.g., by revising the workload), modifying the partially completed ES (e.g., by changing the distribution of database and non-database data), or modifying the CS (e.g., by adding a new relationship). If a path can be found, it is added into the workload sequence for the ES.

The resulting database workload should be represented in the data dictionary by a sequence of programs or modules interacting with the database objects. Three kinds of interactions with entities must be represented:

- Data use--an entity instance is accessed because various attributes are needed for some computation, report, or control purpose.

- Data update--an entity instance is added or modified.

- Data access--an entity instance is part of a path but has no directly relevant attributes. The entity might be removed from the path, with an improvement in database performance, if the Internal Schema has an appropriate relationship to bypass the entity.

As noted in step number 4.3.5, there are two types of interactions with attributes:

- Entity retrieval--an attribute is needed to determine whether an entity instance is needed by the function.

- Attribute selection--an attribute instance is required for a computation, report, control, or update purpose.

There is one type of interaction with relationships:

- Path component--the relationship is part of a path. Note that the direction is important.

The paths may also be represented graphically by an overlay on an ES or CS diagram [MART84, MCCL84, SUST84]. This provides a simple representation that can be easily understood and verified by application specialists, but is not a substitute for the data dictionary.

```
-----------------------------------------------------------
| Step 7.3.2    Develop workload with respect to ES       |
|                                                          |
| Function:      Specifications for physical design       |
|                                                          |
| Output:        Workload specifications                  |
|                                                          |
| Team Members:  User - Programmers, analysts, and DBA    |
|                Developer - Analysts, DA and DBA         |
|                                                          |
| Symbology:     E-R-A diagram with path overlay          |
|                                                          |
| Tools:         Update DD to add workload information    |
|                                                          |
| Guidelines:    Identify access path to avoid errors     |
-----------------------------------------------------------
```

7.3.3 Add Local Constraints to the ES.

The purpose of this step is to add any unique constraints imposed on or by the LIM. Examples of such constraints include security and privacy restrictions, local rules for edit and validation, and local integrity constraints.

```
-----------------------------------------------------------
| Step 7.3.3    Add local constraints to the ES           |
|                                                          |
| Function:      Add local constraints to each ES         |
|                                                          |
| Output:        Updated E-R-A diagrams and updated DD    |
|                                                          |
| Team Members:  User - Programmers, analysts, and DBA    |
|                Developer - DA and DBA                   |
|                                                          |
| Symbology:     E-R-A diagrams                           |
|                                                          |
| Tools:         Update DD to add constraints             |
|                                                          |
| Guidelines:    Identify unique constraints imposed      |
|                on or by the LIM                         |
-----------------------------------------------------------
```

8. CONCLUSIONS

This report presents a Logical Database Design methodology with the following characteristics:

o There are four phases: Local Information-flow Modeling, Global Information-flow Modeling, Conceptual Schema Design, and External Schema Modeling.

o The phases are executed iteratively to control complexity and to provide a means for verifying the results of the different phases against one another.

o Analysis is performed from different points of view (organization, function, and event) in order to ensure that the logical database design accurately reflects all reasonable information requirements of the organization.

o The methodology recommends computer support from a Data Dictionary System, in order to conveniently and accurately handle the volume and complexity of design documentation and analysis, and to provide ready access to work already accomplished.

o Logical database design is integrated into the complete system life cycle.

The purpose of this methodology is to assist in the design of very large and complex information systems, where the effects of poor logical database structures can result in expensive, time-consuming system development efforts whose end results are ineffective and inefficient. The methodology emphasizes both the need for speed, so that the design will be completed in time to be useful, and the need for quality control, to ensure that the design is consistent, complete, and satisfies the eventual users.

APPENDIX A

Agency Financial Management System

INTRODUCTION

A Federal agency is designing a financial management system. None of the applications systems offered by software vendors seem to gracefully accommodate the agency's code structure and its cost accounting procedures for its reimbursable divisions. As a matter of fact, although the individuals on the team surveying these packages are each expert in a particular subject area, they lack a good overview of what their agency's requirements are, or should be.

A primary objective of the design effort is to gain an organizational perspective of the agency's financial data. The logical database design can then be used to develop a system (either in-house or on contract), purchase a system (once requirements are understood) or specify modifications which would be needed if a system were purchased from a vendor or obtained from another agency.

An important consideration in the logical database design project is that the agency's appropriation from Congress constitutes only 63% of the operating budget. Additional income is provided by contracts with other government agencies and the sale of goods and services to the public sector. The financial management system must be able to charge back costs to customers. Another important consideration is that there is an existing payroll system which must interface with the financial management system.

An example of a reimbursable division is Instrument Fabrication Division, IFD, whose income from services to other government agencies represents 8% of the agency's budget. IFD relies on other divisions within the agency for functions such as procurement and accounting. IFD finances all management and support services by applying a fixed-rate surcharge to the labor base in some of its own units.

The following examples are intended to show some of the types of documentation which are gathered or produced in a logical database design.

These examples have been simplified so that the amount of detail does not obscure the intent of the example. However, in some instances enough detail is left in so that the reader may appreciate the sheer volume of the items of information to be gathered, analyzed and organized in logical database design. The result is, unfortunately, an uneven level of detail.

Even the sample system chosen, "Agency Financial Management System," is limited in scope, showing some aspects of normal in-house financial management for a service-oriented agency. Other federal agencies, whose mission is to administer or disburse government funds, would consider this example system a minor subsystem. In general, logical database design for financial management should consider the unique mission of the agency and the extent to which financial data can be used to support that mission.

INSTRUMENT FABRICATION DIVISION
Organizational Chart

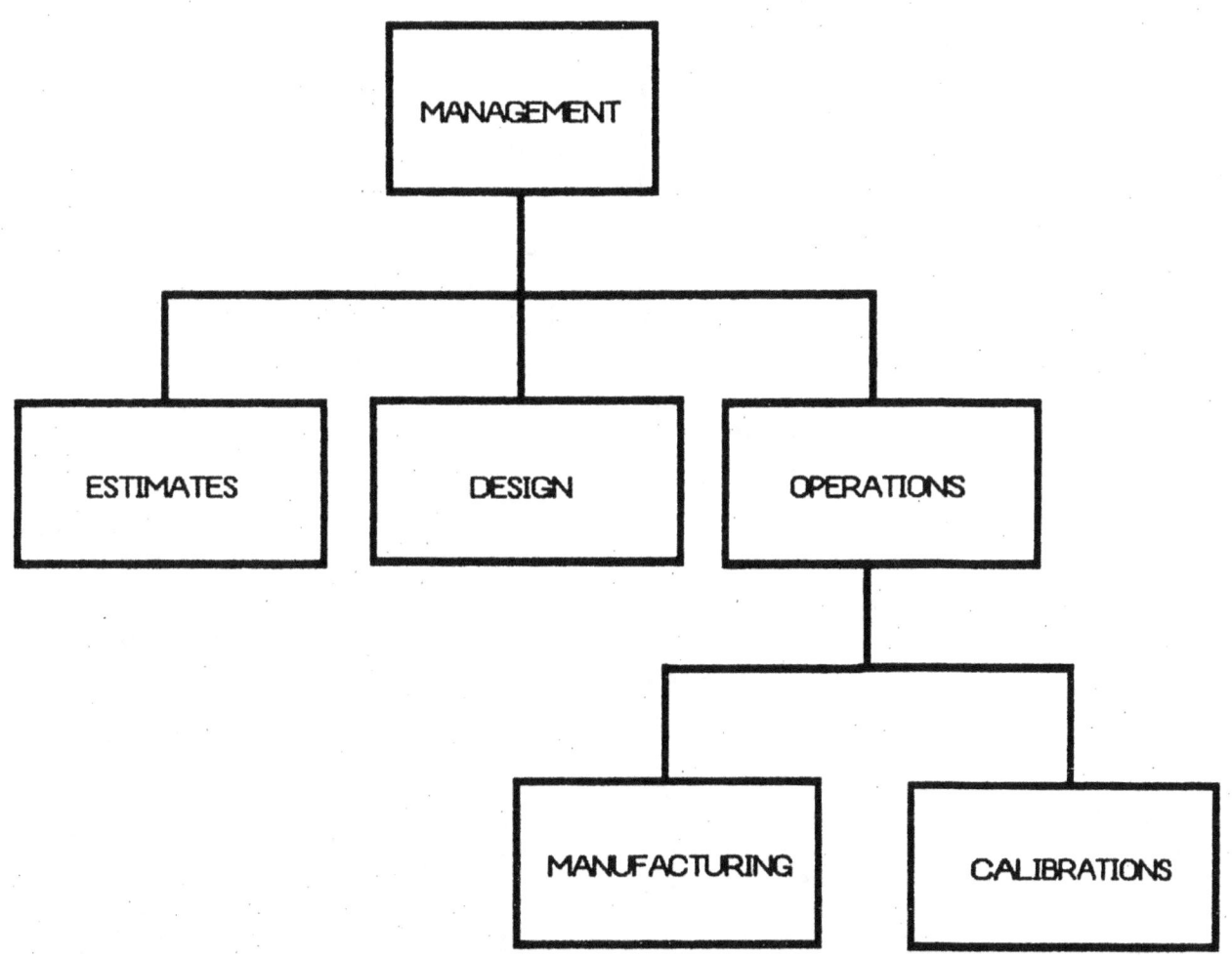

MISSION

The mission of Instrument Fabrication Division is to design and manufacture high-precision, one-of-a kind instruments in support of the agency's scientific research divisions. This service is available to other government agencies as well as the public. All instruments are manufactured on a reimbursable basis.

INSTRUMENT FABRICATION DIVISION

High Level Local Information-flow Model

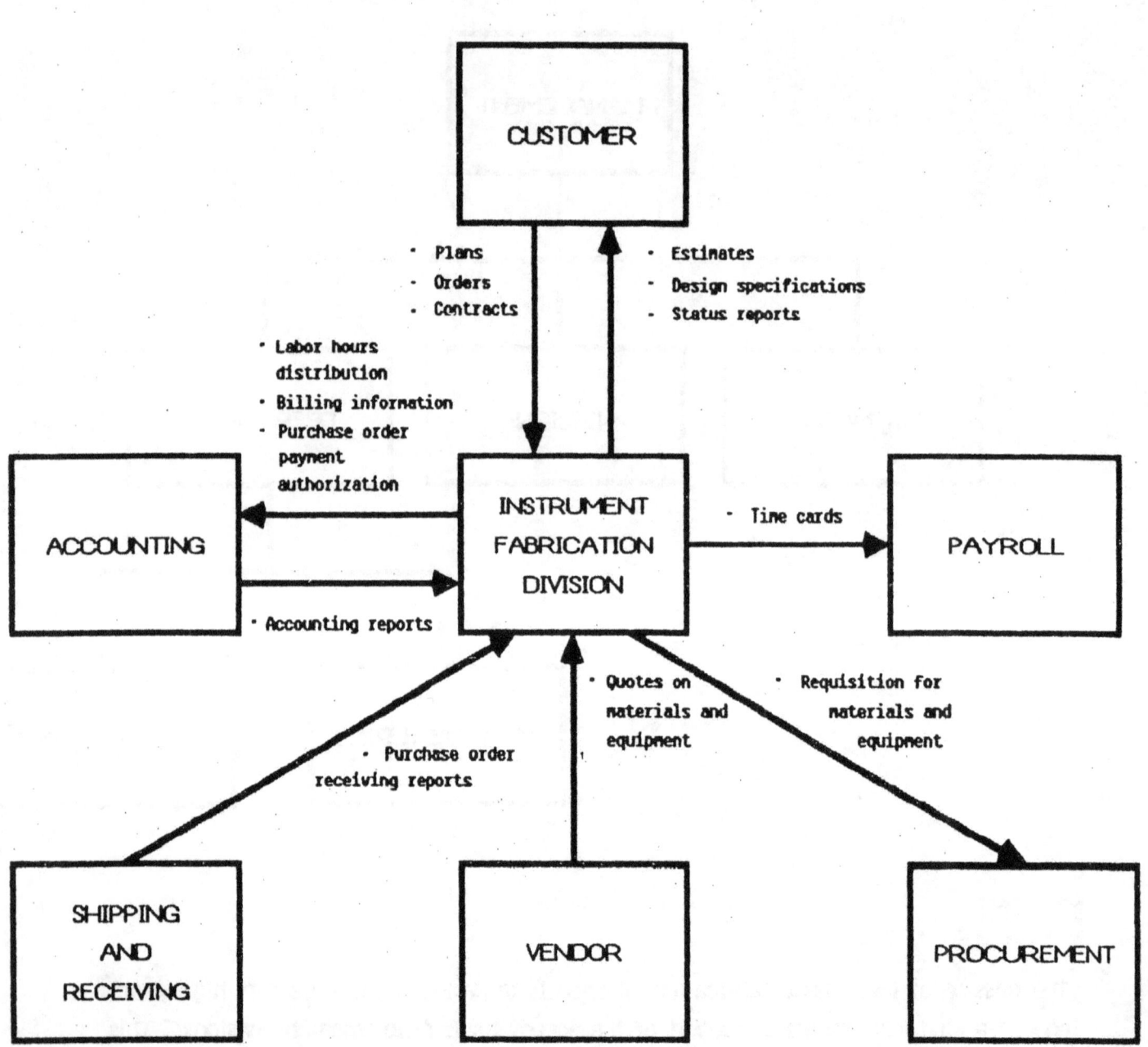

INSTRUMENT FABRICATION DIVISION
Local Information-flow Model
ESTIMATES Unit

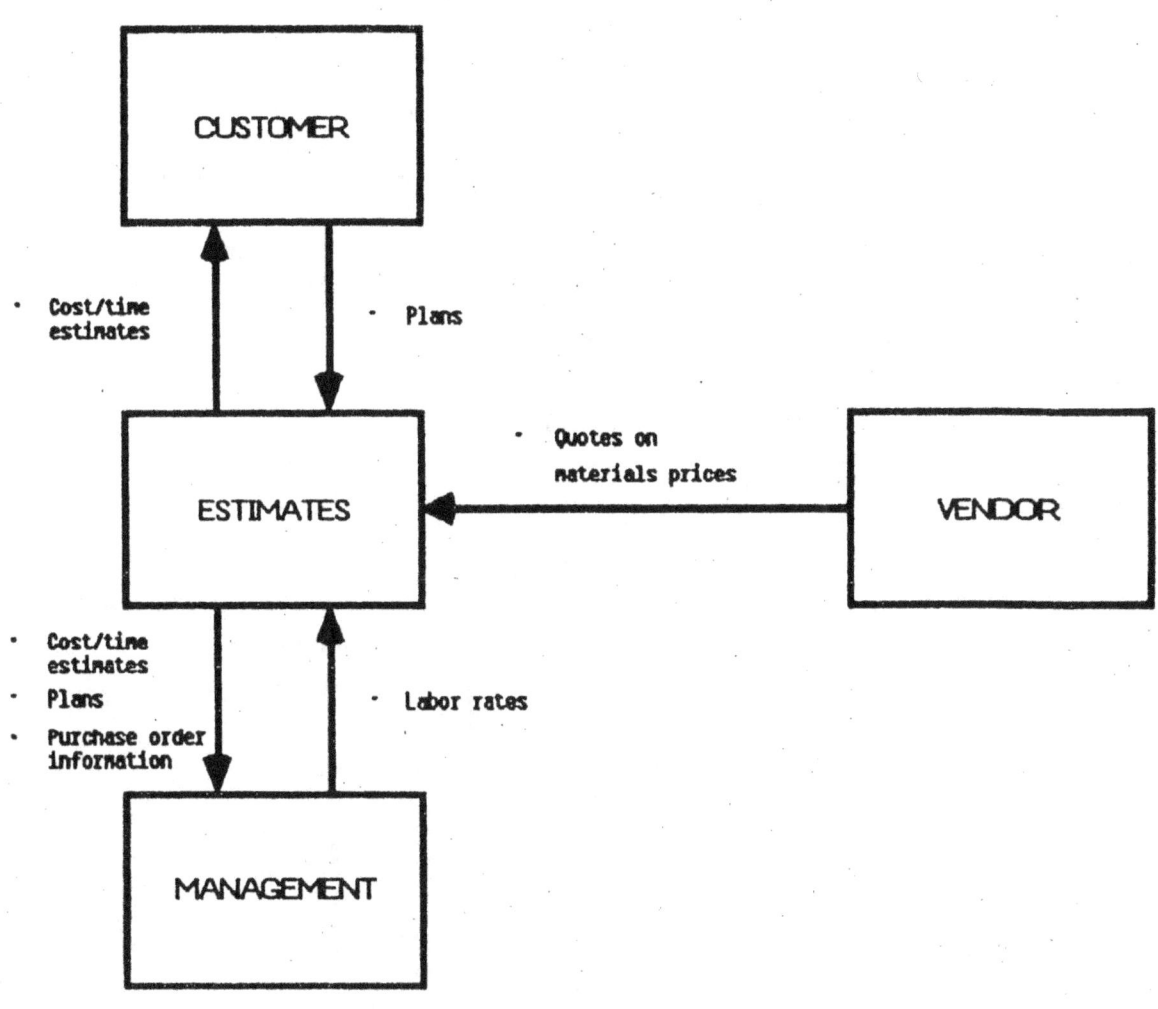

NOTES

Estimates are free to customers. The ESTIMATES unit is not reimbursed directly for services.

INSTRUMENT FABRICATION DIVISION
Local Information-flow Model
OPERATIONS Unit

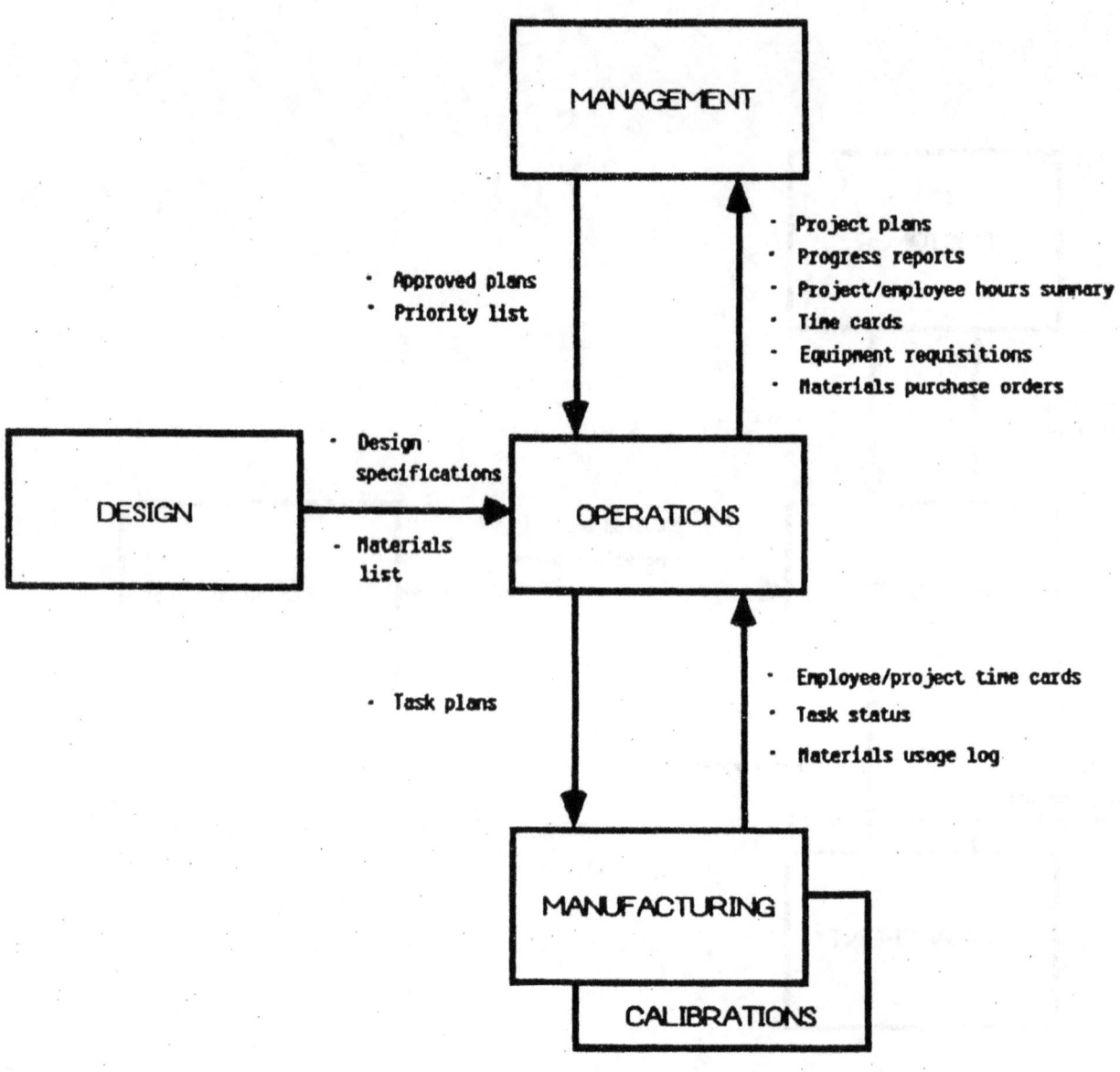

NOTES

OPERATIONS is responsible for coordinating the efforts of MANUFACTURING and CALIBRATIONS, scheduling tasks, ordering materials and equipment, reporting material and labor spent on each project.

INSTRUMENT FABRICATION DIVISION
Local Information-flow Model

Function : Close Out Work Order

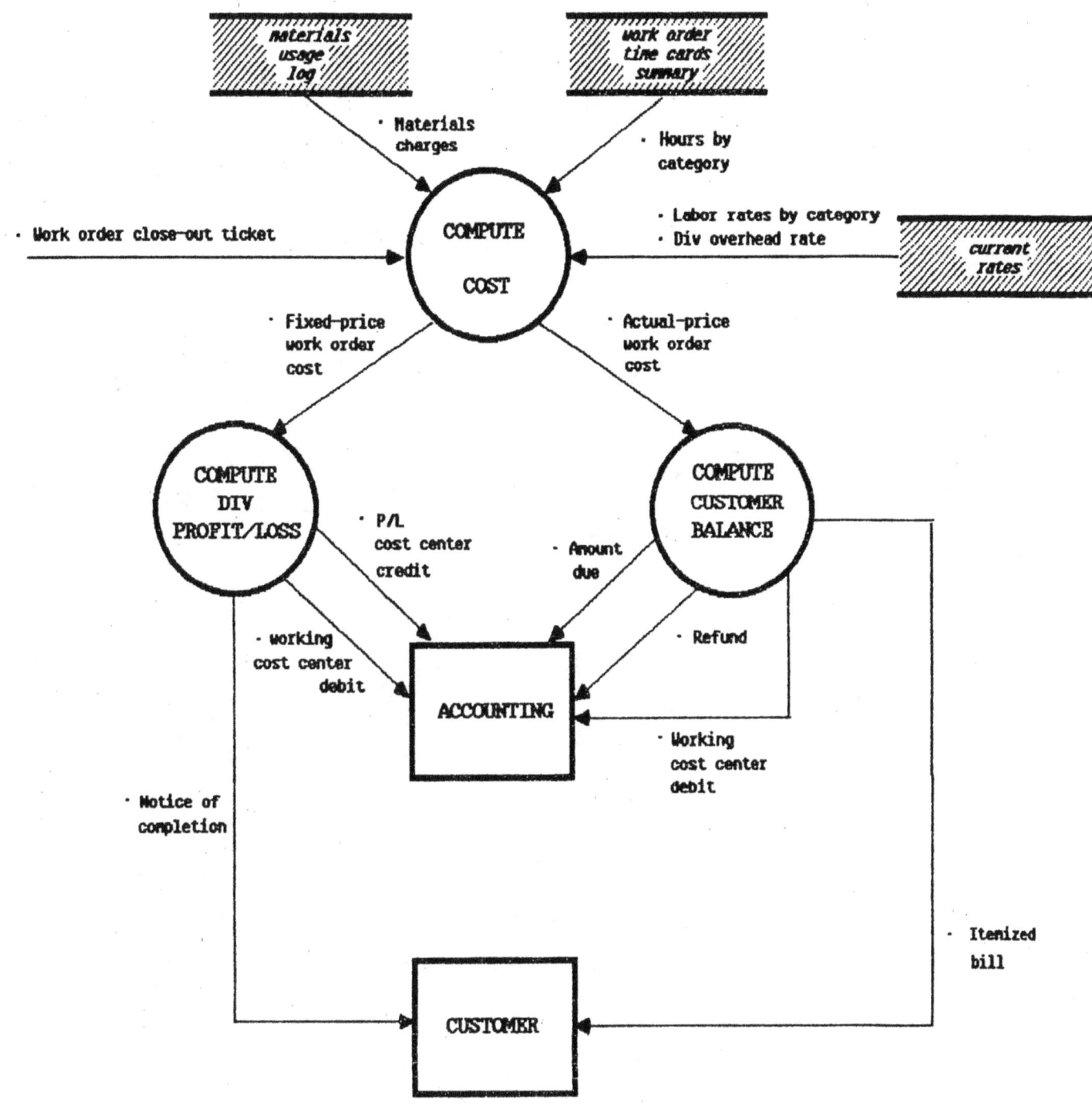

AGENCY FINANCIAL MANAGEMENT SYSTEM
Global Information-flow Model

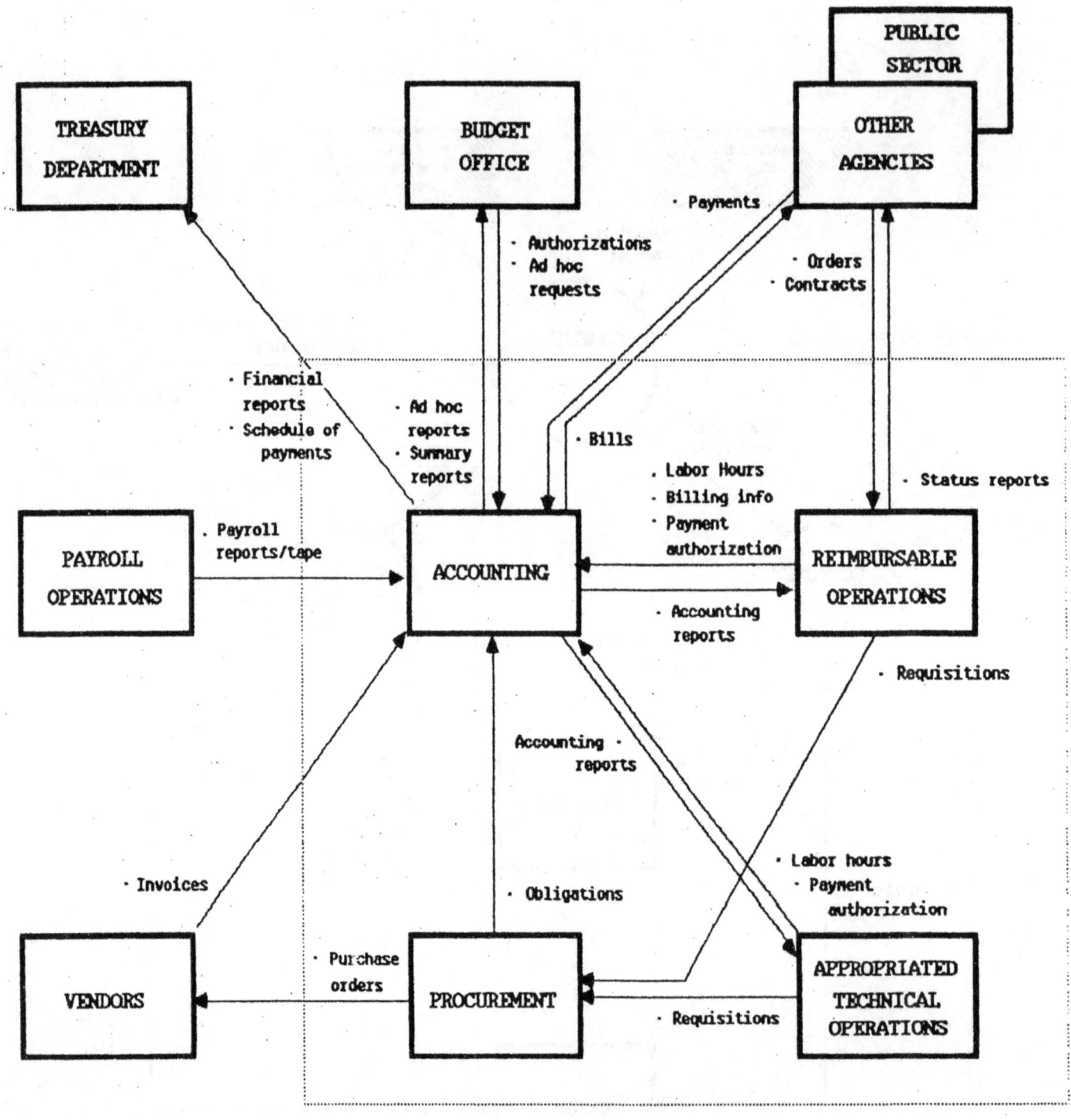

Boundary of Automation

AGENCY FINANCIAL MANAGEMENT SYSTEM
ENTITY-RELATIONSHIP DIAGRAM
OF CONCEPTUAL SCHEMA

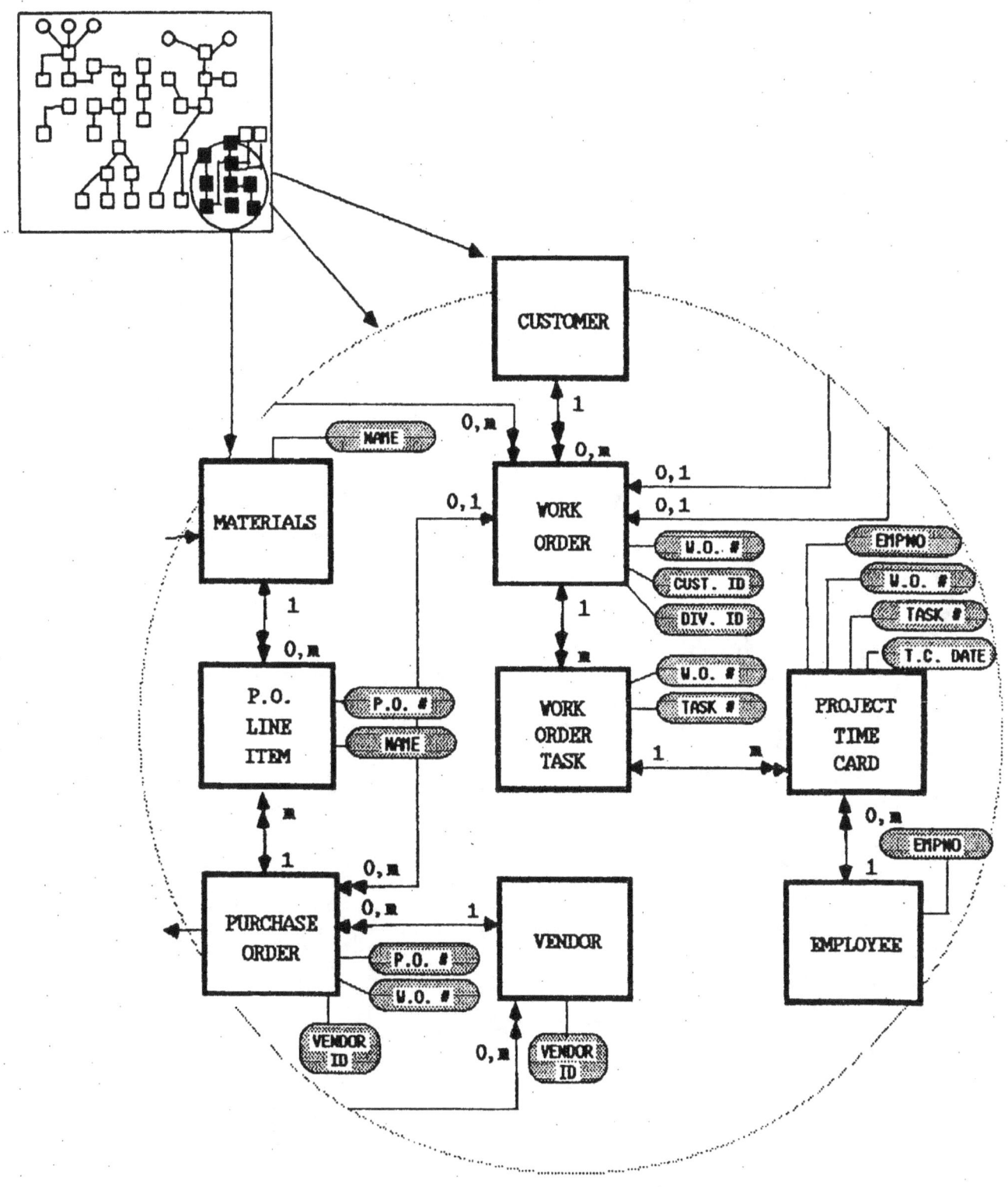

NOTES: Non-key attributes are not shown.
Data dictionary reports list all attributes.

Data Dictionary Display

Relationship : Time Charged To Task

```
QUERY> SHOW TIME-CHARGED-TO-TASK
QUERY> SHOW ENT
        WITH KEYWORD = ENTITY
        USED-BY
        TIME-CHARGED-TO-TASK
```

```
         TIME-CHARGED-TO-TASK
         ---CLASSIFICATION CATEGORY---
         RELATIONSHIP, MANY-TO-ONE
         ---DESCRIPTION CATEGORY---
    10   HOURS AND LABOR CATEGORIES ASSOCIATED WITH
    20   THE TASK ARE USED TO COMPUTE THE FINAL
    30   COST OF THE WORK ORDER.
         ---STRUCTURE CATEGORY---
         CATALOGUE NAME
         PROJECT-TIME-CARD
         WORK-ORDER-TASK
```

```
WORK-ORDER-TASK
         ---CLASSIFICATION CATEGORY---
    10   ENTITY
         ---DESCRIPTION CATEGORY---
    10   A TASK IS A DISCRETE UNIT OF WORK NEEDED TO
    20   COMPLETE A WORK ORDER.
    30   TASKS ARE PART OF THE PROJECT PLAN
    40   AND CARRY INDIVIDUAL STATUS CODES.
         ---STRUCTURE CATEGORY---
         CATALOGUE NAME
    10   WORK-ORDER-NUMBER            INDEXED BY=KEY
    20   TASK-NUMBER                  INDEXED BY=KEY
    30   TASK-DESCRIPTION
    40   TASK-RESPONSIBLE-GROUP
    50   TASK-ESTIMATED-HOURS
    60   TASK-DUE-DATE
    70   TASK-STATUS
    80   TASK-START-DATE
    90   TASK-END-DATE
```

```
PROJECT-TIME-CARD
         ---CLASSIFICATION CATEGORY---
    10   ENTITY
         ---DESCRIPTION CATEGORY---
         EMPLOYEES IN REIMBURSABLE UNITS SUBMIT A DAILY
         TIME CARD SHOWING HOW TIME HAS BEEN SPENT ON
         THE VARIOUS WORK-ORDER/TASKS IN THE UNIT.
         DIVISION LABOR CATEGORY SPECIFIES VARIOUS SKILL
         LEVELS OR EQUIPMENT USAGE.
         ---STRUCTURE CATEGORY---
         CATALOGUE NAME
    10   EMPNO                        INDEXED BY=KEY
    20   WORK-ORDER-NUMBER            INDEXED BY=KEY
    30   TASK-NUMBER                  INDEXED BY=KEY
    40   TIME-CARD-DATE               INDEXED BY=KEY
    50   TIME-CARD-HOURS
    60   DIV-LABOR-CATEGORY
```

AGENCY FINANCIAL MANAGEMENT SYSTEM
EXTERNAL SCHEMA

Function : Close Out Work Order

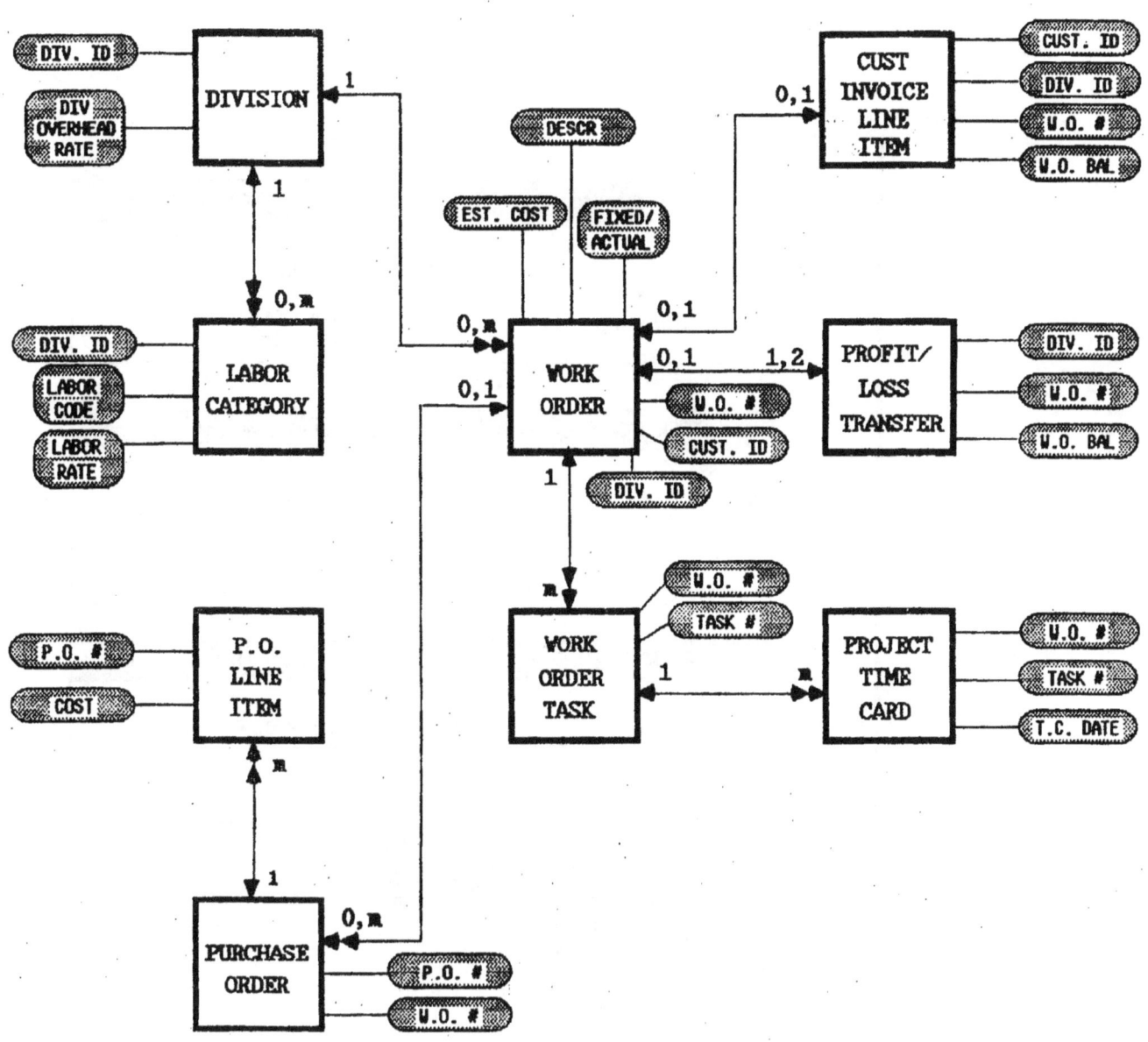

NOTE : Entities, relationships and attributes not used by this function are not shown. Complete details are available from the data dictionary.

EXTERNAL SCHEMA "OVERLAY" WORKLOAD FOR FUNCTION

"Close Out Work Order"
Biweekly Statistics for All Reimbursable Divisions

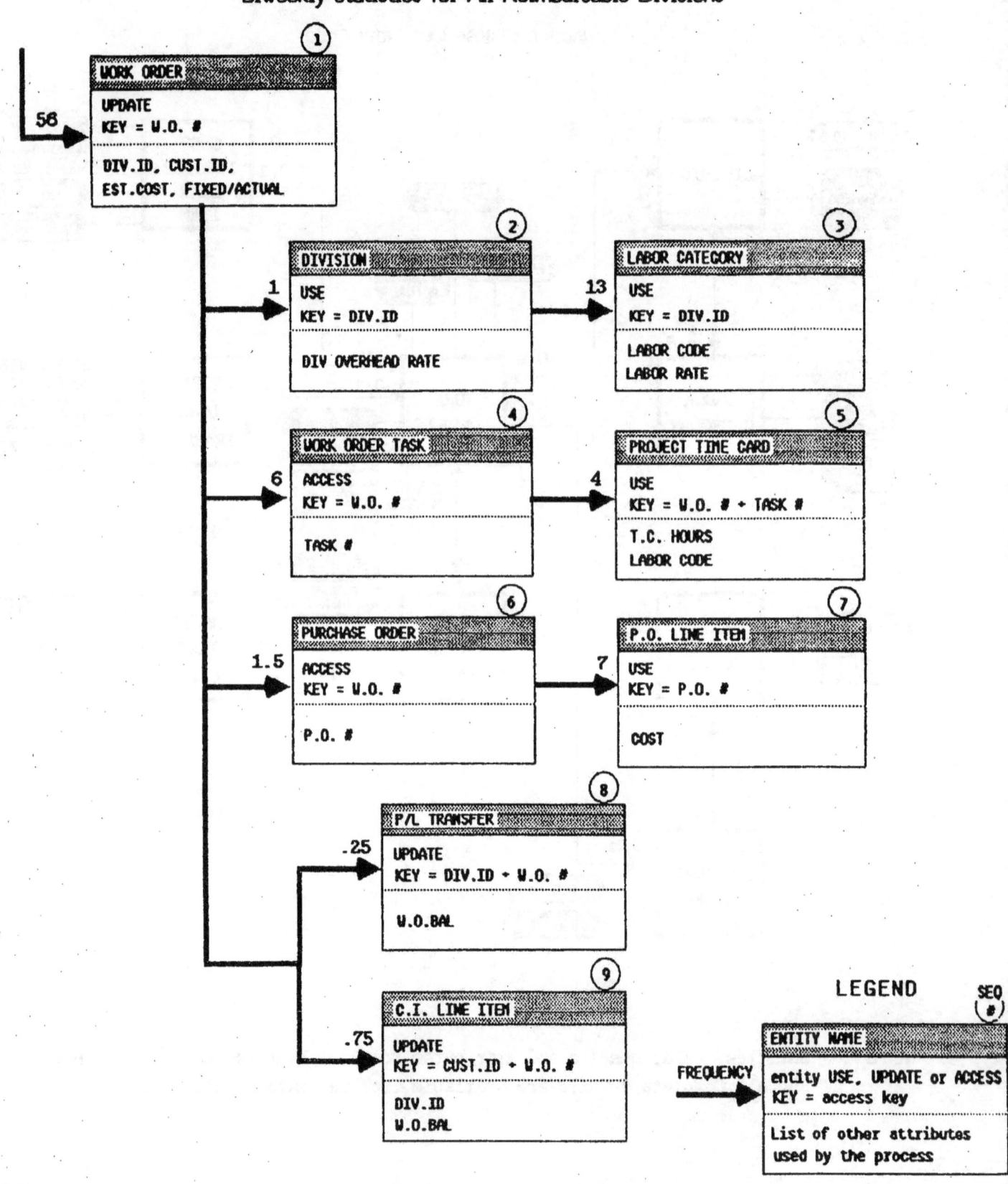

-A.13-

DATA DICTIONARY DISPLAY

WORKLOAD FOR FUNCTION

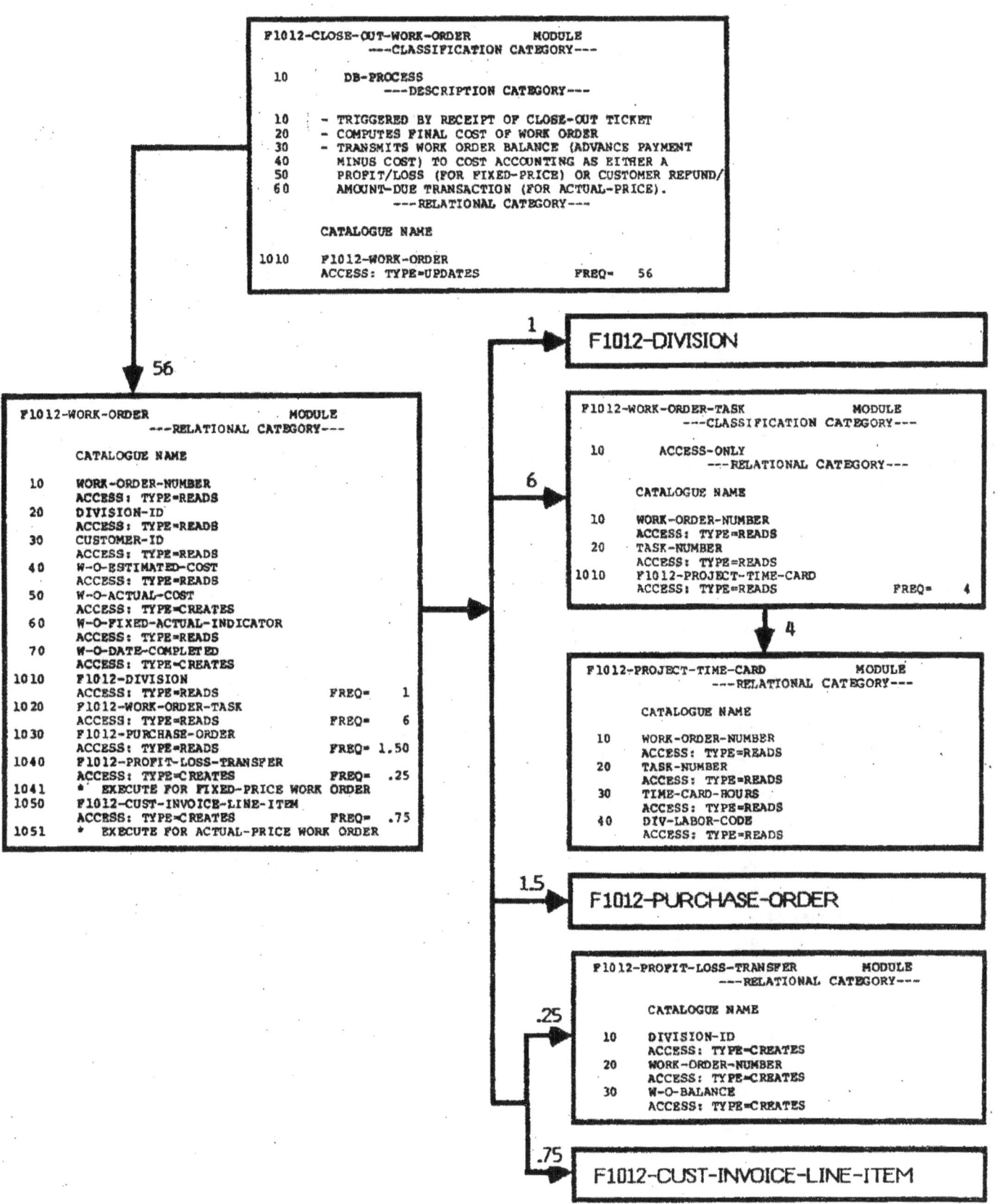

INDENTED INDEX
EXTERNAL SCHEMA FOR FUNCTION

F1012-CLOSE-OUT-WORK-ORDER

RELATIVE LEVEL/DATA CATALOGUE NAME	ENTRY TYPE	PAGE
. F1012-CLOSE-OUT-WORK-ORDER	MODULE	2
. . F1012-WORK-ORDER	MODULE	3
. . . WORK-ORDER-NUMBER	ELEMENT	4
. . . DIVISION-ID	ELEMENT	5
. . . CUSTOMER-ID	ELEMENT	6
. . . W-O-ESTIMATED-COST	ELEMENT	7
. . . W-O-ACTUAL-COST	ELEMENT	8
. . . W-O-FIXED-ACTUAL-INDICATOR	ELEMENT	9
. . . W-O-DATE-COMPLETED	ELEMENT	10
. . . F1012-DIVISION	MODULE	11
. . . . DIVISION-ID	ELEMENT	12
. . . . DIV-OVERHEAD-RATE	ELEMENT	13
. . . . F1012-DIV-LABOR-CATEGORY	MODULE	14
. . . . . DIVISION-ID	ELEMENT	15
. . . . . DIV-LABOR-CODE	ELEMENT	16
. . . . . DIV-LABOR-RATE	ELEMENT	17
. . . F1012-WORK-ORDER-TASK	MODULE	18
. . . . WORK-ORDER-NUMBER	ELEMENT	19
. . . . TASK-NUMBER	ELEMENT	20
. . . . F1012-PROJECT-TIME-CARD	MODULE	21
. . . . . WORK-ORDER-NUMBER	ELEMENT	22
. . . . . TASK-NUMBER	ELEMENT	23
. . . . . TIME-CARD-HOURS	ELEMENT	24
. . . . . DIV-LABOR-CODE	ELEMENT	25
. . . F1012-PURCHASE-ORDER	MODULE	26
. . . . WORK-ORDER-NUMBER	ELEMENT	27
. . . . PURCHASE-ORDER-NUMBER	ELEMENT	28
. . . . F1012-PURCHASE-ORDER-LINE-ITEM	MODULE	29
. . . . . PURCHASE-ORDER-NUMBER	ELEMENT	30
. . . . . P-O-LINE-ITEM-COST	ELEMENT	31
. . F1012-PROFIT-LOSS-TRANSFER	MODULE	32
. . . DIVISION-ID	ELEMENT	33
. . . WORK-ORDER-NUMBER	ELEMENT	34
. . . W-O-BALANCE	ELEMENT	35
. . F1012-CUST-INVOICE-LINE-ITEM	MODULE	36
. . . CUSTOMER-ID	ELEMENT	37
. . . WORK-ORDER-NUMBER	ELEMENT	38
. . . DIVISION-ID	ELEMENT	39
. . . W-O-BALANCE	ELEMENT	40

*** END OF INDEX ***

GLOSSARY OF COMPUTER TERMS

Contents

Basic   Page

application & app----disk	1
drive----function keys	2
graphics----modem	3
monitor----PDA	4
platform----www	5

Reference

65xx----Amiga	6
AmigaOS----ASCII	7
ASK----BeOS	8
beta byte	9
bytecode ----character set	10
CISC---- Cray	11
crippleware---- DRM	12
DTML----FAQ	13
Fire Wire----FTP	14
Gateway----HP-UX	15
HTML----interactive fiction	16
interpreted----JavaScript	17.
jiffy----Llinux	18
Lisp----Mac OS X	19
machine language----MIME	20
MMX----NetBSD	21
netiquette----object-oriented	22
ObjectiveC & ObjC ---- partition	23
Pascal----Power PC	24
proprietary----RISC	25
robot----server	26
SGML----Sugar	27
SunOS----UNIX	28
upload----VAX	29
vector----VRML	30
W3C----Windows 3.1	31
Windows CE----WYSIWYM	32
X-Face----XUL	33
Y2K----Z-Machine	34
Z80----Zoomer	35

GLOSSARY OF COMPUTER TERMS

Basic

application & app
An application (often called "app" for short) is simply a program with a GUI. Note that it is different from an applet.

boot
Starting up an OS is booting it. If the computer is already running, it is more often called rebooting.

browser
A browser is a program used to browse the web. Some common browsers include Netscape, MSIE (Microsoft Internet Explorer), Safari, Lynx, Mosaic, Amaya, Arena, Chimera, Opera, Cyberdog, HotJava, etc.

bug
A bug is a mistake in the design of something, especially software. A really severe bug can cause something to crash.

chat
Chatting is like e-mail, only it is done instantaneously and can directly involve multiple people at once. While e-mail now relies on one more or less standard protocol, chatting still has a couple competing ones. Of particular note are IRC and Instant Messenger. One step beyond chatting is called MUDding.

click
To press a mouse button. When done twice in rapid succession, it is referred to as a double-click.

cursor
A point of attention on the computer screen, often marked with a flashing line or block. Text typed into the computer will usually appear at the cursor.

database
A database is a collection of data, typically organized to make common retrievals easy and efficient. Some common database programs include Oracle, Sybase, Postgres, Informix, Filemaker, Adabas, etc.

desktop
A desktop system is a computer designed to sit in one position on a desk somewhere and not move around. Most general purpose computers are desktop systems. Calling a system a desktop implies nothing about its platform. The fastest desktop system at any given time is typically either an Alpha or PowerPC based system, but the SPARC and PA-RISC based systems are also often in the running. Industrial strength desktops are typically called workstations.

directory
Also called "folder", a directory is a collection of files typically created for organizational purposes. Note that a directory is itself a file, so a directory can generally contain other directories. It differs in this way from a partition.

disk
A disk is a physical object used for storing data. It will not forget its data when it loses power. It is always used in conjunction with a disk drive. Some disks can be removed from their drives, some cannot. Generally it is possible to write new information to a disk in addition to reading data from it, but this is not always the case.

drive
A device for storing and/or retrieving data. Some drives (such as disk drives, zip drives, and tape drives) are typically capable of having new data written to them, but some others (like CD-ROMs or DVD-ROMs) are not. Some drives have random access (like disk drives, zip drives, CD-ROMs, and DVD-ROMs), while others only have sequential access (like tape drives).

e-book
The concept behind an e-book is that it should provide all the functionality of an ordinary book but in a manner that is (overall) less expensive and more environmentally friendly. The actual term e-book is somewhat confusingly used to refer to a variety of things: custom software to play e-book titles, dedicated hardware to play e-book titles, and the e-book titles themselves. Individual e-book titles can be free or commercial (but will always be less expensive than their printed counterparts) and have to be loaded into a player to be read. Players vary wildly in capability level. Basic ones allow simple reading and bookmarking; better ones include various features like hypertext, illustrations, audio, and even limited video. Other optional features allow the user to mark-up sections of text, leave notes, circle or diagram things, highlight passages, program or customize settings, and even use interactive fiction. There are many types of e-book; a couple popular ones include the Newton book and Palm DOC.

e-mail
E-mail is short for electronic mail. It allows for the transfer of information from one computer to another, provided that they are hooked up via some sort of network (often the Internet. E-mail works similarly to FAXing, but its contents typically get printed out on the other end only on demand, not immediately and automatically as with FAX. A machine receiving e-mail will also not reject other incoming mail messages as a busy FAX machine will; rather they will instead be queued up to be received after the current batch has been completed. E-mail is only seven-bit clean, meaning that you should not expect anything other than ASCII data to go through uncorrupted without prior conversion via something like uucode or bcode. Some mailers will do some conversion automatically, but unless you know your mailer is one of them, you may want to do the encoding manually.

file
A file is a unit of (usually named) information stored on a computer.

firmware
Sort of in-between hardware and software, firmware consists of modifiable programs embedded in hardware. Firmware updates should be treated with care since they can literally destroy the underlying hardare if done improperly. There are also cases where neglecting to apply a firmware update can destroy the underlying hardware, so user beware.

floppy
An extremely common type of removable disk. Floppies do not hold too much data, but most computers are capable of reading them. Note though that there are different competing format used for floppies, so that a floppy written by one type of computer might not directly work on another. Also sometimes called "diskette".

format
The manner in which data is stored; its organization. For example, VHS, SVHS, and Beta are three different formats of video tape. They are not 100% compatible with each other, but information can be transferred from one to the other with the proper equipment (but not always without loss; SVHS contains more information than either of the other two). Computer information can be stored in literally hundreds of different formats, and can represent text, sounds, graphics, animations, etc. Computer information can be exchanged via different computer types provided both computers can interpret the format used.

function keys
On a computer keyboard, the keys that start with an "F" that are usually (but not always) found on the top row. They are meant to perform user-defined tasks.

graphics
Anything visually displayed on a computer that is not text.
hardware
The physical portion of the computer.
hypertext
A hypertext document is like a text document with the ability to contain pointers to other regions of (possibly other) hypertext documents.
Internet
The Internet is the world-wide network of computers. There is only one Internet, and thus it is typically capitalized (although it is sometimes referred to as "the 'net"). It is different from an intranet.
keyboard
A keyboard on a computer is almost identical to a keyboard on a typewriter. Computer keyboards will typically have extra keys, however. Some of these keys (common examples include Control, Alt, and Meta) are meant to be used in conjunction with other keys just like shift on a regular typewriter. Other keys (common examples include Insert, Delete, Home, End, Help, function keys,etc.) are meant to be used independently and often perform editing tasks. Keyboards on different platforms will often look slightly different and have somewhat different collections of keys. Some keyboards even have independent shift lock and caps lock keys. Smaller keyboards with only math-related keys are typically called "keypads".
language
Computer programs can be written in a variety of different languages. Different languages are optimized for different tasks. Common languages include Java, C, C++, ForTran, Pascal, Lisp, and BASIC. Some people classify languages into two categories, higher-level and lower-level. These people would consider assembly language and machine language lower-level languages and all other languages higher-level. In general, higher-level languages can be either interpreted or compiled; many languages allow both, but some are restricted to one or the other. Many people do not consider machine language and assembly language at all when talking about programming languages.
laptop
A laptop is any computer designed to do pretty much anything a desktop system can do but run for a short time (usually two to five hours) on batteries. They are designed to be carried around but are not particularly convenient to carry around. They are significantly more expensive than desktop systems and have far worse battery life than PDAs. Calling a system a laptop implies nothing about its platform. By far the fastest laptops are the PowerPC based Macintoshes.
memory
Computer memory is used to temporarily store data. In reality, computer memory is only capable of remembering sequences of zeros and ones, but by utilizing the binary number system it is possible to produce arbitrary rational numbers and through clever formatting all manner of representations of pictures, sounds, and animations. The most common types of memory are RAM, ROM, and flash.
MHz & megahertz
One megahertz is equivalent to 1000 kilohertz, or 1,000,000 hertz. The clock speed of the main processor of many computers is measured in MHz, and is sometimes (quite misleadingly) used to represent the overall speed of a computer. In fact, a computer's speed is based upon many factors, and since MHz only reveals how many clock cycles the main processor has per second (saying nothing about how much is actually accomplished per cycle), it can really only accurately be used to gauge two computers with the same generation and family of processor plus similar configurations of memory, co-processors, and other peripheral hardware.
modem
A modem allows two computers to communicate over ordinary phone lines. It derives its name

from **mod**ulate / **dem**odulate, the process by which it converts digital computer data back and forth for use with an analog phone line.

monitor
The screen for viewing computer information is called a monitor.

mouse
In computer parlance a mouse can be both the physical object moved around to control a pointer on the screen, and the pointer itself. Unlike the animal, the proper plural of computer mouse is "mouses".

multimedia
This originally indicated a capability to work with and integrate various types of things including audio, still graphics, and especially video. Now it is more of a marketing term and has little real meaning. Historically the Amiga was the first multimedia machine. Today in addition to AmigaOS, IRIX and Solaris are popular choices for high-end multimedia work.

NC
The term **n**etwork **c**omputer refers to any (usually desktop) computer system that is designed to work as part of a network rather than as a stand-alone machine. This saves money on hardware, software, and maintenance by taking advantage of facilities already available on the network. The term "Internet appliance" is often used interchangeably with NC.

network
A network (as applied to computers) typically means a group of computers working together. It can also refer to the physical wire etc. connecting the computers.

notebook
A notebook is a small laptop with similar price, performance, and battery life.

organizer
An organizer is a tiny computer used primarily to store names, addresses, phone numbers, and date book information. They usually have some ability to exchange information with desktop systems. They boast even better battery life than PDAs but are far less capable. They are extremely inexpensive but are typically incapable of running any special purpose applications and are thus of limited use.

OS
The **o**perating **s**ystem is the program that manages a computer's resources. Common OSes include Windows '95, MacOS, Linux, Solaris, AmigaOS, AIX, Windows NT, etc.

PC
The term **p**ersonal **c**omputer properly refers to any desktop, laptop, or notebook computer system. Its use is inconsistent, though, and some use it to specifically refer to x86 based systems running MS-DOS, MS-Windows, GEOS, or OS/2. This latter use is similar to what is meant by a WinTel system.

PDA
A **p**ersonal **d**igital **a**ssistant is a small battery-powered computer intended to be carried around by the user rather than left on a desk. This means that the processor used ought to be power-efficient as well as fast, and the OS ought to be optimized for hand-held use. PDAs typically have an instant-on feature (they would be useless without it) and most are grayscale rather than color because of battery life issues. Most have a pen interface and come with a detachable stylus. None use mouses. All have some ability to exchange data with desktop systems. In terms of raw capabilities, a PDA is more capable than an organizer and less capable than a laptop (although some high-end PDAs beat out some low-end laptops). By far the most popular PDA is the Pilot, but other common types include Newtons, Psions, Zauri, Zoomers, and Windows CE hand-helds. By far the fastest current PDA is the Newton (based around a StrongARM RISC processor). Other PDAs are optimized for other tasks; few computers are as personal as PDAs and care must be taken in their purchase. Feneric's PDA / Handheld Comparison Page is perhaps the most detailed comparison of PDAs and handheld computers

to be found anywhere on the web.

platform
Roughly speaking, a platform represents a computer's family. It is defined by both the processor type on the hardware side and the OS type on the software side. Computers belonging to different platforms cannot typically run each other's programs (unless the programs are written in a language like Java).

portable
If something is portable it can be easily moved from one type of computer to another. The verb "to port" indicates the moving itself.

printer
A printer is a piece of hardware that will print computer information onto paper.

processor
The processor (also called central processing unit, or CPU) is the part of the computer that actually works with the data and runs the programs. There are two main processor types in common usage today: CISC and RISC. Some computers have more than one processor and are thus called "multiprocessor". This is distinct from multitasking. Advertisers often use megahertz numbers as a means of showing a processor's speed. This is often extremely misleading; megahertz numbers are more or less meaningless when compared across different types of processors.

program
A program is a series of instructions for a computer, telling it what to do or how to behave. The terms "application" and "app" mean almost the same thing (albeit applications generally have GUIs). It is however different from an applet. Program is also the verb that means to create a program, and a programmer is one who programs.

run
Running a program is how it is made to do something. The term "execute" means the same thing.

software
The non-physical portion of the computer; the part that exists only as data; the programs. Another term meaning much the same is "code".

spreadsheet
An program used to perform various calculations. It is especially popular for financial applications. Some common spreadsheets include Lotus 123, Excel, OpenOffice Spreadsheet, Octave, Gnumeric, AppleWorks Spreadsheet, Oleo, and GeoCalc.

user
The operator of a computer.

word processor
A program designed to help with the production of textual documents, like letters and memos. Heavier duty work can be done with a desktop publisher. Some common word processors include MS-Word, OpenOffice Write, WordPerfect, AbiWord, AppleWorks Write, and GeoWrite.

www
The World-Wide-Web refers more or less to all the publically accessible documents on the Internet. It is used quite loosely, and sometimes indicates only HTML files and sometimes FTP and Gopher files, too. It is also sometimes just referred to as "the web".

Reference

65xx
The 65xx series of processors includes the 6502, 65C02, 6510, 8502, 65C816, 65C816S, etc. It is a CISC design and is not being used in too many new stand-alone computer systems, but is still being used in embedded systems, game systems (such as the Super NES), and processor enhancement add-ons for older systems. It was originally designed by MOS Technologies, but is now produced by The Western Design Center, Inc. It was the primary processor for many extremely popular systems no longer being produced, including the Commodore 64, the Commodore 128, and all the Apple][series machines.

68xx
The 68xx series of processors includes the 6800, 6805, 6809, 68000, 68020, 68030, 68040, 68060, etc. It is a CISC design and is not being used in too many new stand-alone computer systems, but is still being used heavily in embedded systems. It was originally designed by Motorola and was the primary processor for older generations of many current machines, including Macintoshes, Amigas, Sun workstations, HP workstations, etc. and the primary processor for many systems no longer being produced, such as the TRS-80. The PowerPC was designed in part to be its replacement.

a11y
Commonly used to abbreviate the word "accessibility". There are eleven letters between the "a" and the "y".

ADA
An object-oriented language at one point popular for military and some academic software. Lately C++ and Java have been getting more attention.

AI
Artificial intelligence is the concept of making computers do tasks once considered to require thinking. AI makes computers play chess, recognize handwriting and speech, helps suggest prescriptions to doctors for patients based on imput symptoms, and many other tasks, both mundane and not.

AIX
The industrial strength OS designed by IBM to run on PowerPC and x86 based machines. It is a variant of UNIX and is meant to provide more power than OS/2.

AJaX
AJaX is a little like DHTML, but it adds asynchronous communication between the browser and Web site via either XML or JSON to achieve performance that often rivals desktop applications.

Alpha
An Alpha is a RISC processor invented by Digital and currently produced by Digital/Compaq and Samsung. A few different OSes run on Alpha based machines including Digital UNIX, Windows NT, Linux, NetBSD, and AmigaOS. Historically, at any given time, the fastest processor in the world has usually been either an Alpha or a PowerPC (with sometimes SPARCs and PA-RISCs making the list), but Compaq has recently announced that there will be no further development of this superb processor instead banking on the release of the somewhat suspect Merced.

AltiVec
AltiVec (also called the "Velocity Engine") is a special extension built into some PowerPC CPUs to provide better performance for certain operations, most notably graphics and sound. It is similar to MMX on the x86 CPUs. Like MMX, it requires special software for full performance benefits to be realized.

Amiga

A platform originally created and only produced by Commodore, but now owned by Gateway 2000 and produced by it and a few smaller companies. It was historically the first multimedia machine and gave the world of computing many innovations. It is now primarily used for audio / video applications; in fact, a decent Amiga system is less expensive than a less capable video editing system. Many music videos were created on Amigas, and a few television series and movies had their special effects generated on Amigas. Also, Amigas can be readily synchronized with video cameras, so typically when a computer screen appears on television or in a movie and it is not flickering wildly, it is probably an Amiga in disguise. Furthermore, many coin-operated arcade games are really Amigas packaged in stand-up boxes. Amigas have AmigaOS for their OS. New Amigas have either a PowerPC or an Alpha for their main processor and a 68xx processor dedicated to graphics manipulation. Older (and low end) Amigas do everything with just a 68xx processor.

AmigaOS

The OS used by Amigas. AmigaOS combines the functionality of an OS and a window manager and is fully multitasking. AmigaOS boasts a pretty good selection of games (many arcade games are in fact written on Amigas) but has limited driver support. AmigaOS will run on 68xx, Alpha, and PowerPC based machines.

Apple][

The Apple][computer sold millions of units and is generally considered to have been the first home computer with a 1977 release date. It is based on the 65xx family of processors. The earlier Apple I was only available as a build-it-yourself kit.

AppleScript

A scripting language for Mac OS computers.

applet

An applet differs from an application in that is not meant to be run stand-alone but rather with the assistance of another program, usually a browser.

AppleTalk

AppleTalk is a protocol for computer networks. It is arguably inferior to TCP/IP.

Aqua

The default window manager for Mac OS X.

Archie

Archie is a system for searching through FTP archives for particular files. It tends not to be used too much anymore as more general modern search engines are significantly more capable.

ARM

An ARM is a RISC processor invented by Advanced RISC Machines, currently owned by Intel, and currently produced by both the above and Digital/Compaq. ARMs are different from most other processors in that they were not designed to maximize speed but rather to maximize speed per power consumed. Thus ARMs find most of their use on hand-held machines and PDAs. A few different OSes run on ARM based machines including Newton OS, JavaOS, and (soon) Windows CE and Linux. The StrongARM is a more recent design of the original ARM, and it is both faster and more power efficient than the original.

ASCII

The ASCII character set is the most popular one in common use. People will often refer to a bare text file without complicated embedded format instructions as an ASCII file, and such files can usually be transferred from one computer system to another with relative ease. Unfortunately there are a few minor variations of it that pop up here and there, and if you receive a text file that seems subtly messed up with punctuation marks altered or upper and lower case reversed, you are probably encountering one of the ASCII variants. It is usually fairly straightforward to translate from one ASCII variant to another, though. The ASCII character set is seven bit while pure binary is usually eight bit, so transferring a binary file through ASCII channels will result in corruption and loss of data. Note also that the ASCII character set is a

subset of the Unicode character set.
ASK
A protocol for an infrared communications port on a device. It predates the IrDA compliant infrared communications protocol and is not compatible with it. Many devices with infrared communications support both, but some only support one or the other.

assembly language
Assembly language is essentially machine language that has had some of the numbers replaced by somewhat easier to remember mnemonics in an attempt to make it more human-readable. The program that converts assembly language to machine language is called an assembler. While assembly language predates FORTRAN, it is not typically what people think of when they discuss computer languages.

Atom
Atom is an intended replacement for RSS and like it is used for syndicating a web site's content. It is currently not nearly as popular or well-supported by software applications, however.

authoring system
Any GUIs method of designing new software can be called an authoring system. Any computer language name with the word "visual" in front of it is probably a version of that language built with some authoring system capabilities. It appears that the first serious effort to produce a commercial quality authoring system took place in the mid eighties for the Amiga.

AWK
AWK is an interpreted language developed in 1977 by Aho, Weinberger, & Kernighan. It gets its name from its creators' initials. It is not particularly fast, but it was designed for creating small throwaway programs rather than full-blown applications -- it is designed to make the writing of the program fast, not the program itself. It is quite portable with versions existing for numerous platforms, including a free GNU version. Plus, virtually every version of UNIX in the world comes with AWK built-in.

BASIC
The **B**eginners' **A**ll-purpose **S**ymbolic **I**nstruction **C**ode is a computer language developed by Kemeny & Kurtz in 1964. Although it is traditionally interpreted, compilers exist for many platforms. While the interpreted form is typically fairly slow, the compiled form is often quite fast, usually faster than Pascal. The biggest problem with BASIC is portability; versions for different machines are often completely unlike each other; Amiga BASIC at first glance looks more like Pascal, for example. Portability problems actually go beyond even the cross platform level; in fact, most machines have multiple versions of incompatible BASICs available for use. The most popular version of BASIC today is called Visual BASIC. Like all BASICs it has portability issues, but it has some of the advantages of an authoring system so it is relatively easy to use.

baud
A measure of communications speed, used typically for modems indicating how many bits per second can be transmitted.

BBS
A **b**ulletin **b**oard **s**ystem is a computer that can be directly connected to via modem and provides various services like e-mail, chatting, newsgroups, and file downloading. BBSs have waned in popularity as more and more people are instead connecting to the Internet, but they are still used for product support and local area access. Most current BBSs provide some sort of gateway connection to the Internet.

bcode
Identical in intent to uucode, bcode is slightly more efficient and more portable across different computer types. It is the preferred method used by MIME.

BeOS
A lightweight OS available for both PowerPC and x86 based machines. It is often referred to simply as "Be".

beta
A beta version of something is not yet ready for prime time but still possibly useful to related developers and other interested parties. Expect beta software to crash more than properly released software does. Traditionally beta versions (of commercial software) are distributed only to selected testers who are often then given a discount on the proper version after its release in exchange for their testing work. Beta versions of non-commercial software are more often freely available to anyone who has an interest.

binary
There are two meanings for binary in common computer usage. The first is the name of the number system in which there are only zeros and ones. This is important to computers because all computer data is ultimately a series of zeros and ones, and thus can be represented by binary numbers. The second is an offshoot of the first; data that is not meant to be intepreted through a common character set (like ASCII) is typically referred to as binary data. Pure binary data is typically eight bit data, and transferring a binary file through ASCII channels without prior modification will result in corruption and loss of data. Binary data can be turned into ASCII data via uucoding or bcoding.

bit
A bit can either be on or off; one or zero. All computer data can ultimately be reduced to a series of bits. The term is also used as a (very rough) measure of sound quality, color quality, and even procesor capability by considering the fact that series of bits can represent binary numbers. For example (without getting too technical), an eight bit image can contain at most 256 distinct colors while a sixteen bit image can contain at most 65,536 distinct colors.

bitmap
A bitmap is a simplistic representation of an image on a computer, simply indicating whether or not pixels are on or off, and sometimes indicating their color. Often fonts are represented as bitmaps. The term "pixmap" is sometimes used similarly; typically when a distinction is made, pixmap refers to color images and bitmap refers to monochrome images.

blog
Short for web log, a blog (or weblog, or less commonly, 'blog) is a web site containing periodic (usually frequent) posts. Blogs are usually syndicated via either some type of RSS or Atom and often supports TrackBacks. It is not uncommon for blogs to function much like newspaper columns. A blogger is someone who writes for and maintains a blog.

boolean
Boolean algebra is the mathematics of base two numbers. Since base two numbers have only two values, zero and one, there is a good analogy between base two numbers and the logical values "true" & "false". In common usage, booleans are therefore considered to be simple logical values like true & false and the operations that relate them, most typically "and", "or" and "not". Since everyone has a basic understanding of the concepts of true & false and basic conjunctions, everyone also has a basic understanding of boolean concepts -- they just may not realize it.

byte
A byte is a grouping of bits. It is typically eight bits, but there are those who use non-standard byte sizes. Bytes are usually measured in large groups, and the term "kilobyte" (often abbreviated as K) means one-thousand twenty-four (1024) bytes; the term "megabyte" (often abbreviated as M) means one-thousand twenty-four (1024) K; the term gigabyte (often abbreviated as G) means one-thousand twenty-four (1024) M; and the term "terabyte" (often abbreviated as T) means one-thousand twenty-four (1024) G. Memory is typically measured in kilobytes or megabytes, and disk space is typically measured in megabytes or gigabytes. Note that the multipliers here are 1024 instead of the more common 1000 as would be used in the metric system. This is to make it easier to work with the binary number system. Note also that some hardware manufacturers will use the smaller 1000 multiplier on M & G quantities to make

their disk drives seem larger than they really are; buyer beware.

bytecode
Sometimes computer languages that are said to be either interpreted or compiled are in fact neither and are more accurately said to be somewhere in between. Such languages are compiled into bytecode which is then interpreted on the target system. Bytecode tends to be binary but will work on any machine with the appropriate runtime environment (or virtual machine) for it.

C
C is one of the most popular computer languages in the world, and quite possibly *the* most popular. It is a compiled langauge widely supported on many platforms. It tends to be more portable than FORTRAN but less portable than Java; it has been standardized by ANSI as "ANSI C" -- older versions are called either "K&R C" or "Kernighan and Ritchie C" (in honor of C's creators), or sometimes just "classic C". Fast and simple, it can be applied to all manner of general purpose tasks. C compilers are made by several companies, but the free GNU version (gcc) is still considered one of the best. Newer C-like object-oriented languages include both Java and C++.

C#
C# is a compiled object-oriented language based heavily on C++ with some Java features.

C++
C++ is a compiled object-oriented language. Based heavily on C, C++ is nearly as fast and can often be thought of as being just C with added features. It is currently probably the second most popular object-oriented language, but it has the drawback of being fairly complex -- the much simpler but somewhat slower Java is probably the most popular object-oriented language. Note that C++ was developed independently of the somewhat similar Objective-C; it is however related to Objective-C++.

C64/128
The Commodore 64 computer to this day holds the record for being the most successful model of computer ever made with even the lowest estimates being in the tens of millions. Its big brother, the Commodore 128, was not quite as popular but still sold several million units. Both units sported ROM-based BASIC and used it as a default "OS". The C128 also came with CP/M (it was a not-often-exercized option on the C64). In their later days they were also packaged with GEOS. Both are based on 65xx family processors. They are still in use today and boast a friendly and surprisingly active user community. There is even a current effort to port Linux to the C64 and C128 machines.

CDE
The **c**ommon **d**esktop **e**nvironment is a popular commercial window manager (and much more -- as its name touts, it is more of a desktop environment) that runs under X-Windows. Free work-alike versions are also available.

chain
Some computer devices support chaining, the ability to string multiple devices in a sequence plugged into just one computer port. Often, but not always, such a chain will require some sort of terminator to mark the end. For an example, a SCSI scanner may be plugged into a SCSI CD-ROM drive that is plugged into a SCSI hard drive that is in turn plugged into the main computer. For all these components to work properly, the scanner would also have to have a proper terminator in use. Device chaining has been around a long time, and it is interesting to note that C64/128 serial devices supported it from the very beginning. Today the most common low-cost chainable devices in use support USB while the fastest low-cost chainable devices in use support FireWire.

character set
Since in reality all a computer can store are series of zeros and ones, representing common things like text takes a little work. The solution is to view the series of zeros and ones instead as

a sequence of bytes, and map each one to a particular letter, number, or symbol. The full mapping is called a character set. The most popular character set is commonly referred to as ASCII. The second most popular character set these days is Unicode (and it will probably eventually surpass ASCII). Other fairly common character sets include EBCDIC and PETSCII. They are generally quite different from one another; programs exist to convert between them on most platforms, though. Usually EBCDIC is only found on really old machines.

CISC
Complex instruction set computing is one of the two main types of processor design in use today. It is slowly losing popularity to RISC designs; currently all the fastest processors in the world are RISC. The most popular current CISC processor is the x86, but there are also still some 68xx, 65xx, and Z80s in use.

CLI
A command-line interface is a text-based means of communicating with a program, especially an OS. This is the sort of interface used by MS-DOS, or a UNIX shell window.

COBOL
The Common Business Oriented Language is a language developed back in 1959 and still used by some businesses. While it is relatively portable, it is still disliked by many professional programmers simply because COBOL programs tend to be physically longer than equivalent programs written in almost any other language in common use.

compiled
If a program is compiled, its original human-readable source has been converted into a form more easily used by a computer prior to it being run. Such programs will generally run more quickly than interpreted programs, because time was pre-spent in the compilation phase. A program that compiles other programs is called a compiler.

compression
It is often possible to remove redundant information or capitalize on patterns in data to make a file smaller. Usually when a file has been compressed, it cannot be used until it is uncompressed. Image files are common exceptions, though, as many popular image file formats have compression built-in.

cookie
A cookie is a small file that a web page on another machine writes to your personal machine's disk to store various bits of information. Many people strongly detest cookies and the whole idea of them, and most browsers allow the reception of cookies to be disabled or at least selectively disabled, but it should be noted that both Netscape and MSIE have silent cookie reception enabled by default. Sites that maintain shopping carts or remember a reader's last position have legitimate uses for cookies. Sites without such functionality that still spew cookies with distant (or worse, non-existent) expiration dates should perhaps be treated with a little caution.

CP/M
An early DOS for desktops, CP/M runs on both Z80 and the x86 based machines. CP/M provides only a CLI and there really is not any standard way to get a window manager to run on top of it. It is fairly complex and tricky to use. In spite of all this, CP/M was once the most popular DOS and is still in use today.

crash
If a bug in a program is severe enough, it can cause that program to crash, or to become inoperable without being restarted. On machines that are not multitasking, the entire machine will crash and have to be rebooted. On machines that are only partially multitasking the entire machine will sometimes crash and have to be rebooted. On machines that are fully multitasking, the machine should never crash and require a reboot.

Cray
A Cray is a high-end computer used for research and frequently heavy-duty graphics applications. Modern Crays typically have Solaris for their OS and sport sixty-four RISC

processors; older ones had various other configurations. Current top-of-the-line Crays can have over 2000 processors.

crippleware
Crippleware is a variant of shareware that will either self-destruct after its trial period or has built-in limitations to its functionality that get removed after its purchase.

CSS
Cascading style sheets are used in conjunction with HTML and XHTML to define the layout of web pages. While CSS is how current web pages declare how they should be displayed, it tends not to be supported well (if at all) by ancient browsers. XSL performs this same function more generally.

desktop publisher
A program for creating newspapers, magazines, books, etc. Some common desktop publishing programs include FrameMaker, PageMaker, InDesign, and GeoPublish.

DHTML
Dynamic HTML is simply the combined use of both CSS and JavaScript together in the same document; a more extreme form is called AJaX. Note that DHTML is quite different from the similarly named DTML.

dict
A protocol used for looking up definitions across a network (in particular the Internet).

digital camera
A digital camera looks and behaves like a regular camera, except instead of using film, it stores the image it sees in memory as a file for later transfer to a computer. Many digital cameras offer additional storage besides their own internal memory; a few sport some sort of disk but the majority utilize some sort of flash card. Digital cameras currently lack the resolution and color palette of real cameras, but are usually much more convenient for computer applications. Another related device is called a scanner.

DIMM
A physical component used to add RAM to a computer. Similar to, but incompatible with, SIMMs.

DNS
Domain name service is the means by which a name (like www.saugus.net or ftp.saugus.net) gets converted into a real Internet address that points to a particular machine.

DoS
In a denial of service attack, many individual (usually compromised) computers are used to try and simultaneously access the same public resource with the intent of overburdening it so that it will not be able to adequately serve its normal users.

DOS
A disk operating system manages disks and other system resources. Sort of a subset of OSes, sort of an archaic term for the same. MS-DOS is the most popular program currently calling itself a DOS. CP/M was the most popular prior to MS-DOS.

download
To download a file is to copy it from a remote computer to your own. The opposite is upload.

DR-DOS
The DOS currently produced by Caldera (originally produced by Design Research as a successor to CP/M) designed to work like MS-DOS. While similar to CP/M in many ways, it utilizes simpler commands. It provides only a CLI, but either Windows 3.1 or GEOS may be run on top of it to provide a GUI. It only runs on x86 based machines.

driver
A driver is a piece of software that works with the OS to control a particular piece of hardware, like a printer or a scanner or a mouse or whatever.

DRM

Depending upon whom you ask, DRM can stand for either Digital Rights Management or Digital Restrictions Management. In either case, DRM is used to place restrictions upon the usage of digital media ranging from software to music to video.

DTML

The **D**ocument **T**emplate **M**ark-up **L**anguage is a subset of SGML and a superset of HTML used for creating documents that dynamically adapt to external conditions using its own custom tags and a little bit of Python. Note that it is quite different from the similarly named DHTML.

EDBIC

The EDBIC character set is similar to (but less popular than) the ASCII character set in concept, but is significantly different in layout. It tends to be found only on old machines..

emacs

Emacs is both one of the most powerful and one of the most popular text editing programs in existence. Versions can be found for most platforms, and in fact multiple companies make versions, so for a given platform there might even be a choice. There is even a free GNU version available. The drawback with emacs is that it is not in the least bit lightweight. In fact, it goes so far in the other direction that even its advocates will occasionally joke about it. It is however extremely capable. Almost anything that one would need to relating to text can be done with emacs and is probably built-in. Even if one manages to find something that emacs was not built to do, emacs has a built-in Lisp interpreter capable of not only extending its text editing capabilities, but even of being used as a scripting language in its own right.

embedded

An embedded system is a computer that lives inside another device and acts as a component of that device. For example, current cars have an embedded computer under the hood that helps regulate much of their day to day operation.

An embedded file is a file that lives inside another and acts as a portion of that file. This is frequently seen with HTML files having embedded audio files; audio files often embedded in HTML include AU files, MIDI files, SID files, WAV files, AIFF files, and MOD files. Most browsers will ignore these files unless an appropriate plug-in is present.

emulator

An emulator is a program that allows one computer platform to mimic another for the purposes of running its software. Typically (but not always) running a program through an emulator will not be quite as pleasant an experience as running it on the real system.

endian

A processor will be either "big endian" or "little endian" based upon the manner in which it encodes multiple byte values. There is no difference in performance between the two encoding methods, but it is one of the sources of difficulty when reading binary data on different platforms.

environment

An environment (sometimes also called a runtime environment) is a collection of external variable items or parameters that a program can access when run. Information about the computer's hardware and the user can often be found in the environment.

EPOC

EPOC is a lightweight OS. It is most commonly found on the Psion PDA.

extension

Filename extensions originate back in the days of CP/M and basically allow a very rough grouping of different file types by putting a tag at the end of the name. To further complicate matters, the tag is sometimes separated by the name proper by a period "." and sometimes by a tab. While extensions are semi-enforced on CP/M, MS-DOS, and MS-Windows, they have no real meaning aside from convention on other platforms and are only optional.

FAQ

A **f**requently **a**sked **q**uestions file attempts to provide answers for all commonly asked questions related to a given topic.

FireWire
An incredibly fast type of serial port that offers many of the best features of SCSI at a lower price. Faster than most types of parallel port, a single FireWire port is capable of chaining many devices without the need of a terminator. FireWire is similar in many respects to USB but is significantly faster and somewhat more expensive. It is heavily used for connecting audio/video devices to computers, but is also used for connecting storage devices like drives and other assorted devices like printers and scanners.

fixed width
As applied to a font, fixed width means that every character takes up the same amount of space. That is, an "i" will be just as wide as an "m" with empty space being used for padding. The opposite is variable width. The most common fixed width font is Courier.

flash
Flash memory is similar to RAM. It has one significant advantage: it does not lose its contents when power is lost; it has two main disadvantages: it is slower, and it eventually wears out. Flash memory is frequently found in PCMCIA cards.

font
In a simplistic sense, a font can be thought of as the physical description of a character set. While the character set will define what sets of bits map to what letters, numbers, and other symbols, the font will define what each letter, number, and other symbol looks like. Fonts can be either fixed width or variable width and independently, either bitmapped or vectored. The size of the large characters in a font is typically measured in points.

Forth
A language developed in 1970 by Moore. Forth is fairly portable and has versions on many different platforms. While it is no longer an very popular language, many of its ideas and concepts have been carried into other computer programs. In particular, some programs for doing heavy-duty mathematical and engineering work use Forth-like interfaces.

FORTRAN
FORTRAN stands for **for**mula **tran**slation and is the oldest computer language in the world. It is typically compiled and is quite fast. Its primary drawbacks are portability and ease-of-use -- often different FORTRAN compilers on different platforms behave quite differently in spite of standardization efforts in 1966 (FORTRAN 66 or FORTRAN IV), 1978 (FORTRAN 77), and 1991 (FORTRAN 90). Today languages like C and Java are more popular, but FORTRAN is still heavily used in military software. It is somewhat amusing to note that when FORTRAN was first released back in 1958 its advocates thought that it would mean the end of software bugs. In truth of course by making the creation of more complex software practical, computer languages have merely created new types of software bugs.

FreeBSD
A free variant of Berkeley UNIX available for Alpha and x86 based machines. It is not as popular as Linux.

freeware
Freeware is software that is available for free with no strings attached. The quality is often superb as the authors are also generally users.

FTP
The **f**ile **t**ransfer **p**rotocol is one of the most commonly used methods of copying files across the Internet. It has its origins on UNIX machines, but has been adapted to almost every type of computer in existence and is built into many browsers. Most FTP programs have two modes of operation, ASCII, and binary. Transmitting an ASCII file via the ASCII mode of operation is more efficient and cleaner. Transmitting a binary file via the ASCII mode of operation will result in a broken binary file. Thus the FTP programs that do not support both modes of operation will typically only do the binary mode, as binary transfers are capable of transferring both kinds of

data without corruption.
gateway
A gateway connects otherwise separate computer networks.
GEOS
The **g**raphic **e**nvironment **o**perating **s**ystem is a lightweight OS with a GUI. It runs on several different processors, including the 65xx (different versions for different machines -- there are versions for the C64, the C128, and the Apple][, each utilizing the relevant custom chip sets), the x86 (although the x86 version is made to run on top of MS-DOS (or PC-DOS or DR-DOS) and is not strictly a full OS or a window manager, rather it is somewhat in between, like Windows 3.1) and numerous different PDAs, embedded devices, and hand-held machines. It was originally designed by Berkeley Softworks (no real relation to the Berkeley of UNIX fame) but is currently in a more interesting state: the company GeoWorks develops and promotes development of GEOS for hand-held devices, PDAs, & and embedded devices and owns (but has ceased further development on) the x86 version. The other versions are owned (and possibly still being developed) by the company CMD.
GHz & gigahertz
One gigahertz is equivalent to 1000 megahertz, or 1,000,000,000 hertz.
Glulx
A virtual machine optimized for running interactive fiction, interactive tutorials, and other interactive things of a primarily textual nature. Glulx has been ported to several platforms, and in in many ways an upgrade to the Z-machine.
GNOME
The **G**NU **n**etwork **o**bject **m**odel **e**nvironment is a popular free window manager (and much more -- as its name touts, it is more of a desktop environment) that runs under X-Windows. It is a part of the GNU project.
GNU
GNU stands for GNU's not UNIX and is thus a recursive acronym (and unlike the animal name, the "G" here is pronounced). At any rate, the GNU project is an effort by the Free Software Foundation (FSF) to make all of the traditional UNIX utilities free for whoever wants them. The Free Software Foundation programmers know their stuff, and the quality of the GNU software is on par with the best produced commercially, and often better. All of the GNU software can be downloaded for free or obtained on CD-ROM for a small service fee. Documentation for all GNU software can be downloaded for free or obtained in book form for a small service fee. The Free Software Foundation pays its bills from the collection of service fees and the sale of T-shirts, and exists mostly through volunteer effort. It is based in Cambridge, MA.
gopher
Though not as popular as FTP or http, the gopher protocol is implemented by many browsers and numerous other programs and allows the transfer of files across networks. In some respects it can be thought of as a hybrid between FTP and http, although it tends not to be as good at raw file transfer as FTP and is not as flexible as http. The collection of documents available through gopher is often called "gopherspace", and it should be noted that gopherspace is older than the web. It should also be noted that gopher is not getting as much attention as it once did, and surfing through gopherspace is a little like exploring a ghost town, but there is an interesting VR interface available for it, and some things in gopherspace still have not been copied onto the web.
GUI
A **g**raphical **u**ser **i**nterface is a graphics-based means of communicating with a program, especially an OS or window manager. In fact, a window manager can be thought of as a GUI for a CLI OS.
HP-UX
HP-UX is the version of UNIX designed by Hewlett-Packard to work with their PA-RISC and

68xx based machines.

HTML
The **H**ypertext **M**ark-up **L**anguage is the language currently most frequently used to express web pages (although it is rapidly being replaced by XHTML). Every browser has the built-in ability to understand HTML. Some browsers can additionally understand Java and browse FTP areas. HTML is a proper subset of SGML.

http
The **h**ypertext **t**ransfer **p**rotocol is the native protocol of browsers and is most typically used to transfer HTML formatted files. The secure version is called "https".

Hurd
The Hurd is the official GNU OS. It is still in development and is not yet supported on too many different processors, but promises to be the most powerful OS available. It (like all the GNU software) is free.

Hz & hertz
Hertz means cycles per second, and makes no assumptions about what is cycling. So, for example, if a fluorescent light flickers once per jiffy, it has a 60 Hz flicker. More typical for computers would be a program that runs once per jiffy and thus has a 60 Hz frequency, or larger units of hertz like kHz, MHz, GHz, or THz.

i18n
Commonly used to abbreviate the word "internationalization". There are eighteen letters between the "i" and the "n". Similar to (and often used along with) i18n.

iCalendar
The iCalendar standard refers to the format used to store calendar type information (including events, to-do items, and journal entries) on the Internet. iCalendar data can be found on some World-Wide-Web pages or attached to e-mail messages.

icon
A small graphical display representing an object, action, or modifier of some sort.

IDE
Loosely speaking, a disk format sometimes used by MS-Windows, Mac OS, AmigaOS, and (rarely) UNIX. EIDE is enhanced IDE; it is much faster. Generally IDE is inferior (but less expensive) to SCSI, but it varies somewhat with system load and the individual IDE and SCSI components themselves. The quick rundown is that: SCSI-I and SCSI-II will almost always outperform IDE; EIDE will almost always outperform SCSI-I and SCSI-II; SCSI-III and UltraSCSI will almost always outperform EIDE; and heavy system loads give an advantage to SCSI. Note that although loosely speaking it is just a format difference, it is deep down a hardware difference.

Inform
A compiled, object-oriented language optimized for creating interactive fiction.

infrared communications
A device with an infrared port can communicate with other devices at a distance by beaming infrared light signals. Two incompatible protocols are used for infrared communications: IrDA and ASK. Many devices support both.

Instant Messenger
AOL's Instant Messenger is is a means of chatting over the Internet in real-time. It allows both open group discussions and private conversations. Instant Messenger uses a different, proprietary protocol from the more standard IRC, and is not supported on as many platforms.

interactive fiction
Interactive fiction (often abbreviated "IF" or "I-F") is a form of literature unique to the computer. While the reader cannot influence the direction of a typical story, the reader plays a more active role in an interactive fiction story and completely controls its direction. Interactive fiction works come in all the sizes and genres available to standard fiction, and in fact are not always even

fiction per se (interactive tutorials exist and are slowly becoming more common).
interpreted
If a program is interpreted, its actual human-readable source is read as it is run by the computer. This is generally a slower process than if the program being run has already been compiled.
intranet
An intranet is a private network. There are many intranets scattered all over the world. Some are connected to the Internet via gateways.
IP
IP is the family of protocols that makes up the Internet. The two most common flavors are TCP/IP and UDP/IP.
IRC
Internet relay chat is a means of chatting over the Internet in real-time. It allows both open group discussions and private conversations. IRC programs are provided by many different companies and will work on many different platforms. AOL's Instant Messenger utilizes a separate incompatible protocol but is otherwise very similar.
IrDA
The Infrared Data Association (IrDA) is a voluntary organization of various manufacturers working together to ensure that the infrared communications between different computers, PDAs, printers, digital cameras, remote controls, etc. are all compatible with each other regardless of brand. The term is also often used to designate an IrDA compliant infrared communications port on a device. Informally, a device able to communicate via IrDA compliant infrared is sometimes simply said to "have IrDA". There is also an earlier, incompatible, and usually slower type of infrared communications still in use called ASK.
IRI
An Internationalized Resource Identifier is just a URI with i18n.
IRIX
The variant of UNIX designed by Silicon Graphics, Inc. IRIX machines are known for their graphics capabilities and were initially optimized for multimedia applications.
ISDN
An integrated service digital network line can be simply looked at as a digital phone line. ISDN connections to the Internet can be four times faster than the fastest regular phone connection, and because it is a digital connection a modem is not needed. Any computer hooked up to ISDN will typically require other special equipment in lieu of the modem, however. Also, both phone companies and ISPs charge more for ISDN connections than regular modem connections.
ISP
An Internet service provider is a company that provides Internet support for other entities. AOL (America Online) is a well-known ISP.
Java
A computer language designed to be both fairly lightweight and extremely portable. It is tightly bound to the web as it is the primary language for web applets. There has also been an OS based on Java for use on small hand-held, embedded, and network computers. It is called JavaOS. Java can be either interpreted or compiled. For web applet use it is almost always interpreted. While its interpreted form tends not to be very fast, its compiled form can often rival languages like C++ for speed. It is important to note however that speed is not Java's primary purpose -- raw speed is considered secondary to portabilty and ease of use.
JavaScript
JavaScript (in spite of its name) has nothing whatsoever to do with Java (in fact, it's arguably more like Newton Script than Java). JavaScript is an interpreted language built into a browser to provide a relatively simple means of adding interactivity to web pages. It is only supported on a few different browsers, and tends not to work exactly the same on different versions. Thus its

use on the Internet is somewhat restricted to fairly simple programs. On intranets where there are usually fewer browser versions in use, JavaScript has been used to implement much more complex and impressive programs.

jiffy
A jiffy is 1/60 of a second. Jiffies are to seconds as seconds are to minutes.

joystick
A joystick is a physical device typically used to control objects on a computer screen. It is frequently used for games and sometimes used in place of a mouse.

JSON
The JSON is used for data interchange between programs, an area in which the ubiquitous XML is not too well-suited. JSON is lightweight and works extremely cleanly with languages languages including JavaScript, Python, Java, C++, and many others.

JSON-RPC
JSON-RPC is like XML-RPC but is significantly more lightweight since it uses JSON in lieu of XML.

KDE
The **K** **d**esktop **e**nvironment is a popular free window manager (and much more -- as its name touts, it is more of a desktop environment) that runs under X-Windows.

Kerberos
Kerberos is a network authentication protocol. Basically it preserves the integrity of passwords in any untrusted network (like the Internet). Kerberized applications work hand-in-hand with sites that support Kerberos to ensure that passwords cannot be stolen.

kernel
The very heart of an OS is often called its kernel. It will usually (at minimum) provide some libraries that give programmers access to its various features.

kHz & kilohertz
One kilohertz is equivalent to 1000 hertz. Some older computers have clock speeds measured in kHz.

l10n
Commonly used to abbreviate the word "localization". There are ten letters between the "l" and the "n". Similar to (and often used along with) i18n.

LDAP
The **L**ightweight **D**irectory **A**ccess **P**rotocol provides a means of sharing address book type of information across an intranet or even across the Internet. Note too that "address book type of information" here is pretty broad; it often includes not just human addresses, but machine addresses, printer configurations, and similar.

library
A selection of routines used by programmers to make computers do particular things.

lightweight
Something that is lightweight will not consume computer resources (such as RAM and disk space) too much and will thus run on less expensive computer systems.

Linux
Believe it or not, one of the fastest, most robust, and powerful multitasking OSes is available for free. Linux can be downloaded for free or be purchased on CD-ROM for a small service charge. A handful of companies distribute Linux including Red Hat, Debian, Caldera, and many others. Linux is also possibly available for more hardware combinations than any other OS (with the possible exception of NetBSD. Supported processors include: Alpha, PowerPC, SPARC, x86, and 68xx. Most processors currently not supported are currently works-in-progress or even available in beta. For example, work is currently underway to provide support for PA-RISC, 65xx, StrongARM, and Z80. People have even successfully gotten Linux working on PDAs. As you may have guessed, Linux can be made quite lightweight. Linux is a variant of UNIX and as

such, most of the traditional UNIX software will run on Linux. This especially includes the GNU software, most of which comes with the majority of Linux distributions. Fast, reliable, stable, and inexpensive, Linux is popular with ISPs, software developers, and home hobbyists alike.

Lisp

Lisp stands for **list processing** and is the second oldest computer language in the world. Being developed in 1959, it lost the title to FORTRAN by only a few months. It is typically interpreted, but compilers are available for some platforms. Attempts were made to standardize the language, and the standard version is called "Common Lisp". There have also been efforts to simplify the language, and the results of these efforts is another language called Scheme. Lisp is a fairly portable language, but is not particularly fast. Today, Lisp is most widely used with AI software.

load

There are two popular meanings for load. The first means to fetch some data or a program from a disk and store it in memory. The second indicates the amount of work a component (especially a processor) is being made to do.

Logo

Logo is an interpreted language designed by Papert in 1966 to be a tool for helping people (especially kids) learn computer programming concepts. In addition to being used for that purpose, it is often used as a language for controlling mechanical robots and other similar devices. Logo interfaces even exist for building block / toy robot sets. Logo uses a special graphics cursor called "the turtle", and Logo is itself sometimes called "Turtle Graphics". Logo is quite portable but not particularly fast. Versions can be found on almost every computer platform in the world. Additionally, some other languages (notably some Pascal versions) provide Logo-like interfaces for graphics-intensive programming.

lossy

If a process is lossy, it means that a little quality is lost when it is performed. If a format is lossy, it means that putting data into that format (or possibly even manipulating it in that format) will cause some slight loss. Lossy processes and formats are typically used for performance or resource utilization reasons. The opposite of lossy is lossless.

Lua

Lua is a simple interpreted language. It is extremely portable, and free versions exist for most platforms.

Mac OS

Mac OS is the OS used on Macintosh computers. There are two distinctively different versions of it; everything prior to version 10 (sometimes called Mac OS Classic) and everything version 10 or later (called Mac OS X).

Mac OS Classic

The OS created by Apple and originally used by Macs is frequently (albeit slightly incorrectly) referred to as Mac OS Classic (officially Mac OS Classic is this original OS running under the modern Mac OS X in emulation. Mac OS combines the functionality of both an OS and a window manager and is often considered to be the easiest OS to use. It is partially multitasking but will still sometimes crash when dealing with a buggy program. It is probably the second most popular OS, next only to Windows 'XP (although it is quickly losing ground to Mac OS X) and has excellent driver support and boasts a fair selection of games. Mac OS will run on PowerPC and 68xx based machines.

Mac OS X

Mac OS X (originally called Rhapsody) is the industrial strength OS produced by Apple to run on both PowerPC and x86 systems (replacing what is often referred to as Mac OS Classic. Mac OS X is at its heart a variant of UNIX and possesses its underlying power (and the ability to run many of the traditional UNIX tools, including the GNU tools). It also was designed to mimic other OSes on demand via what it originally refered to as "boxes" (actually high-performance emulators); it has the built-in capability to run programs written for older Mac OS (via its "BlueBox", officially called Mac OS Classic) and work was started on making it also run Windows '95 / '98 / ME software (via what was called its "YellowBox"). There are also a few rumors going around that future versions may even be able to run Newton software (via the "GreenBox"). It provides a selection of two window managers built-in: Aqua and X-Windows (with Aqua being the default).

machine language
Machine language consists of the raw numbers that can be directly understood by a particular processor. Each processor's machine language will be different from other processors' machine language. Although called "machine language", it is not usually what people think of when talking about computer languages. Machine language dressed up with mnemonics to make it a bit more human-readable is called assembly language.

Macintosh
A Macintosh (or a Mac for short) is a computer system that has Mac OS for its OS. There are a few different companies that have produced Macs, but by far the largest is Apple. The oldest Macs are based on the 68xx processor; somewhat more recent Macs on the PowerPC processor, and current Macs on the x86 processor. The Macintosh was really the first general purpose computer to employ a GUI.

MacTel
An x86 based system running some flavor of Mac OS.

mainframe
A mainframe is any computer larger than a small piece of furniture. A modern mainframe is more powerful than a modern workstation, but more expensive and more difficult to maintain.

MathML
The **Math M**ark-up **L**anguage is a subset of XML used to represent mathematical formulae and equations. Typically it is found embedded within XHTML documents, although as of this writing not all popular browsers support it.

megahertz
A million cycles per second, abbreviated MHz. This is often used misleadingly to indicate processor speed, because while one might expect that a higher number would indicate a faster processor, that logic only holds true within a given type of processors as different types of processors are capable of doing different amounts of work within a cycle. For a current example, either a 200 MHz PowerPC or a 270 MHz SPARC will outperform a 300 MHz Pentium.

Merced
The Merced is a RISC processor developed by Intel with help from Hewlett-Packard and possibly Sun. It is just starting to be released, but is intended to eventually replace both the x86 and PA-RISC processors. Curiously, HP is recommending that everyone hold off using the first release and instead wait for the second one. It is expected some day to be roughly as fast as an Alpha or PowerPC. It is expected to be supported by future versions of Solaris, Windows-NT, HP-UX, Mac OS X, and Linux. The current semi-available Merced processor is called the Itanium. Its overall schedule is way behind, and some analysts predict that it never will really be released in significant quanitities.

MFM
Loosely speaking, An old disk format sometimes used by CP/M, MS-DOS, and MS-Windows. No longer too common as it cannot deliver close to the performance of either SCSI or IDE.

middleware
Software designed to sit in between an OS and applications. Common examples are Java and Tcl/Tk.

MIME
The **m**ulti-purpose **I**nternet **m**ail **e**xtensions specification describes a means of sending non-

ASCII data (such as images, sounds, foreign symbols, etc.) through e-mail. It commonly utilizes bcode.
MMX
Multi**m**edia e**x**tensions were built into some x86 CPUs to provide better performance for certain operations, most notably graphics and sound. It is similar to AltiVec on the PowerPC CPUs. Like AltiVec, it requires special software for full performance benefits to be realized.
MOB
A **mo**vable **ob**ject is a graphical object that is manipulated separately from the background. These are seen all the time in computer games. When implemented in hardware, MOBs are sometimes called sprites.
Modula-2 & Modula-3
Modula-2 is a procedural language based on Pascal by its original author in around the 1977 - 1979 time period. Modula-3 is an intended successor that adds support for object-oriented constructs (among other things). Modula-2 can be either compiled or interpreted, while Modula-3 tends to be just a compiled language.
MOTD
A **m**essage **o**f **t**he **d**ay. Many computers (particularly more capable ones) are configured to display a MOTD when accessed remotely.
Motif
Motif is a popular commercial window manager that runs under X-Windows. Free work-alike versions are also available.
MS-DOS
The DOS produced by Microsoft. Early versions of it bear striking similarities to the earlier CP/M, but it utilizes simpler commands. It provides only a CLI, but either OS/2, Windows 3.1, Windows '95, Windows '98, Windows ME, or GEOS may be run on top of it to provide a GUI. It only runs on x86 based machines.
MS-Windows
MS-Windows is the name collectively given to several somewhat incompatible OSes all produced by Microsoft. They are: Windows CE, Windows NT, Windows 3.1, Windows '95, Windows '98, Windows ME, Windows 2000, and Windows XP.
MUD
A **m**ulti-**u**ser **d**imension (also sometimes called multi-user dungeon, but in either case abbreviated to "MUD") is sort of a combination between the online chatting abilities provided by something like IRC and a role-playing game. A MUD built with object oriented principles in mind is called a "Multi-user dimension object-oriented", or MOO. Yet another variant is called a "multi-user shell", or MUSH. Still other variants are called multi-user role-playing environments (MURPE) and multi-user environments (MUSE). There are probably more. In all cases the differences will be mostly academic to the regular user, as the same software is used to connect to all of them. Software to connect to MUDs can be found for most platforms, and there are even Java based ones that can run from within a browser.
multitasking
Some OSes have built into them the ability to do several things at once. This is called multitasking, and has been in use since the late sixties / early seventies. Since this ability is built into the software, the overall system will be slower running two things at once than it will be running just one thing. A system may have more than one processor built into it though, and such a system will be capable of running multiple things at once with less of a performance hit.
nagware
Nagware is a variant of shareware that will frequently remind its users to register.
NetBSD
A free variant of Berkeley UNIX available for Alpha, x86, 68xx, PA-RISC, SPARC, PowerPC, ARM, and many other types of machines. Its emphasis is on portability.

netiquette
The established conventions of online politeness are called netiquette. Some conventions vary from site to site or online medium to online medium; others are pretty standard everywhere. Newbies are often unfamiliar with the conventional rules of netiquette and sometimes embarrass themselves accordingly. Be sure not to send that incredibly important e-mail message before reading about netiquette.

newbie
A newbie is a novice to the online world or computers in general.

news
Usenet news can generally be thought of as public e-mail as that is generally the way it behaves. In reality, it is implemented by different software and is often accessed by different programs. Different newsgroups adhere to different topics, and some are "moderated", meaning that humans will try to manually remove off-topic posts, especially spam. Most established newsgroups have a FAQ, and people are strongly encouraged to read the FAQ prior to posting.

Newton
Although Newton is officially the name of the lightweight OS developed by Apple to run on its MessagePad line of PDAs, it is often used to mean the MessagePads (and compatible PDAs) themselves and thus the term "Newton OS" is often used for clarity. The Newton OS is remarkably powerful; it is fully multitasking in spite of the fact that it was designed for small machines. It is optimized for hand-held use, but will readily transfer data to all manner of desktop machines. Historically it was the first PDA. Recently Apple announced that it will discontinue further development of the Newton platform, but will instead work to base future hand-held devices on either Mac OS or Mac OS X with some effort dedicated to making the new devices capable of running current Newton programs.

Newton book
Newton books provide all the functionality of ordinary books but add searching and hypertext capabilities. The format was invented for the Newton to provide a means of making volumes of data portable, and is particularly popular in the medical community as most medical references are available as Newton books and carrying around a one pound Newton is preferable to carrying around twenty pounds of books, especially when it comes to looking up something. In addition to medical books, numerous references, most of the classics, and many contemporary works of fiction are available as Newton books. Most fiction is available for free, most references cost money. Newton books are somewhat more capable than the similar Palm DOC; both are specific types of e-books.

Newton Script
A intepreted, object-oriented language for Newton MessagePad computers.

nybble
A nybble is half a byte, or four bits. It is a case of computer whimsy; it only stands to reason that a small byte should be called a nybble. Some authors spell it with an "i" instead of the "y", but the "y" is the original form.

object-oriented
While the specifics are well beyond the scope of this document, the term "object-oriented" applies to a philosophy of software creation. Often this philosophy is referred to as object-oriented design (sometimes abbreviated as OOD), and programs written with it in mind are referred to as object-oriented programs (often abbreviated OOP). Programming languages designed to help facilitate it are called object-oriented languages (sometimes abbreviated as OOL) and databases built with it in mind are called object-oriented databases (sometimes abbreviated as OODB or less fortunately OOD). The general notion is that an object-oriented approach to creating software starts with modeling the real-world problems trying to be solved in familiar real-world ways, and carries the analogy all the way down to structure of the program. This is of course a great over-simplification. Numerous object-oriented programming languages

exist including: Java, C++, Modula-2, Newton Script, and ADA.
Objective-C & ObjC
Objective-C (often called "ObjC" for short) is a compiled object-oriented language. Based heavily on C, Objective-C is nearly as fast and can often be thought of as being just C with added features. Note that it was developed independently of C++; its object-oriented extensions are more in the style of Smalltalk. It is however related to Objective-C++.
Objective-C++ & ObjC++
Objective-C++ (often called "ObjC++" for short) is a curious hybrid of Objective-C and C++, allowing the syntax of both to coexist in the same source files.
office suite
An office suite is a collection of programs including at minimum a word processor, spreadsheet, drawing program, and minimal database program. Some common office suites include MS-Office, AppleWorks, ClarisWorks, GeoWorks, Applixware, Corel Office, and StarOffice.
open source
Open source software goes one step beyond freeware. Not only does it provide the software for free, it provides the original source code used to create the software. Thus, curious users can poke around with it to see how it works, and advanced users can modify it to make it work better for them. By its nature, open souce software is pretty well immune to all types of computer virus.
OpenBSD
A free variant of Berkeley UNIX available for Alpha, x86, 68xx, PA-RISC, SPARC, and PowerPC based machines. Its emphasis is on security.
OpenDocument & ODF
OpenDocument (or ODF for short) is the suite of open, XML-based office suite application formats defined by the OASIS consortium. It defines a platform-neutral, non-proprietary way of storing documents.
OpenGL
A low-level 3D graphics library with an emphasis on speed developed by SGI.
OS/2
OS/2 is the OS designed by IBM to run on x86 based machines. It is semi-compatible with MS-Windows. IBM's more industrial strength OS is called AIX.
PA-RISC
The PA-RISC is a RISC processor developed by Hewlett-Packard. It is currently produced only by HP. At the moment only one OS runs on PA-RISC based machines: HP-UX. There is an effort underway to port Linux to them, though.
Palm DOC
Palm DOC files are quite similar to (but slightly less capable than) Newton books. They were designed for Palm Pilots but can now be read on a couple other platforms, too. They are a specific type of e-book.
Palm Pilot
The Palm Pilot (also called both just Palm and just Pilot, officially now just Palm) is the most popular PDA currently in use. It is one of the least capable PDAs, but it is also one of the smallest and least expensive. While not as full featured as many of the other PDAs (such as the Newton) it performs what features it does have quite well and still remains truly pocket-sized.
parallel
Loosely speaking, parallel implies a situation where multiple things can be done simultaneously, like having multiple check-out lines each serving people all at once. Parallel connections are by their nature more expensive than serial ones, but usually faster. Also, in a related use of the word, often multitasking computers are said to be capable of running multiple programs in parallel.
partition
Sometimes due to hardware limitations, disks have to be divided into smaller pieces. These

pieces are called partitions.
Pascal
Named after the mathematician Blaise Pascal, Pascal is a language designed by Niklaus Wirth originally in 1968 (and heavily revised in 1972) mostly for purposes of education and training people how to write computer programs. It is a typically compiled language but is still usually slower than C or FORTRAN. Wirth also created a more powerful object-oriented Pascal-like language called Modula-2.
PC-DOS
The DOS produced by IBM designed to work like MS-DOS. Early versions of it bear striking similarities to the earlier CP/M, but it utilizes simpler commands. It provides only a CLI, but either Windows 3.1 or GEOS may be run on top of it to provide a GUI. It only runs on x86 based machines.
PCMCIA
The **P**ersonal **C**omputer **M**emory **C**ard **I**nternational **A**ssociation is a standards body that concern themselves with PC Card technology. Often the PC Cards themselves are referred to as "PCMCIA cards". Frequently flash memory can be found in PC card form.
Perl
Perl is an interpreted language extremely popular for web applications.
PET
The Commodore PET (**P**ersonal **E**lectronic **T**ransactor) is an early (circa 1977-1980, around the same time as the Apple][) home computer featuring a ROM-based BASIC developed by Microsoft which it uses as a default "OS". It is based on the 65xx family of processors and is the precursor to the VIC-20.
PETSCII
The PETSCII character set gets its name from "**PET ASCII**; it is a variant of the ASCII character set originally developed for the Commodore PET that swaps the upper and lower case characters and adds over a hundred graphic characters in addition to other small changes. If you encounter some text that seems to have uppercase where lowercase is expected and vice-versa, it is probably a PETSCII file.
PHP
Named with a recursive acronym (PHP: Hypertext Preprocessor), PHP provides a means of creating web pages that dynamically modify themselves on the fly.
ping
Ping is a protocol designed to check across a network to see if a particular computer is "alive" or not. Computers that recognize the ping will report back their status. Computers that are down will not report back anything at all.
pixel
The smallest distinct point on a computer display is called a pixel.
plug-in
A plug-in is a piece of software designed not to run on its own but rather work in cooperation with a separate application to increase that application's abilities.
point
There are two common meanings for this word. The first is in the geometric sense; a position in space without size. Of course as applied to computers it must take up some space in practise (even if not in theory) and it is thus sometimes synonomous with pixel. The other meaning is related most typically to fonts and regards size. The exact meaning of it in this sense will unfortunately vary somewhat from person to person, but will often mean 1/72 of an inch. Even when it does not exactly mean 1/72 of an inch, larger point sizes always indicate larger fonts.
PowerPC
The PowerPC is a RISC processor developed in a collaborative effort between IBM, Apple, and Motorola. It is currently produced by a few different companies, of course including its original

developers. A few different OSes run on PowerPC based machines, including Mac OS, AIX, Solaris, Windows NT, Linux, Mac OS X, BeOS, and AmigaOS. At any given time, the fastest processor in the world is usually either a PowerPC or an Alpha, but sometimes SPARCs and PA-RISCs make the list, too.

proprietary
This simply means to be supplied by only one vendor. It is commonly misused. Currently, most processors are non-proprietary, some systems are non-proprietary, and every OS (except for arguably Linux) is proprietary.

protocol
A protocol is a means of communication used between computers. As long as both computers recognize the same protocol, they can communicate without too much difficulty over the same network or even via a simple direct modem connection regardless whether or not they are themselves of the same type. This means that WinTel boxes, Macs, Amigas, UNIX machines, etc., can all talk with one another provided they agree on a common protocol first.

Psion
The Psion is a fairly popular brand of PDA. Generally, it is in between a Palm and a Newton in capability. It runs the EPOC OS.

Python
Python is an interpreted, object-oriented language popular for Internet applications. It is extremely portable with free versions existing for virtually every platform.

queue
A queue is a waiting list of things to be processed. Many computers provide printing queues, for example. If something is being printed and the user requests that another item be printed, the second item will sit in the printer queue until the first item finishes printing at which point it will be removed from the queue and get printed itself.

QuickDraw
A high-level 3D graphics library with an emphasis on quick development time created by Apple.

RAM
Random access memory is the short-term memory of a computer. Any information stored in RAM will be lost if power goes out, but the computer can read from RAM far more quickly than from a drive.

random access
Also called "dynamic access" this indicates that data can be selected without having to skip over earlier data first. This is the way that a CD, record, laserdisc, or DVD will behave -- it is easy to selectively play a particular track without having to fast forward through earlier tracks. The other common behavior is called sequential access.

RDF
The Resource Description Framework is built upon an XML base and provides a more modern means of accessing data from Internet resources. It can provide metadata (including annotations) for web pages making (among other things) searching more capable. It is also being used to refashion some existing formats like RSS and iCalendar; in the former case it is already in place (at least for newer RSS versions), but it is still experimental in the latter case.

real-time
Something that happens in real-time will keep up with the events around it and never give any sort of "please wait" message.

Rexx
The Restructured Extended Executor is an interpreted language designed primarily to be embedded in other applications in order to make them consistently programmable, but also to be easy to learn and understand.

RISC
Reduced instruction set computing is one of the two main types of processor design in use

today, the other being CISC. The fastest processors in the world today are all RISC designs. There are several popular RISC processors, including Alphas, ARMs, PA-RISCs, PowerPCs, and SPARCs.

robot
A robot (or 'bot for short) in the computer sense is a program designed to automate some task, often just sending messages or collecting information. A spider is a type of robot designed to traverse the web performing some task (usually collecting data).

robust
The adjective robust is used to describe programs that are better designed, have fewer bugs, and are less likely to crash.

ROM
Read-only memory is similar to RAM only cannot be altered and does not lose its contents when power is removed.

RSS
RSS stands for either Rich Site Summary, Really Simple Syndication, or RDF Site Summary, depending upon whom you ask. The general idea is that it can provide brief summaries of articles that appear in full on a web site. It is well-formed XML, and newer versions are even more specifically well-formed RDF.

Ruby
Ruby is an interpreted, object-oriented language. Ruby was fairly heavily influenced by Perl, so people familiar with that language can typically transition to Ruby easily.

scanner
A scanner is a piece of hardware that will examine a picture and produce a computer file that represents what it sees. A digital camera is a related device. Each has its own limitations.

Scheme
Scheme is a typically interpreted computer language. It was created in 1975 in an attempt to make Lisp simpler and more consistent. Scheme is a fairly portable language, but is not particularly fast.

script
A script is a series of OS commands. The term "batch file" means much the same thing, but is a bit dated. Typically the same sort of situations in which one would say DOS instead of OS, it would also be appropriate to say batch file instead of script. Scripts can be run like programs, but tend to perform simpler tasks. When a script is run, it is always interpreted.

SCSI
Loosely speaking, a disk format sometimes used by MS-Windows, Mac OS, AmigaOS, and (almost always) UNIX. Generally SCSI is superior (but more expensive) to IDE, but it varies somewhat with system load and the individual SCSI and IDE components themselves. The quick rundown is that: SCSI-I and SCSI-II will almost always outperform IDE; EIDE will almost always outperform SCSI-I and SCSI-II; SCSI-III and UltraSCSI will almost always outperform EIDE; and heavy system loads give an advantage to SCSI. Note that although loosely speaking it is just a format difference, it is deep down a hardware difference.

sequential access
This indicates that data cannot be selected without having to skip over earlier data first. This is the way that a cassette or video tape will behave. The other common behavior is called random access.

serial
Loosely speaking, serial implies something that has to be done linearly, one at a time, like people being served in a single check-out line. Serial connections are by their nature less expensive than parallel connections (including things like SCSI) but are typically slower.

server
A server is a computer designed to provide various services for an entire network. It is typically

either a workstation or a mainframe because it will usually be expected to handle far greater loads than ordinary desktop systems. The load placed on servers also necessitates that they utilize robust OSes, as a crash on a system that is currently being used by many people is far worse than a crash on a system that is only being used by one person.

SGML
The **S**tandard **G**eneralized **M**ark-up **L**anguage provides an extremely generalized level of mark-up. More common mark-up languages like HTML and XML are actually just popular subsets of SGML.

shareware
Shareware is software made for profit that allows a trial period before purchase. Typically shareware can be freely downloaded, used for a period of weeks (or sometimes even months), and either purchased or discarded after it has been learned whether or not it will satisfy the user's needs.

shell
A CLI designed to simplify complex OS commands. Some OSes (like AmigaOS, the Hurd, and UNIX) have built-in support to make the concurrent use of multiple shells easy. Common shells include the Korn Shell (ksh), the Bourne Shell (sh or bsh), the Bourne-Again Shell, (bash or bsh), the C-Shell (csh), etc.

SIMM
A physical component used to add RAM to a computer. Similar to, but incompatible with, DIMMs.

Smalltalk
Smalltalk is an efficient language for writing computer programs. Historically it is one of the first object-oriented languages, and is not only used today in its pure form but shows its influence in other languages like Objective-C.

Solaris
Solaris is the commercial variant of UNIX currently produced by Sun. It is an industrial strength, nigh bulletproof, powerful multitasking OS that will run on SPARC, x86, and PowerPC based machines.

spam
Generally spam is unwanted, unrequested e-mail or Usenet news. It is typically sent out in bulk to huge address lists that were automatically generated by various robots endlessly searching the Internet and newsgroups for things that resemble e-mail addresses. The legality of spam is a topic of much debate; it is at best only borderline legal, and spammers have been successfully persecuted in some states.

SPARC
The SPARC is a RISC processor developed by Sun. The design was more or less released to the world, and it is currently produced by around a dozen different companies too numerous to even bother mentioning. It is worth noting that even computers made by Sun typically sport SPARCs made by other companies. A couple different OSes run on SPARC based machines, including Solaris, SunOS, and Linux. Some of the newer SPARC models are called UltraSPARCs.

sprite
The term sprite originally referred to a small MOB, usually implemented in hardware. Lately it is also being used to refer to a single image used piecemeal within a Web site in order to avoid incurring the time penalty of downloading multiple files.

SQL
SQL (pronounced **Sequel**) is an interpreted language specially designed for database access. It is supported by virtually every major modern database system.

Sugar
The window manager used by the OLPC XO. It is made to run on top of Linux.

SunOS
SunOS is the commercial variant of UNIX formerly produced (but still supported) by Sun.

SVG
Scalable **V**ector **G**raphics data is an XML file that is used to hold graphical data that can be resized without loss of quality. SVG data can be kept in its own file, or even embedded within a web page (although not all browsers are capable of displaying such data).

Tcl/Tk
The **T**ool **C**ommand **L**anguage is a portable interpreted computer language designed to be easy to use. Tk is a GUI toolkit for Tcl. Tcl is a fairly popular language for both integrating existing applications and for creating Web applets (note that applets written in Tcl are often called Tcklets). Tcl/Tk is available for free for most platforms, and plug-ins are available to enable many browsers to play Tcklets.

TCP/IP
TCP/IP is a protocol for computer networks. The Internet is largely built on top of TCP/IP (it is the more reliable of the two primary Internet Protocols -- TCP stands for **T**ransmission **C**ontrol **P**rotocol).

terminator
A terminator is a dedicated device used to mark the end of a device chain (as is most typically found with SCSI devices). If such a chain is not properly terminated, weird results can occur.

TEX
TEX (pronounced "tek") is a freely available, industrial strength typesetting program that can be run on many different platforms. These qualities make it exceptionally popular in schools, and frequently software developed at a university will have its documentation in TEX format. TEX is not limited to educational use, though; many professional books were typeset with TEX. TEX's primary drawback is that it can be quite difficult to set up initially.

THz & terahertz
One terahertz is equivalent to 1000 gigahertz.

TrackBack
TrackBacks essentially provide a means whereby different web sites can post messages to one another not just to inform each other about citations, but also to alert one another of related resources. Typically, a blog may display quotations from another blog through the use of TrackBacks.

UDP/IP
UDP/IP is a protocol for computer networks. It is the faster of the two primary **I**nternet **P**rotocols. UDP stands for **U**ser **D**atagram **P**rotocol.

Unicode
The Unicode character set is a superset of the ASCII character set with provisions made for handling international symbols and characters from other languages. Unicode is sixteen bit, so takes up roughly twice the space as simple ASCII, but is correspondingly more flexible.

UNIX
UNIX is a family of OSes, each being made by a different company or organization but all offering a very similar look and feel. It can not quite be considered non-proprietary, however, as the differences between different vendor's versions can be significant (it is still generally possible to switch from one vendor's UNIX to another without too much effort; today the differences between different UNIXes are similar to the differences between the different MS-Windows; historically there were two different UNIX camps, Berkeley / BSD and AT&T / System V, but the assorted vendors have worked together to minimize the differences). The free variant Linux is one of the closest things to a current, non-proprietary OS; its development is controlled by a non-profit organization and its distribution is provided by several companies. UNIX is powerful; it is fully multitasking and can do pretty much anything that any OS can do (look to the Hurd if you need a more powerful OS). With power comes complexity, however, and

UNIX tends not to be overly friendly to beginners (although those who think UNIX is difficult or cryptic apparently have not used CP/M). Window managers are available for UNIX (running under X-Windows) and once properly configured common operations will be almost as simple on a UNIX machine as on a Mac. Out of all the OSes in current use, UNIX has the greatest range of hardware support. It will run on machines built around many different processors. Lightweight versions of UNIX have been made to run on PDAs, and in the other direction, full featured versions make full advantage of all the resources on large, multi-processor machines. Some different UNIX versions include Solaris, Linux, IRIX, AIX, SunOS, FreeBSD, Digital UNIX, HP-UX, NetBSD, OpenBSD, etc.

upload
To upload a file is to copy it from your computer to a remote computer. The opposite is download.

UPS
An **u**ninterrupted **p**ower **s**upply uses heavy duty batteries to help smooth out its input power source.

URI
A **U**niform **R**esource **I**dentifier is basically just a unique address for almost any type of resource. It is similar to but more general than a URL; in fact, it may also be a URN.

URL
A **U**niform **R**esource **L**ocator is basically just an address for a file that can be given to a browser. It starts with a protocol type (such as http, ftp, or gopher) and is followed by a colon, machine name, and file name in UNIX style. Optionally an octothorpe character "#" and and arguments will follow the file name; this can be used to further define position within a page and perform a few other tricks. Similar to but less general than a URI.

URN
A **U**niform **R**esource **N**ame is basically just a unique address for almost any type of resource unlike a URL it will probably not resolve with a browser.

USB
A really fast type of serial port that offers many of the best features of SCSI without the price. Faster than many types of parallel port, a single USB port is capable of chaining many devices without the need of a terminator. USB is much slower (but somewhat less expensive) than FireWire.

uucode
The point of uucode is to allow 8-bit binary data to be transferred through the more common 7-bit ASCII channels (most especially e-mail). The facilities for dealing with uucoded files exist for many different machine types, and the most common programs are called "uuencode" for encoding the original binary file into a 7-bit file and "uudecode" for restoring the original binary file from the encoded one. Sometimes different uuencode and uudecode programs will work in subtly different manners causing annoying compatibility problems. Bcode was invented to provide the same service as uucode but to maintain a tighter standard.

variable width
As applied to a font, variable width means that different characters will have different widths as appropriate. For example, an "i" will take up much less space than an "m". The opposite of variable width is fixed width. The terms "proportional width" and "proportionally spaced" mean the same thing as variable width. Some common variable width fonts include Times, Helvetica, and Bookman.

VAX
The VAX is a computer platform developed by Digital. Its plural is VAXen. VAXen are large expensive machines that were once quite popular in large businesses; today modern UNIX workstations have all the capability of VAXen but take up much less space. Their OS is called VMS.

vector
This term has two common meanings. The first is in the geometric sense: a vector defines a direction and magnitude. The second concerns the formatting of fonts and images. If a font is a vector font or an image is a vector image, it is defined as lines of relative size and direction rather than as collections of pixels (the method used in bitmapped fonts and images). This makes it easier to change the size of the font or image, but puts a bigger load on the device that has to display the font or image. The term "outline font" means the same thing as vector font.

Veronica & Veronica2
Although traditionally written as a proper name, Veronica is actually an acronym for "**v**ery **e**asy **r**odent-**o**riented **n**etwide **i**ndex to **c**omputerized **a**rchives", where the "rodent" refers to gopher. The acronym was obviously a little forced to go along with the pre-existing (and now largely unused) Archie, in order to have a little fun with a comic book reference. Regardless, Veronica (or these days more likely Veronica2) is essentially a search engine for gopher resources.

VIC-20
The Commodore VIC-20 computer sold millions of units and is generally considered to have been the first affordable home computer. It features a ROM-based BASIC and uses it as a default "OS". It is based on the 65xx family of processors. VIC (in case you are wondering) can stand for either **v**ideo **i**nterface **c** or **v**ideo **i**nterface **c**omputer. The VIC-20 is the precursor to the C64/128.

virtual machine
A virtual machine is a machine completely defined and implemented in software rather than hardware. It is often referred to as a "runtime environment"; code compiled for such a machine is typically called bytecode.

virtual memory
This is a scheme by which disk space is made to substitute for the more expensive RAM space. Using it will often enable a comptuer to do things it could not do without it, but it will also often result in an overall slowing down of the system. The concept of swap space is very similar.

virtual reality
Virtual reality (often called VR for short) is generally speaking an attempt to provide more natural, human interfaces to software. It can be as simple as a pseudo 3D interface or as elaborate as an isolated room in which the computer can control the user's senses of vision, hearing, and even smell and touch.

virus
A virus is a program that will seek to duplicate itself in memory and on disks, but in a subtle way that will not immediately be noticed. A computer on the same network as an infected computer or that uses an infected disk (even a floppy) or that downloads and runs an infected program can itself become infected. A virus can only spread to computers of the same platform. For example, on a network consisting of a WinTel box, a Mac, and a Linux box, if one machine acquires a virus the other two will probably still be safe. Note also that different platforms have different general levels of resistance; UNIX machines are almost immune, Win '95 / '98 / ME / XP is quite vulnerable, and most others lie somewhere in between.

VMS
The industrial strength OS that runs on VAXen.

VoIP
VoIP means "Voice over IP" and it is quite simply a way of utilizing the Internet (or even in some cases intranets) for telephone conversations. The primary motivations for doing so are cost and convenience as VoIP is significantly less expensive than typical telephone long distance packages, plus one high speed Internet connection can serve for multiple phone lines.

VRML
A **V**irtual **R**eality **M**odeling **L**anguage file is used to represent VR objects. It has essentially been superceded by X3D.

W3C
The World Wide Web Consortium (usually abbreviated W3C) is a non-profit, advisory body that makes suggestions on the future direction of the World Wide Web, HTML, CSS, and browsers.
Waba
An extremely lightweight subset of Java optimized for use on PDAs.
WebDAV
WebDAV stands for Web-based Distributed Authoring and Versioning, and is designed to provide a way of editing Web-based resources in place. It serves as a more modern (and often more secure) replacement for FTP in many cases.
WebTV
A WebTV box hooks up to an ordinary television set and displays web pages. It will not display them as well as a dedicated computer.
window manager
A window manager is a program that acts as a graphical go-between for a user and an OS. It provides a GUI for the OS. Some OSes incorporate the window manager into their own internal code, but many do not for reasons of efficiency. Some OSes partially make the division. Some common true window managers include CDE (Common Desktop Environment), GNOME, KDE, Aqua, OpenWindows, Motif, FVWM, Sugar, and Enlightenment. Some common hybrid window managers with OS extensions include Windows ME, Windows 98, Windows 95, Windows 3.1, OS/2 and GEOS.
Windows '95
Windows '95 is currently the second most popular variant of MS-Windows. It was designed to be the replacement Windows 3.1 but has not yet done so completely partly because of suspected security problems but even more because it is not as lightweight and will not work on all the machines that Windows 3.1 will. It is more capable than Windows 3.1 though and now has excellent driver support and more games available for it than any other platform. It is made to run on top of MS-DOS and will not do much of anything if MS-DOS is not on the system. It is thus not strictly an OS per se, but nor is it a true window manager either; rather the combination of MS-DOS and Windows '95 result in a full OS with GUI. It is partially multitasking but has a much greater chance of crashing than Windows NT does (or probably even Mac OS) if faced with a buggy program. Windows '95 runs only on x86 based machines. Currently Windows '95 has several Y2K issues, some of which have patches that can be downloaded for free, and some of which do not yet have fixes at all.
Windows '98
Windows '98 is quite possibly the second most popular form of MS-Windows, in spite of the fact that its official release is currently a point of legal debate with at least nineteen states, the federal government, and a handful of foreign countries as it has a few questionable features that might restrict the novice computer user and/or unfairly compete with other computer companies. It also has some specific issues with the version of Java that comes prepackaged with it that has never been adequately fixed, and it still has several Y2K issues, most of which have patches that can be downloaded for free (in fact, Microsoft guarantees that it will work properly through 2000 with the proper patches), but some of which do not yet have fixes at all (it won't work properly through 2001 at this point). In any case, it was designed to replace Windows '95.
Windows 2000
Windows 2000 was the intended replacement for Windows NT and in that capacity received relatively lukewarm support. Being based on Windows NT, it inherits some of its driver support problems. Originally it was also supposed to replace Windows '98, but Windows ME was made to do that instead, and the merger between Windows NT and Windows '98 was postponed until Windows XP.
Windows 3.1
Windows 3.1 remains a surprisingly popular variant of MS-Windows. It is lighter weight than

either Windows '95 or Windows NT (but not lighter weight than GEOS) but less capable than the other two. It is made to run on top of MS-DOS and will not do much of anything if MS-DOS is not on the system. It is thus not strictly an OS per se, but nor is it a true window manager, either; rather the combination of MS-DOS and Windows 3.1 result in a full OS with GUI. Its driver support is good, but its game selection is limited. Windows 3.1 runs only on x86 based machines. It has some severe Y2K issues that may or may not be fixed.

Windows CE

Windows CE is the lightweight variant of MS-Windows. It offers the general look and feel of Windows '95 but is targetted primarily for hand-held devices, PDAs, NCs, and embedded devices. It does not have all the features of either Windows '95 or Windows NT and is very different from Windows 3.1. In particular, it will not run any software made for any of the other versions of MS-Windows. Special versions of each program must be made. Furthermore, there are actually a few slightly different variants of Windows CE, and no variant is guaranteed to be able to run software made specifically for another one. Driver support is also fairly poor for all types, and few games are made for it. Windows CE will run on a few different processor types, including the x86 and several different processors dedicated to PDAs, embedded systems, and hand-held devices.

Windows ME

Windows ME is yet another flavor of MS-Windows (specifically the planned replacement for Windows '98). Windows ME currently runs only on the x86 processor.

Windows NT

Windows NT is the industrial-strength variant of MS-Windows. Current revisions offer the look and feel of Windows '95 and older revisions offer the look and feel of Windows 3.1. It is the most robust flavor of MS-Windows and is fully multitasking. It is also by far the most expensive flavor of MS-Windows and has far less software available for it than Windows '95 or '98. In particular, do not expect to play many games on a Windows NT machine, and expect some difficulty in obtaining good drivers. Windows NT will run on a few different processor types, including the x86, the Alpha, and the PowerPC. Plans are in place to port Windows NT to the Merced when it becomes available.

Windows Vista

Windows Vista is the newest flavor of MS-Windows (specifically the planned replacement for Windows XP). Windows Vista (originally known as Longhorn) currently only runs on x86 processors.

Windows XP

Windows XP is yet another flavor of MS-Windows (specifically the planned replacement for both Windows ME and Windows 2000). Windows XP currently only runs on the x86 processors. Windows XP is currently the most popular form of MS-Windows.

WinTel

An x86 based system running some flavor of MS-Windows.

workstation

Depending upon whom you ask, a workstation is either an industrial strength desktop computer or its own category above the desktops. Workstations typically have some flavor of UNIX for their OS, but there has been a recent trend to call high-end Windows NT and Windows 2000 machines workstations, too.

WYSIWYG

What you see is what you get; an adjective applied to a program that attempts to exactly represent printed output on the screen. Related to WYSIWYM but quite different.

WYSIWYM

What you see is what you mean; an adjective applied to a program that does not attempt to exactly represent printed output on the screen, but rather defines how things are used and so will adapt to different paper sizes, etc. Related to WYSIWYG but quite different.

X-Face
X-Faces are small monochrome images embedded in headers for both provides a e-mail and news messages. Better mail and news applications will display them (sometimes automatically, sometimes only per request).
X-Windows
X-Windows provides a GUI for most UNIX systems, but can also be found as an add-on library for other computers. Numerous window managers run on top of it. It is often just called "X".
X3D
Extensible **3D** Graphics data is an XML file that is used to hold three-dimensional graphical data. It is the successor to VRML.
x86
The x86 series of processors includes the Pentium, Pentium Pro, Pentium II, Pentium III, Celeron, and Athlon as well as the 786, 686, 586, 486, 386, 286, 8086, 8088, etc. It is an exceptionally popular design (by far the most popular CISC series) in spite of the fact that even its fastest model is significantly slower than the assorted RISC processors. Many different OSes run on machines built around x86 processors, including MS-DOS, Windows 3.1, Windows '95, Windows '98, Windows ME, Windows NT, Windows 2000, Windows CE, Windows XP, GEOS, Linux, Solaris, OpenBSD, NetBSD, FreeBSD, Mac OS X, OS/2, BeOS, CP/M, etc. A couple different companies produce x86 processors, but the bulk of them are produced by Intel. It is expected that this processor will eventually be completely replaced by the Merced, but the Merced development schedule is somewhat behind. Also, it should be noted that the Pentium III processor has stirred some controversy by including a "fingerprint" that will enable individual computer usage of web pages etc. to be accurately tracked.
XBL
An XML **B**inding **L**anguage document is used to associate executable content with an XML tag. It is itself an XML file, and is used most frequently (although not exclusively) in conjunction with XUL.
XHTML
The **E**xtensible **H**ypertext **M**ark-up **L**anguage is essentially a cleaner, stricter version of HTML. It is a proper subset of XML.
XML
The **E**xtensible **M**ark-up **L**anguage is a subset of SGML and a superset of XHTML. It is used for numerous things including (among many others) RSS and RDF.
XML-RPC
XML-RPC provides a fairly lightweight means by which one computer can execute a program on a co-operating machine across a network like the Internet. It is based on XML and is used for everything from fetching stock quotes to checking weather forcasts.
XO
The energy-efficient, kid-friendly laptop produced by the OLPC project. It runs Sugar for its window manager and Linux for its OS. It sports numerous built-in features like wireless networking, a video camera & microphone, a few USB ports, and audio in/out jacks. It comes with several educational applications (which it refers to as "Activities"), most of which are written in Python.
XSL
The **E**xtensible **S**tylesheet **L**anguage is like CSS for XML. It provides a means of describing how an XML resource should be displayed.
XSLT
XSL Transformations are used to transform one type of XML into another. It is a component of XSL that can be (and often is) used independently.
XUL
An XML **U**ser-**I**nterface **L**anguage document is used to define a user interface for an application

using XML to specify the individual controls as well as the overall layout.
Y2K
The general class of problems resulting from the wrapping of computers' internal date timers is given this label in honor of the most obvious occurrence -- when the year changes from 1999 to 2000 (abbreviated in some programs as 99 to 00 indicating a backwards time movement). Contrary to popular belief, these problems will not all manifest themselves on the first day of 2000, but will in fact happen over a range of dates extending out beyond 2075. A computer that does not have problems prior to the beginning of 2001 is considered "Y2K compliant", and a computer that does not have problems within the next ten years or so is considered for all practical purposes to be "Y2K clean". Whether or not a given computer is "clean" depends upon both its OS and its applications (and in some unfortunate cases, its hardware). The quick rundown on common home / small business machines (roughly from best to worst) is that:

- All Mac OS systems are okay until at least the year 2040. By that time a patch should be available.
- All BeOS systems are okay until the year 2040 (2038?). By that time a patch should be available.
- Most UNIX versions are either okay or currently have free fixes available (and typically would not have major problems until 2038 or later in any case).
- NewtonOS has a problem with the year 2010, but has a free fix available.
- Newer AmigaOS systems are okay; older ones have a problem with the year 2000 but have a free fix available. They also have a year 2077 problem that does not yet have a free fix.
- Some OS/2 systems have a year 2000 problem, but free fixes are available.
- All CP/M versions have a year 2000 problem, but free fixes are available.
- PC-DOS has a year 2000 problem, but a free fix is available.
- DR-DOS has a year 2000 problem, but a free fix is available.
- Different versions of GEOS have different problems ranging from minor year 2000 problems (with fixes in the works) to larger year 2080 problems (that do not have fixes yet). The only problem that may not have a fix in time is the year 2000 problem on the Apple][version of GEOS; not only was that version discontinued, unlike the other GEOS versions it no longer has a parent company to take care of it.
- All MS-Windows versions (except possibly Windows 2000 and Windows ME) have multiple problems with the year 2000 and/or 2001, most of which have free fixes but some of which still lack free fixes as of this writing. Even new machines off the shelf that are labelled "Y2K Compliant" usually are not unless additional software is purchased and installed. Basically WinNT and WinCE can be properly patched, Windows '98 can be patched to work properly through 2000 (possibly not 2001), Windows '95 can be at least partially patched for 2000 (but not 2001) but is not being guaranteed by Microsoft, and Windows 3.1 cannot be fully patched.
- MS-DOS has problems with at least the year 2000 (and probably more). None of its problems have been addressed as of this writing. Possible fixes are to change over to either PC-DOS or DR-DOS.

Results vary wildly for common applications, so it is better to be safe than sorry and check out the ones that you use. It should also be noted that some of the biggest expected Y2K problems will be at the two ends of the computer spectrum with older legacy mainframes (such as power some large banks) and some of the various tiny embedded computers (such as power most burglar alarms and many assorted appliances). Finally, it should also be mentioned that some older WinTel boxes and Amigas may have Y2K problems in their hardware requiring a card addition or replacement.
Z-Machine
A virtual machine optimized for running interactive fiction, interactive tutorials, and other interactive things of a primarily textual nature. Z-Machines have been ported to almost every

platform in use today. Z-machine bytecode is usually called Z-code. The Glulx virtual machine is of the same idea but somewhat more modern in concept.

Z80

The Z80 series of processors is a CISC design and is not being used in too many new stand-alone computer systems, but can still be occasionally found in embedded systems. It is the most popular processor for CP/M machines.

Zaurus

The Zaurus is a brand of PDA. It is generally in between a Palm and a Newton in capability.

zip

There are three common zips in the computer world that are completely different from one another. One is a type of removable removable disk slightly larger (physically) and vastly larger (capacity) than a floppy. The second is a group of programs used for running interactive fiction. The third is a group of programs used for compression.

Zoomer

The Zoomer is a type of PDA. Zoomers all use GEOS for their OS and are / were produced by numerous different companies and are thus found under numerous different names. The "classic" Zoomers are known as the Z-7000, the Z-PDA, and the GRiDpad and were made by Casio, Tandy, and AST respectively. Newer Zoomers include HP's OmniGo models, Hyundai's Gulliver (which may not have actually been released to the general public), and Nokia's Communicator line of PDA / cell phone hybrids.

www.ingramcontent.com/pod-product-compliance
Lightning Source LLC
Chambersburg PA
CBHW081757300426
44116CB00014B/2152